On Rockingham Street

On Rockingham Street

Reclaiming My Family's Jewish Identity—
Our Journey from Vilna to the Suburban South

DAVID R. KUNEY

WIPF & STOCK · Eugene, Oregon

ON ROCKINGHAM STREET
Reclaiming My Family's Jewish Identity—Our Journey from Vilna to the Suburban
South

Wipf & Stock
An Imprint of Wipf and Stock Publishers
199 W. 8th Ave., Suite 3
Eugene, OR 97401

www.wipfandstock.com

PAPERBACK ISBN: 978-1-7252-6573-8
HARDCOVER ISBN: 978-1-7252-6572-1
EBOOK ISBN: 978-1-7252-6574-5

07/01/21

For my wife, Cathy—who made all of this possible.

If you have no sense of the past, no access to the historical narrative, you are afloat, untethered; you cannot see yourself as part of the narrative, you cannot place yourself within a context. You will not have an understanding of time, and a respect for memory and its subtle victory over the remorselessness of time.

—PENELOPE LIVELY, *DANCING FISH AND AMMONITES*

Contents

Acknowledgments

I HAVE BEEN THE fortunate beneficiary of invaluable assistance from friends and colleagues who contributed to this project and to my late-life interest in the topics I have addressed. I acknowledge some of them here, knowing it is impossible to include them all in these pages.

I am grateful to Susan Kristol, with whom I have spent untold hours studying Torah, and who graciously agreed, without hesitation, to read an initial draft of this book, and provided encouragement and insight that convinced me to finish this work.

My thanks as well to Myrna Goldenberg who also read an early draft, and provided much-needed insight and editing suggestions, and who urged me to think carefully about my audience and how to reach that audience.

My thanks to Curt Leviant, the translator of Chaim Grade, who graciously spent more time with me than I could have hoped, and who provided me with stories about Grade, including his secular views of Judaism and the role of his wife in protecting his reputation.

There are many others who deserve my thanks and deep appreciation. Roger Price, who encouraged me to contact Wipf and Stock about publishing this book, and who proved to be key to this undertaking.

Marsha Teichman, who reminded me that one of the keys to Jewish education and Jewish involvement in synagogue life is whether one has the spark—an idea that may indeed explain why Jewish education works for some, but not for all.

Rabbi David Golinkin, President of The Schecter Institute in Jerusalem, kindly allowed me to interview him on one of his visits to Maryland, and, in doing so, provided me with key background material about Vilna, and his father's relationship with Chaim Grade. It was through his insights and learning that I came to understand the underlying tension between the sacred and the profane, an issue that seems to have lingered throughout all of Jewish history.

Many thanks to my cousin, Jo Ellen Kuney, who read key parts of this book and provided me with critically important thoughts about my father, Joseph, and his relationship with his brother, Julius, as well as information about the early history of Anna and Sol.

Jordan Auslander, of Probate & Genealogy Research Associates in New York City, was able to locate the ship manifests for both Sol and Anna, along with a number of the key documents upon which I have drawn in order to make my grandparents' journeys from Vilna to Virginia more vivid and real, both for me and, I hope, the reader.

I am forever grateful to the Board and Officers of the Pardes Institute of Jewish Studies, including Sherwin Pomerantz, Leon Morris, Deborah Shapira, Jamie Bornstein, and Joshua Chadajo, whose leadership in Jewish literacy first prompted me to begin my own study of Jewish texts, and to explore the value of Jewish studies. And special thanks to Tom Barad, a member of the Board, who told me ten years ago when I first met him in Jerusalem that America does not know how much it needs Pardes—words that sparked my own journey into the richness of studying Jewish texts. And, of course, my deep gratitude to Rabbi Meir Schweiger, a great scholar and teacher, whose belief in Jewish education is an example for all of us.

Thanks, too, to my friends and colleagues at the Reconstructionist Rabbinical College, including Rabbi Deborah Waxman, Seth Rosen, David Roberts, and Elsie Stern, who permitted me to serve on their Board for a period of time, and who spent years reminding me of the importance of Jewish education and their holy mission in training young men and women to become rabbis and Jewish leaders, all of which kept me deeply interested and focused on Jewish learning.

I also owe much to the clergy and lay leaders at Adat Shalom Reconstructionist Congregation, including Rabbi Sid Schwarz, Rabbi Fred Dobb, and Rabbi Hazan Rachel Hersh, whose spiritual guidance has convinced me that there is indeed something profoundly important about why the Jewish religion must survive. These clergy have been shining examples of what it means to build a Jewish community where commitment to the highest ethical and Jewish ideals is always in the forefront. And a special thanks to Audrey Lyon who has been a leader and a stunning example of selfless devotion to Jewish education for adults who continue to thirst for Jewish learning—all of which has helped me believe that Jewish education for adults is one of the keys to Jewish survival.

My thanks to Ira Ungar, a wonderful Torah scholar and teacher, who has opened up the joys of studying Torah, Rashi and the other great commentators, along with my classmates in Ira's class, Marcia Bordman, Linda Kacser, Art Boyars, Philip Abrams, Bob Barkin, Steve Isaacson and Susan Kristol, all of whom have inspired me with their wisdom and learning. Many thanks to the various people who read one or more versions of this book and provided useful edits and guidance, including Caroline Levitt, Shannon O'Neill, and Jeff Tamarkin. I am grateful for your suggestions and your wisdom.

I could not be more grateful to and for my children (Robert, Daniel, and Jessica), grandchildren (Jacob, Noah, and Joshua) and daughter-in-law (Dana), all of whom listened patiently when I talked about this book during the past three years, and who never once doubted that I would one day finish it and that it was a worthy undertaking. The uncynical enthusiasm that only one's children can bring to life has made this undertaking worthwhile.

And most of all, thank you to my wonderful wife, Cathy, whose unending and tireless efforts provided the critical energy and motivation that both encouraged me to start this book, and then kept me going through all of the dark moments of doubt and frustration. Without Cathy's skilled and unparalleled editing skill, her tireless perseverance, her keen eye and flawless ear for the worthy phrase, and her strict and demanding insistence on proper grammar, I could never have finished this book, nor made it of value to any reader.

PROLOGUE

The Sacred Role of Remembering

MY MOTHER, ESTHER, DIED on a Saturday in May 2005. It was the Friday of Memorial Day weekend when my mother's caregiver called to say death was near. It was not unexpected. Esther was the last of the four of them—Sol and Anna, my grandparents, who had emigrated from Vilna in 1913 and 1916, and their son, Joseph—my father—and now Esther, his wife. All would soon be together again in King David Memorial Garden, just south of Arlington, Virginia, where they had spent most of their adult lives and raised me and my two brothers.

It was Sol and Anna who had started the journey from Vilna to Arlington—from the Jerusalem of Lithuania to America's suburban South, which did not even have a synagogue of its own until almost 1950. A journey that transformed everything and covered every epoch, from Old Country to New, from Jewish to secular, from one tradition to another—but always the journey, the essential act of being Jewish—leaving one's homeland and going into exile and assimilation and the casting off and deliberate forgetting of the past. This modern notion of exile, with its seeming insistence on forgetting, played out in the suburban South of Virginia.

Napoleon first called Vilna the Jerusalem of the North in 1812. But what did he know of Jerusalem? By that point, the temple had been twice destroyed, and Jews had been exiled from their homeland in 70 CE and would not return until Napoleon had been dead for well over a century. Certainly Napoleon had no concept of the Vilna that Sol and Anna knew—the Vilna of the great and learned Rabbi Eliyahu, the Vilna Gaon, the Great

Synagogue, and the Jewish Enlightenment, and then the murderous pogroms from which Sol and Anna would flee for fear of their lives, and in which Anna's mother lost hers.

When my wife Cathy and I arrived that Saturday morning, we found my mother had not waited for us. Death had already claimed her. Her passing was a relief of sorts, if not a blessing. Esther had not enjoyed life after Joe—her husband and my father—had died three years earlier. We—my younger brother and I, our wives and our children—were some consolation, but not enough.

When the undertakers put Esther on a gurney and wheeled her down the hallway, wrapped in a black plastic body bag, I cried out loud. The men from the funeral home stopped the gurney and looked at me. I hugged her, a body with no life. Then I hugged Cathy and said I was sorry, but I had no idea for what. For everything, I guess.

I had never been told that Jews do not touch the body of a deceased (Lev 21:1). Later, I would learn that relatives, including sons, may touch the dead, but must take care to purify themselves after contact. All to show reverence for the dead and the living, and a sense of separation between the two. This notion of separateness is so central to Judaism, keeping the sacred and the profane apart, but it also signifies a belief in the dignity and even holiness of the small things, the small actions—reverence for all of it, all of life.

No surprise I violated Jewish law; after all, what had Esther and Joe taught me about such things? Sol and Anna, too, were surprisingly silent about things Jewish, once they too had come to live in gentile Arlington. I saw this now as my mother was rolled away, the entire history of my family from 1913 to that day, and how we had given up, surrendered, forgot so much, this being the trajectory of Jewish life in assimilated America, the price of exile in America.

It was then that I first began to realize what it was that I had not taken seriously, and the need to change it: our history, our memory, our role in life, as Jews. Now, the last of the four of them, my parents and grandparents, immigrants and first-generation Jews, was being laid to rest. The burden was being handed to me, to carry on, to remember. Little wonder I cried as she was taken down to the black car, sent to her next stop. Could I be trusted to do this? To make order of it? Give some modest coherence to the chaos of these four lives and what they had done for us?

After the two men from the funeral home had rolled Esther into the black limousine, I called the King David Memorial Garden to see if I could arrange a graveside funeral on a holiday weekend. King David was the largest Jewish cemetery in the Washington, DC area. It sat on beautiful rolling hills just off Lee Highway, a major artery in the Northern Virginia suburb in which I grew up. The highway was named after one of our nation's most notorious traitors—a gifted general, trained at West Point, who took the side of the South and slavery, mostly because his love of Virginia transcended his love of nation.

So, here I am, at the beginning of a holiday weekend, sitting in a condo in suburban Virginia, the son of first-generation American parents, the grandson of Sol and Anna, who somehow had found their way from Vilna to Chicago in the early years of the last century, and from there to Arlington, Virginia, and then to King David, where, if I can manage it, my mother will be buried in the next day or two. Contradictions abound. A family of Jews from the Old World who wound up in the American South, where so much of our lives had happened, where the inexplicable blandness of suburbia eagerly embraced the dry monotony of secular life. This corner of the world felt devoid of the spiritual: undemanding, unrelenting.

"Don't people die on holidays?" I asked when the cemetery pushed back against my request for a weekend funeral. But for an extra fee they agreed to make the burial arrangements over the holiday.

It is the Jewish custom to bury our dead immediately—a sign of respect for the dead and a warning to the living to keep their distance. This is all part of the laws of ritual defilement that Moses is said to have given to the Jewish people. We were taught that we must value life in this world, and distance ourselves from idle speculation about what might come next. The mystery of death is too sacred to take lightly, and the living are too vulnerable to dawdle in that zone. We do not open coffins at our services nor do we stare at the deceased. We take care of their souls, sit by their side until burial, and then send them on their way to wherever they are headed. Belief without speculation as to what it all means—such is Judaism.

It rained the day Esther was buried. Rabbi Marvin Bash delivered a graveside eulogy about the more than fifteen years that Esther had worked for him, and for his predecessor, Rabbi Golinkin. Esther had worked for both rabbis at the "Center"—the Arlington-Fairfax Jewish Center. This was where our entire Jewish life had unfolded—there and on Rockingham Street where we lived for all those years. Some of my former classmates from what was then called Hebrew High School showed up for the funeral. Everyone at the Center knew Esther and Joe.

Soon after Esther died, my brother Steve and I hired an auction house to sell the modest furniture in their home. We had offered their things to our own children for their homes, but there was no interest. It was all old and used. People came to the condo and looked things over, fingered through the small kitchen items, the trinkets, the IBM typewriter from the 1960s, the color TV. What else is one to do with a life's collection of things, once so dear, and now to be abandoned?

But there were files Joe had maintained in a carefully labelled old metal file cabinet. Joe was always meticulous, with a neat handwriting style I tried without success to copy when I was younger. So, we packed up their files into cardboard boxes. No real system; little marking. Of course, this was part of a larger issue. One might well ask how we could forget so much, be so inattentive to the past, so careless with the things we had taken out of their home, packed up, and sent for a time to Steve's home in Fairfax. There the boxes stayed for a few years, until Steve and his wife moved to Jackson, Wyoming, and there they stayed for several more years. Their voices were silent, like the boxes. Inert. None of this felt right.

Steve and I talked about the boxes from time to time. We never talked about what might be in the boxes, but only where to store them. Years passed. The boxes were a bit too much clutter for Steve's otherwise orderly and modern home in Jackson. "Send the boxes to me," I suggested. I had ample room to store them, yet I still had not thought much about what they might contain. When the boxes arrived, they sat unopened in my basement. Yet, the boxes had travelled by Priority Mail from Jackson. What was the rush?

I walked past the boxes for days, weeks, months. It had been a little over ten years since we had packed things up. I told myself I should leave them alone. Our friends talk of uncluttering; they are in the process of throwing out old records; old notes that once were the basis for a dissertation; research and lectures; business plans; time records. A Facebook friend, Rabbi B., posts that she has just thrown out 1,500 folders of original notes on the 700-year-old documents she had studied for her PhD dissertation in Barcelona in 1986.

Susan Gubar opens her novel on aging and love, *Late-Life Love*, by throwing out years of records and work, by moving out, moving on, shredding and trashing the past. Should I do the same? I take a quick look inside one of the boxes but put the cover back on. Should I open them, peer into the time and history of those who have gone? For what purpose? Not now, I think.

At some point, as I walk past the still unopened boxes, I begin to think about the concept of duty and whether I had any obligation to open the boxes, to study their contents, and try to make sense of whatever I found. I had fallen lately into the habit of framing my conversations with myself, of which there were far too many, in terms of my Judaism and my obligations as a Jew. But duty can be a bit dry, cold, and hard; things get done or not done, but where is the heart?

But doing nothing meant that Esther and Joe—not to mention Sol and Anna—would be forgotten over time, their memory would vanish, and none of us—including our children and grandchildren, not to mention ourselves—would remember much about them. I was uneasy with the thought; too much forgetting.

The Hebrew verb to remember, *zahkor*, is repeated over 160 times in the Bible and appears more than any verb other than "to say." No wonder. God seems to talk endlessly. "And God said . . ." "And Moses said . . ." And on and on, almost without end, coupled with the duty to remember. So much talk; so much to remember.

Jewish scholars insist that remembering is a duty, an obligation. Sacred perhaps. Yosef Yerushalmi, a well-known Jewish scholar, writes, "Moreover, only in Judaism is the injunction to remember [*zakhor*] 'felt as a religious imperative to an entire people.'"[1] "Remember these things, O Jacob, for you, O Israel are My servant" (Isa 44:21).

Rabbi Lord Jonathan Sacks, knighted by Queen Elizabeth for his contributions to Jewish thought, writes that the ability to remember is what places a value on life itself: "To most humans at most times, there seems to be no meaning in history. We live, we die, and it is as if we had never been. The universe gives no sign of any interest in our existence. Time seems to obliterate all meaning. Nothing lasts. Nothing endures." This view, says Sacks, is exactly what Judaism rejected, and instead gave to the world and mankind an entirely different view of the meaning of history and hence of memory. Thus, "[f]or the first time, we find affirmed and increasingly accepted the idea that historical events have a value in themselves."[2]

But I could still ignore all this, I think. We have ample storage room and what would be the harm in simply labeling the boxes and putting them on the shelves? With good labels, there was at least a chance that one day I would return to them.

And then I discovered how forgetting can get out of hand. I attended a *minyan* (the early morning Jewish service, usually lightly attended) at what is now called Etz Hayim ("tree of life") but which was the Arlington-Fairfax Jewish Center when I was a boy. The Center, as we called it, was the first real synagogue in Arlington, the place where, after years of exile and assimilation, Sol and Anna and Esther and Joseph would ultimately go to pray.

While in the synagogue, I walked over to the Memorial Board, now filled with several hundred names of deceased members spanning the years, and looked for the Kuneys who had passed away. I had lost count. Yet, where

1. Yerushalemi, quoted in Singer, "Zakhor," para. 1.
2. Sacks, "God Who Acts in History," 7:30–8:11.

Esther's name should have been, in the space below Joseph, there was only a sign with the single word "reserved." How odd, given that she had been the rock, the source of strength, the person who kept the place running for nearly two decades. Had Esther been here still, the place for her name would not have been unmarked. She never forgot. Yet, had I not chanced to attend the *minyan*, almost on a whim, I never would have seen this omission of her name. No one had called to tell us about the missing plaque. Had we forgotten to purchase it? How had she disappeared, given all that she had done? This missing plaque weighed on me.

Standing there, that day, and in the days that followed, I had a gnawing sense of forgotten history. Who would now give voice to the meaning of the journey they had made? Sol and Anna had gotten us here, but who knew how or why or what it all meant? There was a story here and I began to feel it needed to be told. I wanted to understand what their lives meant, and what they may have been trying to teach me, when we were still three brothers, this before Richard, the eldest of the three, had decided to take his own life. Even more, I wanted to know what they had laid aside, forgotten, and discarded in their own sense of Jewishness and how it had played out decades later in suburban America.

Leaving the Center that day, walking away from the long list of names of those who are now speechless, and seeing again the small details outside—the street where Esther and Joe always parked when they arrived early, the wide expanse of Arlington Boulevard on which the Center sat, the sidewalk on which we walked after High Holiday services for so many years, I wanted to make some sense of all this, to sort it out, accurately and faithfully, and to come to terms with it. Not only with who they were, and what they tried to say to us, to me, but also with the words we never heard, or they never uttered, which still shaped our lives at the deepest level—we, the faithless transcribers.

Returning home, I opened the boxes. What I saw was this: manila file folders, loose documents, pictures, diplomas—the few items remaining from the estate of my parents. And fragments, too few of course, of Anna and Sol, who made the journey, disparate items from the past, no rhyme or reason for what remained and what was gone: binoculars in a well-worn leather case; yellowing black-and-white photographs of unknown distant relatives from the nineteenth century; a marriage license from 1939; a stamp collection with stamps from 1890, for one cent, two cents, a mere penny to carry a letter from east to west, and more. There was a death certificate, a letter to our daughter, deeds from buying a home and then selling the same home, yearbooks from the 1930s, a baby book recording every month of my (now long gone) older brother's first few years, scholarly articles, more photographs, some in color, of family events, of Rockingham Street, of Arlington, Virginia, others from Chicago. Some from another country—Lithuania, it seems. And still more.

Once started, there is no stopping. I ask myself: if I understand my history, will I know anything more about myself?

Going through the boxes, fragments of the Jewish life of Sol and Anna, and of Esther and Joe, emerge. A *tallit* in a small blue bag, but no *tefillin*. No old prayer book. Apprently, we did not save the *mezuzah* from their front door, the small piece of Torah that Jews are supposed to keep on their doorposts, so that wherever they go they are reminded to think of Torah, of Jewish learning. So easy to forget otherwise. Looking at these objects, and seeing as well what was missing, I wondered what had become of their Jewishness, and how it had changed our lives, all of us—me, my brothers, and now our children.

Going through the boxes revealed something else I had not expected: I began to see more clearly a problem about my own Jewishness that had weighed on me for years. I had come of age in suburban Virginia, suburban America in truth, where so much of Jewish custom and learning had been cast aside, and now was mostly forgotten. This experience had left me with doubts about my own authenticity, because in truth I had not objected to the laying aside of so much—even if now I struggled to recapture, recreate, and rejoin a tradition that I barely understood.

The question of assimilation and exile also weighed on me. Did my family's life story and journey mirror the larger, universal journey of the immigrant? Newly landed on fresh shores, they had to pick and choose what should be remembered and what could be forgotten, celebrated or discarded. Did they know they were making choices for all of us, so that my identity today is shaped by their inner struggle? And had the same thing happened to the friends of my youth, here in suburban America, where being Jewish had lost so much of its distincive qualities that it was hard to say why it mattered anymore? The question of separateness, the basis for holiness, had now dissolved into the bland sameness of suburban life.

Here in these boxes was part of the story of Sol and Anna, and Esther and Joe, of me and my brothers, but it was more than that. It was the story of the tension between belief and doubt in all things Jewish. When Sol and Anna's journey to America began in 1913, it was not at all clear they would bring their Jewish heritage with them. When I look back, I am struck both by how much and how little strict Jewishness they brought with them, and how their values flowed through the generations. Was Sol happy to be far from the Yiddish he spoke in Vilna, the orthodoxy that surrounded him as a child and young man, often suffocating perhaps in too much insistence, and the shadow of the Great Synagogue? Two sets of dishes and a third for Passover, and yet, not a word was ever said to us, their grandchildren, about Torah or Jewish text. We could see the customs played out, but the mysterious foundation for it was left unexplained and thus became easy to ignore.

But the photographs, the few notes, and the recollections, coming back to me, forced me to confront the same issues they had confronted. No longer was it an issue of the Old Country versus the New Country. They had brought with them enough skepticism and doubt to survive through generations, certainly through Esther and Joe, and their children, including me—skeptic and believer, trying to get a firm grasp on what it means to be Jewish.

I wonder if they set in motion, along with millions like them, this casting off of so much Jewish custom and text, so that now we are left with so few memories, so few customs, and no true feeling for whatever great mysteries might be answered within the text of the Torah. We cling to our Judaism and at the same time are not sure what it is we are clinging to. After all the leaving, stripping away, and belonging to another nation, what then is the irreducible minimum that made the generations that followed Sol and Anna still Jewish?

In writing this memoir, I had other hopes as well. I was searching for answers to my own Judaism, and where and how I had wound up where I was. I wanted to know not just where we had been—Sol and Anna and the rest of us—but where we might now be headed. Was there something to be done? I had for years wondered about this: How was it that I had turned—at age sixty-five no less—to a more methodical study of things Jewish, of Torah, of Jewish history, and of Hebrew—three trips now to Jerusalem to study with some of the greatest Jewish scholars, dazzled always, almost breathless with new insights? Was there something more I should be doing other than taking note that we were hanging by a thread, and then simply moving on to the next task?

What I had begun to see in this late-life study was the great wisdom and guidance of the narrative of Jewish writings, virtually no match found elsewhere: difficult to access; complex; troubling, but of immense value. And yet, within the Jewish community that I saw almost daily, it was largely ignored. Not just custom and tradition, but text, words, language as the essence of life, all drifting away. The carpool parents on Shabbat sit outside in their cars, waiting for services to end before picking up their children, and then wonder why belief is so fragile.

I began to see that my family, like many others, had been steadfastly on this same path—of laying things aside, Jewish things, and moving on, step by step to get ahead—without giving any Jewish shape to our lives. But it was more complicated than that, more nuanced; more contradictions than firm answers. How was I to make sense of the fact that Esther and Joe, neither of whom ever joined a synagogue in their own youth, had come to be president (Joe) of Arlington's only synagogue, and executive administrator for the Rabbi (Esther) for almost two decades? All this when neither could read Hebrew or tell you what the weekly Torah portion was. Nor had they given up bacon, ever kept kosher, or thought for a second about the kind of work one can and cannot do on Shabbat.

More worrisome, why was it that my own children seemed only sometimes interested in things Jewish? Why was it that I was so often at Shabbat services alone, davening alone at home on weekdays, praying alone at Saturday services, but my children mostly unaware? Not quite indifferent, but not yet ready to make a commitment. Not yet ready to join a synagogue, but at least not drifting into the gentile faiths, or believing in Jesus as had some of Esther's siblings after they have moved to Los Angeles.

So then, in truth, I am writing this book for several reasons: to honor the memory of Sol and Anna and Esther and Joe, but also to try to find the words that have eluded me for so long; the words that express my own belief in the Jewish notion of God: that somewhere in our collective ancient history, we were all at Sinai, all of us Jews, and that we entered into a covenant with God that imposed on us a life-long obligation of duty and commitment, that same duty that made me devote so much of my life to causes of economic justice, and compelled me to serve on Jewish boards. It is this unshakeable belief, for which I have never found the right words when said out loud to those around me, that was trying to find its voice in the memory of those who came before me. Was it possible that by writing about Sol and Anna and Esther and Joe, some part of this would emerge for me as well? If I could explain some part of their lives, then perhaps I could explain a part of my own. After all, were not Sol and Anna and Esther and Joe with all of us at Sinai? Isn't that what they would have wanted me to say, if they, too, had found their voice when there was still time?

Making Sol and Anna reappear here has required both research, memory, and imagination. I don't know their words, not exactly, but in some way my imagination fills the void. I see their faces and I learn their history and, with each new fact, each new piece of geography, I hear more and understand better. And so I become their advocate; their voice, and I can turn, at last, to the story and arguments of those who got me here. This is what I owe them. Because, other than memory, if Jewish law teaches us anything, it is that gratitude for the life given to us, and to those who put all of this into motion, is what truly makes us human, and gives us a sense of contentment, of peace.

So then, what exactly were Sol and Anna doing in America, and how did they get here?

Chanukah/Christmas week: December 2017

CHAPTER 1

On Forgetting

Sol on Broadway (Chicago 1930)

IN THE SUMMER OF 1930, if you had been walking down North Broadway Street in Chicago, coming at last to number 2951, at the street's intersection with Wellington Avenue, you might well have spotted Sol Kuney. Sol is by then a moderately prosperous tailor. He is modestly dressed, in dark grey suit pants, white dress shirt and tie, despite the heat, with his jacket folded neatly over his arm. He taught me later how to fold clothes properly. Almost six feet tall and solidly built, he is not quite overweight but not slender either. There is nothing distinctive about his looks. Everyman, in a manner of speaking.

Sol could well have been out for one of his afternoon breaks from his tailor shop, and on his way to pick up the afternoon *Chicago Tribune* and an El Producto cigar, still only a nickel then. There is not much news that day. Herbert Hoover is president and, at his press conference, he announces the appointment of Douglas MacArthur as Chief of Staff of the United States Army. Elsewhere, a local paper in Wapakoneta, Ohio, announces the birth of a baby boy named Neil Armstrong, who will later become the first man to walk on the moon.

Sol makes his way past a three-story low-rise building, with a drug store on the street level, its large canopy providing shade from the hot August sun, with apartments above the retail, all flush with the sidewalk. The landscape is static; time standing still. In fact, almost nothing has changed since Sol's stroll that afternoon, except now the awning reads Bobtail Ice

Cream Company. Other than that one detail, the street looks and feels largely the same today as it did on that summer day in 1930.[1]

Lake Michigan is to the east, and when the mood strikes, it sends a cool wind that creeps over the cement sidewalk, bleached by the sun and heat and by the cold. Chicago weather is unforgiving. The lake has no mercy. In winter, it turns into ice and freezes the wind, and in summer, it selfishly surrenders only the smallest breeze to cool the day.

Nearby is the North Pier and what will later become the Dime Pier and Tony's. In 1930, fried shrimp sold for fifty cents for a brown paper bag overflowing with the daily catch, and the sweet fragrance of the freshly fried shrimp, still dripping with hot grease, would easily make its way to Broadway. Sol could pick up the aroma on his walk, but Anna's two sets of dishes, one for meat and one for dairy, meant the greasy bag with this *trayf* (nonkosher food) was not coming home. Yet Sol, and later Joe, Sol's son, would find their way to the pier more than a few times over the years. Today, however, Sol is alone and is mindful of the greasy bag lest it stain his pants; a tailor cannot be too careful.

Sol and Anna live in the same building where Sol has his shop, a few doors away from the corner, at number 2945 Broadway.[2] I was often there. When I was young, we played catch with our baseball during our short summer trips back "home." A neighbor taught us how to play marbles on the back porch, which was in truth just a large common area for all the residents to share. The porch was gray, ugly, and large, but mostly a fire escape. Still, it was a place where three boys could play for hours on a splintering and weathered-wood frame that was covered with cheap tar, but if we were not careful it would leave dusty black residue on our hands and clothes, and Esther, our mother, would complain. Chicago seemed dirty to us; we were kids of the suburbs, and cities frightened us.

Sol's tailor business, at 2935 Broadway,[3] was across an alley separating two structures. The building is still standing. Of course, there is no plaque reminding passersby that once this was where our family had worked and

1. See Google Maps, 2951 North Broadway, Chicago, Illinois, and 2945 Broadway. The building was constructed in 1911 and although renovated on the inside, appears almost exactly the same as it did over 80 years ago. See Zillow.com for 2951 North Broadway.

2. The 1930 census shows that Sol and Anna lived at 2935 Broadway, and it is possible they lived above the tailor shop until shortly after 1930, when they moved into the larger building across the alley. My recollection from visits while a pre-teen is that they lived and worked in the same structure, with the alley and the wooden balconies in the rear of the building, all still visible today.

3. Sol's draft registration card, filled out in 1942, says his place of business was at 2931 Broadway.

lived. We were too ordinary, our history not worth remembering. Sol was a good tailor, patient and skillful, and his business did well. Customers liked him and they trusted him with their clothes.Today, the retail shop is City Press. Next door is a small Mexican carry-out. In the intervening ninety years or so, the stores have come and gone. So, too, the people. Still, I see Sol standing outside, taking a break from his work, perhaps thinking about his life in Vilna, or perhaps not. Maybe he, too, is in the business of forgetting.

If you asked him, he would say the tailoring business was good. It is the Great Depression, yet Sol is doing reasonably well. Things still need mending. Waistlines grow and shrink. Old clothes need to be repaired. Sol takes care of his family, and they are never forced to move from their home. Sol continues to run his business without interruption despite the stock market crash. We never heard any talk of waiting in line for food, pulling money out of the bank, moving west. Yet, still, the Great Depression has left its mark on Sol and his children. Later, Esther will tell us three brothers that when Joe received a scholarship to attend the University of Chicago he had to turn it down because the family could not spare the daily cost of the trolley fare, then a nickel each way. Had Esther, our mother, made up that story to show us what they had endured? She was given to exaggeration, not one to hew too closely to facts.

Sol would likely introduce himself to you as Sol Kuney—not his given name, though one well-suited for America. He would insist his first name was Sol, not Saul, not Solomon. Hardly a name that his parents—Russian craftsmen or artisans, I am guessing—would have chosen. Solomon was proud to be Jewish; after all, he was King of Judea, the son of King David. Does our Sol think of himself as Jewish? Does he ever see himself at Sinai, part of the great covenant of a chosen people, or does he think of himself only as one of many immigrants from Eastern Europe, from a country with no name or too many names, like himself, not even sure of what to call himself?

Sol has invented a new name for himself in his new country. Sol was born Zelick Kurenitzky. Zelick becomes Sol, just as Kurenitzky becomes Kuney. I spent decades guessing how and when our last name was changed to Kuney. I was all but certain it was the act of some immigration agent, meeting Sol at the dock or harbor, not quite understanding what Sol had said when asked his name, and recording his best guess on the ship manifest.

Yet, this is not what really happened. It turns out that Kurenitzky survived the ocean crossing, and that it was not until 1920, when Sol applied for citizenship, that he asked a federal district court to change his name to Kuney. Perhaps the sound of this new name struck him as more American. Or perhaps he just wanted to forget. Not a mistake, after all, just more erasing of things gone by.

No matter. The old names, the original names are gone, forgotten. *Good riddance*, he might have thought. Sol, then, as I see him in 1930, is unmoored to any fixed beginning, other than his arrival in America, having left Vilna behind. Perhaps he has left his personal history behind as well— no accident this, knowing full well what that means, and intending a new birth here, free from the Old Country, free from whatever responsibility a history means. In some sense, then, Sol is done with the Old Country now that he has been in America since 1913.

He speaks English with a slight accent, just enough so you would know he was not from here. He is a plain person, in some ways entirely suited for the plain-spoken and modest mode of the Midwest, with values that feed themselves into his children's and grandchildren's views and beliefs about what it means to be a person. We learned to live without affectation. No need to call attention to ourselves. Simple clothing. Nothing to stand out. Looking back now, my memory makes Sol sound too plain, I seem to be flattening out his intricacies, because I am failing to look deeply enough at the man he was. Or worse, by some lack of empathy? How we treat the old. Nothing to be proud of.

When I knew him, Sol rarely mentioned the Old Country, perhaps because he knew he could never fully make it come alive for us and better, he thought, to hold his tongue than to seem like a foolish old man. I recall a lingering sadness, a melancholy, unspoken perhaps. And I see it now, never changing, when I look at the photos and the homemade films of him and his two sons, my father and my uncle. An absence of lightheartedness, no easy smile, the joy always somewhat forced. Ours was not a family that smiled much anyway. Leave his memories to himself, he must have thought.

But as a young man in Chicago, Sol had a certain modest grace, and was not averse to talking to strangers. He would not have been offended or surprised if you had asked him where he was from, or when he was born. He would have said "Vilna, Russia, 1892." But on another day, you would probably get a different answer. In fact, he has a different answer each time he is asked. He will tell the 1920 census taker that he was born in 1892. Ten years later, he will tell the census taker he was born in 1893. And, then, in 1940, Sol will manage to change his age yet again, telling the census taker he was born in 1894. All these pieces of history just slip away: the names, the dates, the places. How is one to remember when so much forgetting has already occurred?

If Sol had said he was from Russia, well then, I should warn you not to put too much stock in that answer either. He would have been only partly correct. He is in truth from Lithuania, or what we know as Lithuania today.

Oddly, I never once heard him say Lithuania—only Russia or Poland, with the boundaries somehow changing at will. Lithuania seemed to have been wiped clean from his memory. I never understood how boundaries could change, but I simply let this odd piece of information slip past me without trying to piece together the mystery of a place having two names and two countries attached to it. Do countries disappear? A people can. By the 1940s, all of the Jews of Lithuania had left or been murdered by the Nazis. So maybe this was something Sol simply chose not to remember. Besides, who could have understood the magnitude of what lay frozen in his silenced memory?

What did Sol's parents do to earn their keep? They were peasants perhaps, but the more I learn, the more I think they were likely a bit more prosperous than that. Middle-class tradesmen, more than likely. Why didn't I ask? And now I am left to piece together entire generations from the barest of fragments. Oddly though, I am not deterred. The imagination has its own power, its own truth, and it can traverse time and history without fear of modest error. So then, in this sense, I begin to see, or feel, that Sol's mother and father, whose first names I never learn, are not likely among the poorest of Vilna. They must, after all, have had enough money to afford the passage west for Sol when that time came. Between the cost of the ticket and the bribing of ticket sellers and port agents, the journey was costly.[4]

Sol was an accomplished tailor by the time I meet him in the 1950s. Did his father do the same? Sol never told me. Why was Sol silent about the family that did not join him in America? Did he mourn their loss? His mother, father, and any siblings remain a total mystery to me. Did Sol or Anna have brothers and sisters who were left behind in Vilna when they left? What happened to my great-grandfather and his siblings? Of course, the answer is that none of the Jews of Vilna survived the Nazi invasion. In June 1941, the Nazis invaded the city and were careful and systematic in rounding up and killing every Jew, starting first with the intellectuals, the lawyers, the doctors, and the community leaders—not by gas, but by rifle and machine gun, and then into mass graves, all lost. Still, the Romans kept coming. Were they not finished with us?

What Sol left behind is now gone. Time and place both disappear—good reason, then, to forget it. No going back now. Likewise, the Romans burned Jerusalem to the ground, and then, for completeness' sake, plowed under

---

4. See generally, Diner, *Roads Taken*. Diner, a Jewish scholar, writes of the difference between the peasant class and the peddler class, these being the two poorer groups that lived in Vilna and Eastern Europe.

every remnant of life until even the dogs refused to scrounge for scraps of food. The ground smoldered for years, smoke rising from the buried debris, not to mention the bodies of Jews who had fought each other at least as hard as they fought the Romans, some say harder, and it is that eternal wrangling among the Jews that caused the temple to fall. So now the holy site is gone. Rabbis cry from the distant banks of Babylonia. It will take 2,000 years to repair this history. So, too, later with Vilna. Buildings, cities, worlds—all come and go.

All of this forgetting will have consequences. There is nothing casual about what Sol has done: wiping the slate clean, hoping for a fresh start, the memory of his ancestors and their faith starting to disappear. Soon he loses the ability to transmit this history to his son, my father, and then my father to us. We will always be starting over without a history that we truly understand, stranded in the modern era, unmoored, and without the knowledge of all that preceded us. Too much has been lost. The spoken word was the conversation between generations, and now we cannot hear it.

And Sol is not alone. This is what those who came on those same ships seemed intent on doing. This is the universal forgetting that has given full voice to assimilation, so we can pretend that nothing we needed to know was ever given up.

What Sol left behind, though, was a city of enormous Jewish energy and clashing ideas; different notions of what it meant to be Jewish; ideas that could hardly survive one next to the other; ideas that could give birth to one movement and destroy others; the Jewish Enlightenment tugging away at traditional Judaism. Still fighting among themselves just as in the temple days; only worse, because it is now and not then.

Is this what Moses saw when he came down from Mount Sinai and broke the tablets? Not just a golden calf, but more likely a vision of the future? Maybe he saw an enduring and intractable instinct of men to tear away at one another over what it all means; over this notion of covenant and the chosen people. *Were we not supposed to be a nation of priests*, Moses wonders? He saw how hard it would be to hold us all together, and for a moment, in despair, tried to give it up. Still, he went back up the mountain, and now we are here, like it or not, obligated to make sense of this history. All of it. Still glued to the covenant.

But Sol is on a break from work, in Chicago—an American now—not Sinai.

I wish I had met him that day on Broadway, in August 1930, under the relentlessly hot summer sun. I wish now I had met him as a young man, met him as he saw himself, both then and always. For isn't it true that we tend to see ourselves as young, even as we age? A part of our soul is still the youth inside us. We are saddened and dismayed when we realize that only we see that part of us, that others see us as old, though we know for a certainty this image is untrue, is not us. We yearn for the world to see us as we are, with our immutable youth and all its folly. But such is not how it goes.

Where is Anna while Sol is on North Broadway, now headed back to his tailoring shop? When Sol left that morning, he and Anna had continued their long-standing argument over whether Joe, now almost thirteen years old, needed to attend Hebrew school and have a bar mitzvah. Anna insisted, but Sol had refused to pay. Anna had worried about this from the day they met—that this simple tailor was no scholar. She had kept some money set aside, and Joe would prepare for his bar mitzvah despite Sol.

Sol knows Anna will not be happy with him if he is not home in time for Shabbat. His afternoon break is over. Paper in hand, folded, he walks back to his work. Anna is home getting ready for dinner, preparing to light the Shabbat candles and to serve a festive meal: some meat that had been saved for Friday night, too expensive for weekdays. I am almost certain she lights Shabbat candles, hands covering her eyes, saying the blessing in Hebrew or Yiddish. But beyond that, there is not much in the way of observance. Wine? Challah, maybe. But certainly no synagogue.

Anna has told Sol, yet again, to be home in time to light candles, to turn off the oven because there is no cooking on Shabbat, to wash and clean, and get ready to meet the Sabbath. Sol shrugs it off. His Judaism has become more casual; not a rejection, actually, but not a passion. Still, being from Vilna, he is caught between cultures, between doubt and belief, unable to escape what he saw and heard in the Old Country, no matter how hard he tries.

So here they are, a brief look at them both in Chicago in 1930. But their true journey begins in Vilna, which means we must go back in time and memory to see them, to understand them. There seems to be only one way to get to the bottom of this, and now that the boxes are open, I have no choice but to go back to Vilna myself to see what Sol and Anna were doing before they made the journey to America. If Sol will not tell his own story, then I must try to do it for him.

What then was Vilna? And where was Vilna after all?

CHAPTER 2

Vilna

*The Jerusalem of Lithuania—Intimations
of the Sacred (1890–1910)*

WE MEET ANNA ON SHABBAT IN VILNA:
WHEN THINGS WERE STILL JEWISH

SOMEWHERE IN VILNA, OR perhaps in a nearby village, is a young Jewish girl, the daughter of a Jewish shopkeeper and the shopkeeper's wife. It is 1905, give or take. She is Anna Rudashefsky.[1] Her exact age cannot now be known: parts of Anna's history vanished into the ether of forgetfulness, carelessness, and destruction of documents. Even Anna forgets her true birthday. Once in America, in 1930, Anna will tell the census taker that she was born in 1893. Yet, when she dies, and her son Joseph completes her Certificate of Death, he records her date of birth as May 1894.

As best we can tell, Anna is born in a village near Vilna. "Rudashevskij" means from the village of Rudashi, a name that others tell me was common in Vilna. The names of the land are shared with the people who live on the land; the intimacy between geography and people is thus embedded— meant to be remembered and not forgotten.

And yet it is forgotten or lost. Looking through every atlas we have, I am unable to discover any village called Rudashi. But there is more than the name of her village that is lost, at least to those of us who came two generations later. Anna's father also has seemed to disappear from memory. When the three of us were young, we never saw a picture of him, nor of her mother.

---

1. Note there is an alternate spelling on Ancestry.com which has a "c": Radaschefsky.

So it is a surprise when, years later, in going through the boxes, I discover a black-and-white photograph of a man who looks very much like a Jewish scholar, possibly a rabbi. On the back of the picture, in Joe's handwriting, are the words, "Mom's father—Rudashefsky." He is a European-looking, bearded man, but without a wife by his side. That Joseph knew his last name seems odd; when Anna dies on April 12, 1971, Joseph leaves blank Anna's maiden name on the Certificate of Death.

It is not until the spring of 2019, when I visit what used to be the Arlington-Fairfax Jewish Center, and take a photograph of the memorial plaque containing the names of synagogue members who have passed away, that I notice for the first time Anna's name plaque, and the name of my great-grandfather; the plaque reads, in Hebrew, "Anna daughter of rav Fishel David." I am surprised that Fishel's middle name is David. Have I been named after him? How odd that, at age seventy-three, I first learn the possible origin of my name. If I'd known earlier, things might have been different. Perhaps a question or two more? How was I to carry out whatever secret hopes Esther and Joe may have had when they gave me that name?

Yet, more strikingly, there is the Hebrew letter *resh* before Fishel's name, the Hebrew equivalent of an "R" in English. I am at first told that this is a form of Hebrew shorthand for "rabbi." This information is from a reliably well-educated Jewish scholar. Yet, a further search reveals that the Hebrew letter *resh* before a man's name simply means "mister" and that one needs the full expression, *Ha rav*, to mean "the rabbi." Still, the only remaining photograph I have of Fishel appears to show him with a skull cap, or yarmulke, and looking not a little rabbinic.

Of course, it seems unlikely that Esther and Joe would never mention that Fishel had been a rabbi if this were true, and certainly neither Steve nor I recalls hearing anything like this. When I ask, no one else in the family recalls Anna saying that her father was a rabbi. That this would have escaped everyone's notice seems unlikely.

I find myself wishing he had been a rabbi. I was excited about the prospect of being the great-grandson of a rabbi. I would have been responsible for our heritage; taken care of it. This would have been reason enough not to drift away in those moments of doubt and confusion. There had been a brief time when I considered studying to become a rabbi. But the mere thought of trying to achieve this in my late sixties or early seventies was hardly feasible—not to mention my inexplicably weak skills with Hebrew.

But Fishel was no rabbi, after all. Anna's father was the owner of a grocery store, and presumably the family was part of the thriving economic life of Vilna and the villages surrounding it. The photographs I find in the box suggest they are on the order of the middle class: not wealthy, but not peasants either. There is no talk later, in Arlington, of poverty in the Old Country.

Anna's mother is also a mystery. We never learn either her maiden name or her first name, and we never see a picture of her—at least not until 2019. That is when, after I open the boxes, I discover a picture of what I now believe is Anna's mother. This woman, my great-grandmother, looks more cheerful and light-hearted than Fishel. The photograph, like that of Anna's father, is a studio portrait, so someone had enough money to spend on what must have been something of a luxury. Anna's mother is young and stylishly dressed in a fashion that could well have been recognized in Paris or London or elsewhere in Europe. Her leaning pose is slightly frivolous, as if she were taking a stroll, no hint of piety. She appears instead to be a woman of society, well-groomed and refined.

Anna is well-educated, at least for a young woman of that period. Anna tells the census taker in America that she has completed two years of high school. This is an achievement, as most girls at that time did not attend high school. She is able to read and write, and later will easily learn English and speak fluently, almost without accent. When she meets Sol, she worries that he is not an educated man, merely an apprentice tailor, humble and not learned. At least, this is what she told her son Julius decades later.

Anna has no formal education in things Jewish, however, or if she did, she never says a word about it once she comes to America. She never reads from the Torah, and I am certain she does not speak or read Hebrew. Still, she had a love of things Jewish that we all saw later, in Arlington, when she had long since left Vilna. Had she been able to read the great narratives, she might have seen some part of herself within them. In thinking about Anna now, so long after her death, I see how plainly she walked in the path of these biblical narratives, at times with the courage of a Ruth who followed her mother-in-law to wherever she was headed.

RELIGIOUS LIFE IN VILNA: VILNA AS THE JERUSALEM OF LITHUANIA

I never asked Anna to tell me what her Jewish life was like before she and Sol came to America, even when we sat around the Passover table, many years later, in Arlington. Had I done so, she almost certainly would have told me that Vilna was known as the "Jerusalem of Lithuania."[2] Napoleon named it

---

2. Seltzer, *Jewish People, Jewish Thought,* 484. "Vilna became an important focus of Jewish intellectual life from the mid-eighteenth century until the twentieth century.

"the Jerusalem of the North."[3] Everywhere, it seems, were Jewish neighbors. Jewish ideas were inescapable.

A German scholar, writing years later about Vilna, would recall:

> When I entered the streets all was quiet. For the first time in my life I had an idea of a Sabbath as celebrated by our ancestors in the holy land in times of yore. Heaven and earth, moon and stars, houses and streets, all preached: 'It is the Sabbath, the day consecrated by the Lord.' All the stores were closed: no cart was moving in the street; a holy tranquility reigned everywhere. . . . It was as if the whole city had put on its holiday attire to receive in a dignified manner the heavenly bride of the Sabbath.[4]

In Jewish Vilna, the eye and mind are in constant touch with things Jewish—icons and structures—so unlike what Sol and Anna will later encounter in a very different world once they reach Virginia. But here, in Vilna, Jewish life surrounded them and could not escape their notice.

Towering above all was the Great Synagogue, erected in the 1600s when architects were brought from Italy and Germany to build a synagogue of brick to replace the existing wood-frame structure. The Great Synagogue served as the spiritual center of the Jewish community in Vilna from the 1600s until the 1940s, when the Nazis burnt it to the ground. But, unlike their Roman predecessors, the Nazis neglected to plow it under, leaving intact for future discovery the massive basement and substructure.

Sol and Anna and their neighbors are surrounded by over a hundred synagogues and *Kloizes* or study halls. Vilna had hundreds of Jewish educational institutions, many of them *cheders*—traditional elementary schools that teach Hebrew and other Jewish subjects, in which 13,000 students studied.[5]

Vilna was long a magnet for the leading Jewish scholars and thinkers. In 1768, a 48-year-old scholar, Elijah ben Solomon Zalman, later known as the Vilna Gaon (1720–1797), moves to Vilna. He is considered by some to be among the greatest Jewish scholars in Jewish history.[6] He is revered almost as a saint in Vilna and elsewhere in Europe. He wrote commentaries

---

(Vilna came to be called the Jerusalem of Lithuania—a lively center not only of traditional rabbinic scholarship, but of the nineteenth-century Jewish Enlightenment and Jewish social radicalism as well.)"

   3. "Napoleon Named Vilnius 'Jerusalem of the North.'"

   4. Cutler, *Jews of Chicago*, 45. Dr. Max Lilienthal, a German Jewish scholar, writing in 1941 on his visit to Vilna.

   5. "Beginnings of the Vilna Community."

   6. Zalkin, "Vilnius."

on the Bible, the Mishnah, the Babylonian and Jerusalem Talmuds, the midrash literature, the Zohar, and the Shulhan Arukh. The Gaon focused on Jewish literacy. He stressed the importance of the Jewish canonical texts and mastering Hebrew grammar as well as secular science, because it would promote a better understanding of the devotional text. "His corrections [to prior interpretations] of the Talmud appear in the margin of every edition of the Talmud today."[7]

I doubt that Sol and Anna actually saw much of this observant Judaism in Vilna. Vilna was at once both the home of rabbinic scholarship and the birthplace of Jewish social radicalism.[8] Vilna was a hotbed of dissent.

In truth, there are two Vilnas. Judaism is going through one of its most disruptive periods in Europe when Sol and Anna are there, still young, still impressionable. Unlike what they will later find in suburban America, where religion is often an afterthought, an occasional venture to church or synagogue, in Vilna, how one practiced being Jewish, was the subject of intense debate and even verbal fights within the synagogue. The Jewish community splintered into the deeply observant on the one hand, and those who were seeking a more secular view, one more focused on the daily tasks of making a living—a sense of Judaism that asked little, and required neither great learning nor a study of Torah.

The movement that would likely shape Sol's life and ultimately find its way, however transformed, to Arlington, is known as the Haskalah movement. The word *haskalah* means "rationalism." The Haskalah movement, sometimes known as the Jewish Enlightenment, "found fertile soil in Lithuania."[9]

Haskalah was said to be the "beginning of modern Jewish history."[10] It was described by one scholar as "the Jewish version of the European Enlightenment of the eighteenth century, which substituted this-worldliness, rationalism, universalism for the other-worldliness, authoritarianism, and exclusivism of the medieval world."[11] It was seen as the "hinge on which the European nations turned from the Middle Ages to 'modern' times marking

7. Greenbaum, *Jews of Lithuania*, 84.

8. Seltzer, *Jewish People, Jewish Thought*, 484.

9. Greenbaum, *Jews of Lithuania*, 115.

10. Goldsmith et al., *American Judaism of Mordecai M. Kaplan*, 20.

11. Goldsmith et al., *American Judaism of Mordecai M. Kaplan*, 21.

the passage from a supernaturalistic-mythical-authoritative to a naturalistic-scientific type of thinking."[12]

Haskalah adherents "considered themselves rationalists in the secular humanist sense, and taught that reason was the yardstick by which all should be measured. Such a prescription could only lead to conflict with traditionalist forces."[13] So substantial was the impact of this Jewish Enlightenment, that Rabbi Mordecai Kaplan, who founded the Reconstructionist movement, stated thus: "The conceptions of God, Israel, Torah, human nature, sin, repentenance, messianic redemption, and the world to come in pre-modern Traditional Judaism belong to a radically different universe of thought, or world outlook, from that of the average westernized Jew."[14]

Sol and Anna came of age in Vilna shortly after the Haskalah movement had been most active. Still, its effects lingered, and there is no way to understand Sol and Anna's sense of Judaism, and the sense that they then transmitted to their children, and then to us, first in Arlington and now here in suburban America, without at least some sense of the debates that were ongoing in Vilna when Sol and Anna were there.

THE RAMAYLES YESHIVA:
INTIMATIONS OF DISBELIEF

Only a few years after Sol and Anna left Vilna, two young schoolboys at the Vilna Yeshiva, both of whom later become famous scholars, were arguing with one another over the Talmudic texts—two men whose paths would directly and intimately cross with both Sol and Anna in America.[15] One would become their rabbi in Arlington, Noah Golinkin. The other was Chaim Grade, the brother of Abraham Grade, Sol's first cousin, who took Sol into his home when Sol first arrived in Chicago in 1913.[16]

12. Goldsmith et al., *American Judaism of Mordecai M. Kaplan*, 21.

13. Greenbaum, *Jews of Lithuania*, 115.

14. Kaplan, *Greater Judaism in the Making*, 5.

15. The following is a quote from an introduction, written by David Golinkin, to an English edition of a booklet written by Noah Golinkin: "The rest of his life [Noah's] can be divided into four periods. [1] He spent his formative years ca. 1920–1938, in and around Vilna where he studied at the famous Ramayles Yeshiva together with the Yiddish writer Chaim Grade . . ." (YIVO Institute for Jewish Research, "Center of Jewish Scholarship," para. 2.).

16. Chaim Grade is likely Sol's "half-cousin"—this because Abraham and Chaim have different mothers—although it is decades before we realize the family connection.

Elie Wiesel would later write that Chaim Grade was the greatest living Yiddish writer. In Grade's novel, *The Yeshiva*, he wrote at length about his profound doubts about nearly everything Jewish, including his belief in God. Sol and Anna may well have been influenced by the Grade family, and Chaim's strong and outspoken views on Judaism.

Noah Golinkin, also at the Ramayles Yeshiva, became Chaim Grade's *hevrutah* partner, a practice in which Jewish students study in pairs, and they debated their deeply divergent views. Golinkin, who is strictly observant and a believer in text, will one day leave Vilna and become the rabbi of the Arlington-Fairfax Jewish Center, where he meets Sol and his son Joe. In contrast to Chaim, Golinkin comes to Arlington to resurrect both the Hebrew language and a more observant, conservative adherence to Jewish law and custom.

Noah and Chaim may have been having the same argument that is dividing the Jews in Vilna, if not across all of Eastern Europe. Had Sol and Anna gone inside one of the many *shuls*, including even the Great Synagogue, they could not have missed the sharp division among the Jewish population, and would have likely witnessed some of the more severe outbursts and fighting that was part of Jewish life in Vilna.

So, here then, in the Jerusalem of Lithuania, we see the inevitable—if not eternal—clash between strict obedience to Jewish law and observance on the one hand, and a more secular, rational view on the other. The same arguments that Chaim Grade and Noah Golinkin were likely having in the Yeshiva, the struggle over belief and doubt, were the same arguments that Sol and Anna brought with them to America, along with all of the others who came with small suitcases and a history of questions. Grade's wife would later describe this as the conflict between the sacred and the profane.

By the time Sol and Anna settled in America and had children, the argument had become a quieter resentment, each of the other's view. Yet, you could see it in the small details, if you looked: Anna, with her three sets of dishes, head covered, saying the blessing over the Shabbat candles, insisting that Joe attend Hebrew school and have a bar mitzvah; Sol, ambivalent at best and unwilling to pay for Joe's Jewish education. Sol in the background, leaning against the fireplace while she lights the candles, mind drifting to some work left undone on the sewing machine, having his evening *schnapps*. Sol, with his eye on his tasks, remains tolerant of his wife's Jewish devotion, but is always a few steps behind Anna—never the deep embrace.

These arguments have made their way from Vilna to Arlington and to assimilated America. It was not America that gave rise to assimilation. It was something more ageless, and permanent, a condition of the Jewish soul regardless of time or place. Assimilation in America was nothing more than an extension of beliefs that were deeply rooted in an older country.

We are not a didactic people—we have no pope. Our embrace of God has been one constant argument, and I see no end to this. Sol and Anna, Chaim and Noah, and all of the future generations, all wrapped up in the endless arguments about what Torah means and what God wants of us.

CHAPTER 3

Love and Death in Vilna

Reason Enough to Leave (1911–1913)

THE END OF LITHUANIA-POLAND AND
THE SEEDS OF THE MIGRATION

WHY IS IT THAT when we meet Sol on the streets of Chicago, in 1930, he will say he is from Russia? Vilna is not, of course, in Russia. It is in Lithuania. Sometimes Sol and Anna say that Vilna was part of Poland. But that was never true when Sol and Anna were there. And they never speak of our family history in terms of Poland. Why is it that Sol and Anna never once uttered a word about Lithuania to us—when we were young and often at their table?

Sol and Anna arrive in America and steadfastly declare themselves Russians. Every document Sol signed in the United States claims he was from Russia. It is what Sol told us, although he always obscured this by saying the boundaries kept changing, so that first Vilna was in one country, and then another. How could Vilna have been in three different countries in such a short time span? And did this constant changing of national boundaries have an impact on Sol and Anna's decision to leave Vilna?

Sol and Anna's great-grandparents were from what was once part of the Polish-Lithuanian Commonwealth, a dualistic state ruled by a common monarch who was both the King of Poland and Grand Duke of Lithuania. At its peak in the early seventeenth century, the Commonwealth spanned almost 400,000 square miles and had a multiethnic population of 11 million people.[1] It attracted scholars, universities, and leading Jewish thinkers. Poland-Lithuania was once the largest state in Europe.

Sol and Anna's grandparents (or possibly their great-grandparents) were likely alive to see the end of the Polish-Lithuanian Commonwealth, and the annexation of this Commonwealth by Russia—which explains why Sol and Anna tell us they were from Russia, or "what was once part of Russia." It also explains why there were pogroms, a draft, and then, ultimately, the need to flee Vilna and to become part of the great migration from Eastern Europe to America.

The Polish-Lithuanian Commonwealth was torn apart in "The Great Crime of Empires," ending in 1795, which marked the horrifying "destruction of a state."[2] One scholar describes this as a twenty-year period in which "surrounding empires ate the state of Poland-Lithuania alive."[3]

What is known as the first partition took place in 1772, when Russia, Prussia, and Austria moved in their armies and grabbed territories for themselves. As part of this land grab, Russia gained lands in the east that had been part of Lithuania, and are today's Belarus and parts of Ukraine.

The second partition occurred in 1791 and 1792. It was during this period that Sol and Anna's ancestors became Russian, and lost their sense of national identity as part of the Polish-Lithuanian state. Catherine the Great of Russia grabbed land to the west of Russia's borders, an enormous land mass: "More than a hundred times the size of Great Britain and three times larger than the United States. . . .[I]ts population doubled from about 74 million inhabitants in 1861 to about 150 million by 1905."[4]

Catherine the Great forced the Jews from Russia to move into this newly created Russian territory.[5] This—the Pale of Settlement—is where Sol and Anna's parents made their home.[6] And it is from this Pale of Settle-

---

1. "Commonwealth of Poland," para. 1.

2. Liulevicius, *History of Eastern Europe*, 63.

3. Liulevicius, *History of Eastern Europe*, 63.

4. Merriman, *History of Modern Europe*, 2:716.

5. The Pale of Settlement was huge. It included all of Belarus, Lithuania, and Moldova, much of present-day Ukraine, parts of eastern Latvia, eastern Poland, and some parts of western Russia. In all, it comprised about 20 percent of the territory of European Russia and largely corresponded to the historical lands of the former Polish-Lithuanian Commonwealth, the Cossack Hetmanate, and the Ottoman Empire.

6. Merriman, *History of Modern Europe*, 2:716. Professor Merriman, the Charles Seymour Professor of History at Yale University, writes that by 1855, the Russian Empire stretched from its western border with Austria-Hungary, moving eastward to the Bering Sea, the Sea of Okhotsk, and nearing the Pacific Ocean, with Siberia bordering Mongolia and China. Its easternmost port was at Vladivostok, on the Sea of Japan, not far from the mainland of Japan. Maps of that time showed Poland within the Russian Empire.

ment that Sol and Anna will one day flee—although not without risk and great difficulty.

At its height, the Pale, including the new Polish and Lithuanian territories with a Jewish population of over 5 million, comprised the largest component (40 percent) of the world's Jewish population at that time. Thus, a vast Jewish population found itself in the embrace of the "Russian bear."[7]

The third partition occurred in 1795, and it explains why Sol did not think of himself as Polish. "In 1795, the three empires completed the third and last partition of Poland-Lithuania, gobbling up the remaining territories. With matchless cynicism, the occupying powers also agreed to abolish the memory of Poland—to not use the name for the territory in documents. After 800 years of history, Poland was to be forgotten."[8]

By 1795, the Polish-Lithuanian Commonwealth had been completely erased from the map of Europe. The memory of a separate Lithuania was gone from Sol's memory or at least from the memory he cared to share with us. From 1795 until 1914 (after both Sol and Anna had left Vilna), historic Lithuania—Kaunas, Grodno, Minsk, Moghliev, and Vitebsk—was part of the "Northwest Territory" of the Russian Empire.[9]

And so it was that Sol and Anna would call themselves Russians, and rarely, if ever, mentioned any Polish heritage or ancestry. Lithuania was also forgotten. So forgotten that Sol would never once refer to Lithuania as his native country when filling out forms for the census taker or registering for the draft.

For Sol and Anna, the annexation of their homeland by Russia was the reason they and so many others had to leave Vilna. Through this massive annexation, Russia wound up with a Jewish population that it detested and wanted to be rid of. It was from this that pogroms came, the horrific draft by the tsar, and finally the need to flee, to emigrate. Jews had to leave Vilna because it was the Jerusalem of Lithuania, and if there was anything the Russians hated, it was the Jews.

POGROMS—THE "LONGEST HATRED" IN THE WORLD

Sol told us from time to time about the pogroms. It was a word he used often. We are in Chicago for a family visit, driving with Esther and Joe in their two-door, blue-and-white 1949 Pontiac—the three brothers in the

---

7. Greenbaum, *Jews of Lithuania,* 160.

8. Liulevicius, *History of Eastern Europe,* 67.

9. Greenbaum, *Jews of Lithuania,* 160.

back with Anna. I am seven or eight, and Sol is speaking of things I do not understand.

Driving through the city streets, and listening in the cramped back seat, Sol is telling us about fierce German shepherd dogs that the soldiers trained by beating to make them cruel, and about Cossacks riding horses into the city looking to maim or kill the people who lived there. Sol described the Cossacks as marauding soldiers, high on their horses and carrying large curved swords. *Who were these horrible creatures?* we wondered. A fairy tale of horror. No wonder they left Vilna. No need to tell us more. I stared out the car window at Chicago, itself dismal to our suburban eyes. *From what horrifying place had our strange grandparents come?* we thought. Surely it no longer existed.

Sol's fear of the Cossacks was well-grounded. The Cosssacks were a separate form of terror for Sol and Anna—not always connected to the pogroms. The Cossacks were a people of mixed ethnic origins who had settled mostly in the vast steppe (grassland plains) that stretched from Asia to southern Europe. Their military was particularly fierce and was known for its equestrian skills, courtesy of the Russian military. Indeed, rulers of the Grand Duchy of Moscow and the Polish-Lithuanian Commonwealth employed Cossacks as mobile guards against Tatar raids from what is now Ukraine. By the sixteenth century, the Cossacks were already known as having a unique warrior culture and were conducting raids and pillaging against their neighbors. "The resulting orgy of carnage had few parallels in history at the time. The murder of Jews was *de rigeur.* . . They were only the first victims of widespread slaughter."[10]

Sol's stories about the Cossacks and the pogroms were brief, nothing more than a few words here and there, but he repeated them often. His words were more than enough to frighten us, and left us convinced that whatever Old Country he and Anna came from, we would never want to visit.

I had no way then to understand this long-standing hatred of the Jews. The pogroms and the virulent anti-Semitism of pre-Hitler Europe have been described as the "Longest Hatred" in the world. Attacks occurred throughout the Pale of Settlement. Devastating anti-Jewish pogroms occurred from 1881 to 1883 and from 1903 to 1906, targeting hundreds of communities, assaulting thousands of Jews, and causing widespread property damage.[11] What made the pogroms more serious and sinister than random violence

---

10. Greenbaum, *Jews of Lithuania*, 31.
11. Greenbaum, *Jews of Lithuania*, 187 (discussing "large-scale arson by pogoromists).

is that they were almost always organized and directed by the government, including, at times, senior army officers and court officials.[12]

I wonder now if Sol had been holding back, not wanting to recall this part of his history, and maybe not wanting his grandchildren to know how close the Jews had come to extinction in Eastern Europe, even decades before Hitler.

Sol's stories fail to illuminate the entirety of the pogroms or their unimaginable horror. And they fail to show how the acts of terror in one generation continue to reverberate through future generations; how the wrongs committed in Lithuania against the Jews when Sol was young were followed by the next generation in Lithuania committing similar atrocities. So it is that history is always with us; and when we forget the past, we are in mortal peril.

Under Nicholas II, the last czar of Russia (1894–1917), anti-semitism and pogroms expanded. As one scholar noted, "The many pogroms were a turning point in Russian Jewish History. They brought death, maiming, and suffering on a very large scale and uprooted masses of Jews who suddenly found themselves homeless and with no country of their own to which to turn."[13]

The Kishinev Pogrom occurs when Sol is about twelve years old—a pogrom that will later lead to rallies and protests in Paris, London, and New York.[14] On April 6 to 7, 1903—a savage pogrom rocked Kishinev, the capital of Bessarabia. "Forty-nine Jews were brutally massacred and another 495 were wounded, eight of whom died in the hospital. Seven hundred homes and 600 businesses and shops were looted and destroyed. Over 2,000 families were left homeless."[15]

A group known as the "Black Hundreds" were "murderous gangs responsible for the killing and raping of innumerable Jews. . . . They were proud and happy only when they were able to show proof of having 'killed or mutilated a few peaceful *zhidi*.'"[16]

What Sol saw and heard never really ended—not during his lifetime at least. The hatred of Jews throughout the Russian Empire carried well into the future, and three decades later, in 1941, shortly before the Nazis invaded Lithuania, the locals participated in savage killings of Jews. "Jewish men, women and children were hunted down and butchered savagely in every

---

12. Greenbaum, *Jews of Lithuania*, 187.
13. Greenbaum, *Jews of Lithuania*, 188.
14. Greenbaum, *Jews of Lithuania*, 199.
15. Greenbaum, *Jews of Lithuania*, 198.
16. Greenbaum, *Jews of Lithuania*, 203.

city and townlet where they were found. Synagogues were torched."[17] The killings were carried out by Lithuanians. Photographs of Lithuanian men and women—the men dressed in suits—watched as Jews were killed in the streets, cheering each death in this the Kaunas Pogrom.[18]

On June 25, 1941, Lithuanian partisans "decapitated the Chief Rabbi of Slobodka, Zalman Ossovsky, and displayed his head in the front window of his house. His headless body was discovered in another room, seated near an open volume of the Talmud that he had been studying."[19] Another version of the murder told by Rabbi Ephrian Oshry is even more gruesome.[20]

In Slobodka, "partisans went from house to house searching for Jews. Their victims were thrown into the River Vilja; those who did not drown were shot to death as they swam. Jewish houses were set afire and their occpuants burned alive as partisans blocked the path of approaching firefighters."[21]

Little wonder, then, that when the Nazis finally arrived, they "were blessed and lauded as the liberators of Lithuania . . . [because] the Jews had it coming for having 'collaborated' with the atheist Bolsheviks." Historians could thus write, without exaggeration, that when Sol and Anna lived in Vilna, and when pogroms were commonplace, "[t]he Pale [had begun] to disgorge its desperate Jewish inhabitants."[22]

Sol's stories told during our drives through Chicago come back to me often—both the parts he said and the parts he left unsaid. Years later, in Vienna, Austria, I stood in front of a statue of a Jew on his hands and knees, scrubbing away the blood from the cobblestone street. But what good is that cleaning now that there is no way to wash away the blood? That blood is my ancestors' blood. And that is why I have thrown my lot in with these Jews, those who died in Europe, those whose blood is still on those streets, because that is our blood, my blood, the blood of all times, and no washing will make it go away.

17. Greenbaum, *Jews of Lithuania*, 305.

18. See "Kaunas Pogrom" (photograph showing killing of Jews with well dressed Lithuanians watching). https://en.wikipedia.org/wiki/Kaunas_pogrom#/media/File: Massacre_of_Jews_in_Lietūkis_garage.jpeg.

19. Greenbaum, *Jews of Lithuania*, 307.

20. "According to Rabbi Ephraim Oshry, there were Germans present on the bridge to Slobodka, but it was the Lithuanian volunteers who killed the Jews. The rabbi of Slobodka, Rav Zalman Osovsky, was tied hand and foot to a chair, "then his head was laid upon an open volume of gemora (volume of the Talmud) and [they] sawed his head off, after which they murdered his wife and son. His head was placed in a window of the residence, bearing a sign: 'This is what we'll do to all the Jews'" ("Kaunas Pogrom," para. 3).

21. Greenbaum, *Jews of Lithuania*, 307.

22. Greenbaum, *Jews of Lithuania*, 189.

So, Sol, when were you going to tell me this?

THE CZAR'S DRAFT: ANOTHER WAY TO KILL OFF THE JEWS

Sol tells us about more than pogroms in those rare moments when he talks about the Old Country. Sol tells us about his fear of being drafted, and surely he and Anna knew that being drafted meant years away from one another, and in many cases, death.

In 1865, when Alexander II was coronated, he announced that Jews would be conscripted into the Russian army on equal terms with non-Jews. The term of military service was sixteen years.[23] According to Nicolas I's military law of 1827, Jews were to provide a limited number of recruits at first. Single Jews, like Sol, not heads of households, were the first choice, with the ultimate draft decision being left to communal leaders.[24] But then, after 1874, all male Jews, irrespective of their social status, became subject to the draft.[25] As such, the proportion of Jews in the Russian army grew much larger than their proportion in the general population.

For young Jewish men like Sol, the draft was a near-certain death sentence. A confidential memorandum dated January 4, 1915, from the Russian High Command, "ordered Jewish soldiers on the front lines to be positioned in the most forward positions and, at times of retreat in the rear, always in the first line of fire."[26] An article in a Russian publication, dated August 12, 1914, stated that, "The Jews should be sent to places that may fall into enemy hands. When our army retakes these places, the Jews may then be expelled as foreigners."[27]

Draft evasion becomes rampant. By the time Sol leaves Vilna in 1913, draft evasion is at its peak when approximately 2,400 males fail to report each year.[28] The annual desertion rate between 1895 and 1900 is 18 percent.[29] Sol must know that his chances of being killed in a pogrom or the army are about the same.

---

23. Greenbaum, *Jews of Lithuania*, 180.

24. Balkelis, "Opening Gates," 53.

25. Balkelis, "Opening Gates," 53–54.

26. Greenbaum, *Jews of Lithuania*. 212.

27. Greenbaum, *Jews of Lithuania*, 210.

28. Balkelis, "Opening Gates," 54.

29. Balkelis, "Opening Gates," 54.

THE MURDER OF ANNA'S MOTHER:
EXILE TO SIBERIA (1906)

Anna tells her son Julius, and then Julius tells his daughter Jo Ellen, the story of Anna's mother. Jo Ellen remembers it well.

Anna's parents owned a grocery store in a village outside of Vilna. One night, after the legal hours for liquor sales had ended, a Cossack came in and demanded liquor. Anna's father, Fishel, refused to sell it to him. Anna was fourteen years old, and her mother was pregnant. Enraged, the Cossack beat Anna's mother to death in front of Anna.

Without a wife, and perhaps with his business failing, Fishel is told that he could burn down the store and collect the insurance. Apparently, what he is not told is that he could be prosecuted for this crime and sent to Siberia, which is exactly what happened.

After her father was imprisoned, Anna was sent to Vilna to live with relatives who were more affluent. If she was fourteen when her mother was murdered, it seems likely she moved in with these relatives around the age of fifteen or sixteen, roughly in 1907.

Vilna was a sophisticated city and an arts center at that time. The relatives took care of Anna and sent her to the "gymnasium" (high school), which was unusual for girls of that period. Anna became an educated young woman, and, as her son Julius later claimed, she felt superior to Sol because of her education. Sol lists his "highest grade completed" on the 1940 census as "elementary school, 8th grade."

SOL AND ANNA MEET AND ARE
MARRIED (1910–1913)

What happens to Sol and Anna between 1910 and 1913 is not entirely clear. If Jo Ellen's version is correct, Anna spends two years in Vilna attending the gymnasium, while her father is in Siberia. Sol, and other young Jewish men like him, are thinking of leaving Vilna and going to America.

I do not know when Sol first meets Anna: After she has moved in with relatives and while her father is in Siberia? After her mother's death, and before her father is sent to Siberia—at a time when Fishel is still trying to make a living in his store? Before Fishel has burned down the store?

I could see Sol going to Fishel's shop for some thread or a cloth to make repairs, or to borrow or buy something he lacks. He meets Anna and is interested, but Anna is shy and unsure. In truth, Anna was never sure about Sol. Was he smart enough? Jewish enough? Too withdrawn or too angry?

I doubt they see much of each other before the marriage. Sol is from Vilna, so if Anna is still living in a nearby village, the chance of seeing each other is remote. They never have the time for long talks and never develop a deep intimacy. And yet, for whatever reason, each senses that they could become a couple, work together, perhaps form a family, all of this in the practical way couples must have viewed such things when options were fewer and life much harder.

So then, not love exactly, but maybe affection, and surely something more practical. Given her looks—not a beauty—Anna knows that finding a man to marry her will not be easy. If nothing else, Sol is a good man who has a trade and can make a living.

Sol may have told Anna that they should marry in Vilna. He may have heard that, once in America, he could arrange for her to come as his wife, and that perhaps it would be easier this way, easier to obtain the needed papers to join one's spouse.

There are no surviving documents confirming the marriage. There is no formal marriage certificate or a *ketubah* (the traditional Jewish marriage contract) that they saved for future generations. There are also no marriage records from Chicago.

Did Sol and Anna love one another? I am not sure I ever saw them embracing, kissing, or holding hands—no words of endearment; no pet names. I look for clues elsewhere. I try to hear them speaking to one another, when young, when old, and in the middle years when I knew them best, but I am stymied, as the only voice I can now recreate is their old voice; yet there was a time, was there not, when they spoke with the softness and eagerness of youth?

Love or not, they stayed together and did what was required: they built a life, paid attention to the details, did the small things that lovers do for one another during the day, the things that speak quietly of a true and enduring love. Perhaps they discovered that, from these acts, love finds its footing, develops.

But this is all in the future. After they marry, Sol and Anna must first leave Vilna, the Jerusalem of Lithuania. Sol boards a ship to America and Anna heads for Siberia to try to find her father. It will take three years before their paths cross again.

CHAPTER 4

The Journey

By Land and By Sea (1913)

"G-d said to Avram, 'Go from your land, from your birthplace, and from your father's house, [and go] to the land I will show you. I will make you into a great nation, I will bless you and make your name great; and you will be a blessing.'"

(GEN 12:1, LECH LECHA)

SOL ON THE DOCKS OF ANTWERP: ANNA IS NOT WITH HIM

SOL STANDS ON A dock in Antwerp, Belgium, in July 1913.[1] The dock is on the River Scheldt, linked to the North Sea by the river's Westerschelde estuary. It is about twenty-five miles north of Brussels, and about nine miles south of the Dutch border. The Port of Antwerp is one of the biggest in the world.

---

1. The 1930 census form says Sol arrived in America in 1913. It also says he was twenty when he married, which means he was born in 1893. Anna does not join him until 1916, according to the 1930 census form, when they seem to get the dates in a more logical order. Sol's date of leaving is muddled on the official records. Sol lists his date of immigration in the 1920 census as 1911, when he would have been nineteen years old. He tells the 1930 census taker that he immigrated in 1913, when he would have been twenty (he also changes his birthdate to 1893). 1913 appears to be the more reliable date. Anna tells the 1930 census taker she came to the US in 1917, or four years after Sol. In fact, the ship manifest shows she arrived in December 1916. She also claims she was born in 1893.

The SS Montrose is due to sail to Quebec, Canada. From there, Sol hopes to travel to Detroit, by train, and then to Chicago to meet his cousin, Abraham Grade. He is just twenty-one years old; still slender at 176 pounds, five feet eleven inches. He is about to start a journey to the new world and to create a new generation.

Sol's journey to Antwerp began by land, in a railway station in Vilna. The land journey was made somewhat easier by a sea of honest and not-so-honest agents and others willing to assist. Vilna was described as a "hotbed of migrant recruitment."[2] The agents saw the chance for large profits: "[w]ith an expansion of migration into a mass exodus after 1882, it became also heavily fueled by a vast network of emigration agents and steamship companies who viewed migration as a profitable business and competed for those who wanted to leave."[3]

Once in Antwerp, Sol ventures down to the dock. He has never seen an ocean liner, and in truth, has probably never seen the ocean. The ship he will sail on is likely taller than any structure he has seen in Vilna. The SS Montrose is a 443.3-foot ocean liner, longer than a football field. It was outfitted with seventy second-class berths and 1,800 third-class passenger berths. I am reasonably certain Sol is among the steerage passengers in third class. Many of the other passengers, like Sol, list Yiddish as their native language.

Sol may have seen pictures of the vessel as they circulated frequently throughout Europe. The SS Montrose's maiden voyage was in 1897, sixteen years earlier. It had been a reliable passenger ship ever since. Still, it was just the prior April, in 1912, when the Titanic sank only four days into its maiden voyage, even though it was thought to be unsinkable. Two years later, on May 7, 1915, the Lusitania will be sunk by the Germans. But Sol will find other things to worry about.

The dock that day, as other docks on other days, is crowded with young Yiddish-speaking men from Vilna, many with Sol's same skills as a tailor, and many with parents seeking promises of fidelity to things Jewish as their young sons venture off into an unseen and unknowable world. Rabbi Alex Israel, who now teaches in Jerusalem at the Pardes Institute of Jewish Studies, told me one such young man was his grandfather. While standing on the docks, ready to leave for America, Rabbi Israel's great-grandfather made his son promise that, even though he was leaving his homeland, he would remain faithful to the Jewish traditions. It was an important pledge and his great-grandfather was not about to let Rabbi Israel's grandfather board the ship until the words were spoken, the vow made.

2. Balkelis, "Opening Gates," 59.
3. Balkelis, "Opening Gates," 58.

But for better or worse, there is no one on the dock with Sol that day. And I doubt there is any such vow made by Sol to his father: no promise, no commitment, and hence the tearing of the fabric becomes easier. Sol is about to board and leave the Old Country. No one is there to make him promise to carry on the tradition. There is no struggle over the patriarchal blessing by the father among competing sons. All of this is out of fashion. Nor does Sol, many years later, seek any commitment from his son Joseph, nor even later, Joseph from me or Steve. Blessing and covenant simply fade into an impossible vocabulary, unspeakable words to a modern mind.

THE SHIP MANIFEST

Before Sol can board, the agents for the SS Montrose must complete a manifest, with detailed charts that have been deliniated by an Act of Congress. In 2018, with the help of a genealogist, I discover the ship manifest for Sol's voyage, and though it clarifies some of our family myths it also reveals new mysteries.

The form and content of a ship manifest for immigration purposes between the years 1891 and 1957 was a matter of substantial congressional attention and revision. Passenger lists for this period were called immigration manifests or immigration passenger lists. Collecting them was initially the responsibility of the newly created US Office of Immigration. Standard forms for recording the required information about passengers arriving in the United States came into use in 1893.[4] Indeed, "their size, color, and quality of paper were specified in detail by law, but it was still the responsibility of the individual steamship companies to obtain their own manifests."[5] The number of columns and the required information was specified by law: in 1893, there were twenty-one columns to be filled in; after 1903, when Sol and Anna came to America, the Immigration Act of 1903 had added a twenty-second column called "race of people" (but numbered as column 6). Six more columns were added in 1906, requiring personal descriptive information, and in 1907, a column was added: "name and address of closest living relative in native country." What these columns tell us about Sol and Anna is critical, although the handwriting makes accurate depiction open to some question.

The manifest, column 22, lists Detroit as Sol's ultimate destination, although the Montrose is sailing only to Quebec. Sol's subsequent Petition for

4. Colletta, *They Came in Ships*, 39.
5. Colletta, *They Came in Ships*, 39.

Naturalization confirms that he in fact arrived in Detroit on August 6, 1913, via the Canadian Pacific Railway.[6] Chicago is about 281 miles due west of Detroit and about a four-hour drive on today's roads.

Many families, ours included, have settled upon a myth about how their Americanized names came into being. A common view is that an immigrant's name was changed at Ellis Island, upon arrival, by a port agent who could not understand Yiddish or the other spoken language of the immigrant. Our family myth was that someone at Ellis Island must have misunderstood Sol when he said his name, and changed Kurenitzky to Kuney.

For many, the truth is that their name change occurred not when they arrived in America, but rather when they left their homes. Names were placed on a ship manifest at the port of embarkation before the ship sailed.[7] Though some pursers may have copied the name from a passport or travel papers, or some other document, it appears that many pursers simply asked the passengers their names and wrote down what they heard as best they could.[8] Errors and changes were inevitable, since surnames were transliterated. Sol might have known his own name only in Cyrillic or Yiddish. When an immigrant tells his name to the purser, the official likely Romanizes the name, putting it into Latin letters as he hears and understands it. Three brothers from Vilna coming on three different ships may have been given three different last names, and these are the names that remain with them and are passed on to their children.[9]

Yet, Sol's manifest shows that none of this is true for him. Sol's name change was not the result of an error at embarkation or upon arrival. Sol's name is listed on the ship manifest as Selik Kurenitzki. Not Sol Kuney. He is Kurenitzki (although the correct spelling seems to be with a "y" as the last letter).

Sol's name is changed to Sol Kuney on December 3, 1920, when the US District Court for the Northern District of Illinois signs an Order of Court Admitting Petitioner, granting his request to change his name to Sol Kuney. Why Sol picked Kuney as his new last name I do not know, nor do I know what it may have meant to him. And though I used to think Kuney was unique, I have more recently learned of many others with the same surname.[10]

---

6. See also, Sol's Certificate of Arrival for Naturalization Purposes.

7. Colletta, *They Came in Ships*, 8.

8. Colletta, *They Came in Ships*, 8.

9. Colletta, *They Came in Ships*, 8.

10. For example, Professor George Kuney, teaches bankruptcy law in Tennessee. There also seem to be a lot of Kuney families in Michigan.

The manifest debunks another myth as well. Sol does not go through Ellis Island. The SS Montrose is headed for Quebec. Sol never sees New York on his journey from Vilna.

The ship manifest lists Sol's trade as a tailor and his race as "Hebrew" (See line 15 of ship manifest). The use of the term "Hebrew" is archaic, although when the Jews were in Egypt, still slaves, they were indeed known as the Hebrews. The notion that the Jews were a "race" is also troubling.

Nor was Sol unique. The SS Montrose had other Jewish tailors from Vilna—a ship full of them, it seems, all with thimble and thread. During the period from 1899 to 1910, among Lithuanian Jewish immigrants to the United States, tailors, carpenters, dressmakers and shoemakers made up nearly 63 percent of all skilled Jewish immigrants.[11] "Overall, the social make-up of Jewish migrants reflected their social profile in the Pale where the majority of Jews (38 percent) were involved in manufacturing and mechanical occupations."[12]

And then this. Column 18 asks the passengers to list whether they are going to join a relative or friend, and if so, to identify the name and address of the relative. Here Sol lists Abraham Grade, who lives at 1423 Leavitt Street in Chicago. Abraham is identified as a cousin. Later, I learn that Abraham's younger half brother, Chaim, became a well-known and highly acclaimed Yiddish writer—the same Chaim Grade who had studied with Noah Golinkin in the Yeshiva in Vilna. What this means we must explore later after Sol has arrived in America.

THE JOURNEY WEST: A SHIP OF TAILORS, CARPENTERS, AND DRESSMAKERS

Once the manifest is complete, Sol boards the SS Montrose. And now his journey truly begins.

It takes nine days to sail from Antwerp to the United States, that is, if you are traveling by sea in the late nineteenth or early twentieth century, but then only if you are on the best of the larger, newer boats—those with iron hulls and compound steam engines and screw propulsion. It is not a pleasant journey: cramped spaces, lack of fresh air, little food, to say nothing of the sanitary conditions. First, the treachery of the bribery required to obtain the steerage ticket, now this: worse even for those who had never been on or even seen a large ship, or any vessel on water, nor even the ocean. What,

11. Balkelis, "Opening Gates," 57.
12. Balkelis, "Opening Gates," 57.

after all, did one who labored in a tailor shop know of the water, its ebbs and flows, its disorienting and frightening waves?

But Sol is not on the most modern vessel of its time, and his journey on the SS Montrose takes upwards of twelve days. The ship manifest says that the Montrose left Antwerp on July 25, 1913, and arrived in Quebec in early August, possibly the sixth, according to Sol's Declaration of Intention to become a citizen, although Sol's recollection of dates is notably inconsistent.

I imagine Sol on that ship deck, by himself. Although plans or promises were made, he had no assurance Anna would be joining him in America anytime soon, or at all. He is lonely on the deck and perhaps goes below to look into his small suitcase, all that he brought with him, just a few items, checking them again and again, to make sure he has everything. The other passengers are all strangers, and, although they speak Yiddish, it does nothing to make him feel safe; indeed, he is as far from safe as one can get.

He looks into his suitcase and sees again, for the fourth time, his *tallit*—the white-and-blue cotton prayer shawl that Jews typically wear during the daily morning prayer service. He had not taken it out the whole voyage. Not the yarmulke either—the head covering that Jews wear on the top of the head so that the soul is never exposed. I am almost certain his heart is too heavy even to pray, and besides, he had left Vilna with doubts about his own faith, despite the pervasiveness of all things Jewish in Vilna.

Beneath his one change of clothes, he sees his thimble, threads, and three spools: black, white, and blue. This, then, is what he will rely on. His work at least is certain. The only thing between him and utter dismay is his ability to sew things. The prayerbook he left behind was too heavy to put in the small suitcase. But this, his thimble and thread, they are what define him. Even Anna admires his skill. He will be needed, valued in America, or so he hopes.

If Anna had been with him, he would have been attentive to his morning prayers. Anna had been insistent, and he had gone along—mostly to please her. Better not to bring to the surface too much of their disagreements. Later they would work it out, he thought, make their peace.

It was always Anna, always the woman who guarded the soul, who kept the home kosher, who made sure that the holy was known and seen. Ironic, of course, because Anna, as a Jewish woman, would not be counted as one of the ten persons required for the daily *minyan*, the prayer service. Still it was women who carried the precious soul of the Jewish people from generation to generation. It was women who disobeyed Pharaoh and secretly refused to kill their male babies and throw them in the Nile, as Pharaoh had decreed. It was women who, when the men were fatigued and lifeless, put on perfume and fine clothes and seduced them so that another generation would follow.

Anna would have made him pay attention and would have insisted he pray. But now, alone and unsafe, he was distracted and worried. America? What kind of place was he headed to?

Sol kept no diary, no notes of his journey. Years later, when he talks about the Old Country, he keeps coming back to the same themes and images: the growling dogs; the Cossacks with curved swords drawn at the ready; chains; some formless, dark violence we cannot understand and are grateful is not part of our life. I am too young when I hear this to truly understand, but it leaves me with a firm conviction that whatever kind of world Sol and Anna have left behind, I want no part of it. We three brothers and our young friends turn our backs on all of it, the good and the bad, the Jewish and the secular of the Old World. We never hear of the Vilna Gaon, the Enlightenment, or Haskalah. We close our minds to this terrible past of theirs, and instead of searching for clues and information, we are content to dismiss it, be done with it, be thankful it is over. *Enough*, we think. Some parts of our history are best left alone, lest through imagining them we in some way recreate that same fear of faceless horsemen, swords held high, coming into our town, our homes. Best to keep old traumas at bay.

Sol's journey of twelve days was part of an epic migration, the likes of which the world had never seen before. Masses of people moving west. One scholar estimates that between 1860 and 1914, combined migration from all Polish territories totaled 9 million people.[13] Lithuania lost almost a quarter of its population (635,000) during the period from 1868 to 1914. "This rate of emigration was one of the highest in Europe at the time," with Jews and [ethnic] Lithuanians comprising the majority of migrants from the Lithuanian provinces.[14] Some went to New York, but many headed west to Chicago, making it the city with the largest concentration of Jews anywhere in the world other than New York and Warsaw.

Did Sol see himself as part of this larger Jewish migration—always moving from homeland into exile? In Genesis, God tells Abraham to "go from your land" and to become a nation, and to be a blessing to the world. This central thought underlies so much of Judaism; to go out into the world and be a blessing to all of mankind through good works, through justice. We are the people of the diaspora. Surely, there is a reason for our journey.

It would be easy to think Sol is simply fleeing army service and pogroms and almost certain death wherever he went. But I often wonder if he

13. Balkelis, "Opening Gates," 42.
14. Balkelis, "Opening Gates," 42.

is fleeing his Jewishness. I can tell from what he doesn't talk about later. In the 1950s, when I am old enough to see him as a distinct person, he does not talk to me about being Jewish in the Old Country. There is no mention of Torah, although decades later he will start to go to daily *minyan*. Sol was fleeing: fleeing the draft, fleeing the pogroms, but more largely, fleeing history itself, and perhaps the heavy burden of his Jewishness.

For better or worse, Sol's fleeing and forgetting would set the stage not only for Esther and Joe, but now I think for many in the first generation of Jews born in America following the Great Migration. What I later saw in Arlington was in no small measure the consequence of Sol's journey—the journey without covenant, the journey of a skilled tailor. But then, to give Sol his fair due, if the journey were truly Abrahamic, even if Sol knew nothing of the Torah, even if Sol's lonely journey were conflicted, it was Sol and others like him who, whether they meant to or not, brought the old Jewish world to the New World and then later to me and my brothers in suburban America.

CHAPTER 5

Sol Alone in Chicago (1913–1917)

SOL ARRIVES IN DETROIT alone on August 6, 1913, with twenty-five dollars in his pocket, speaking not a word of English. In Joe's 1994 letter to our daughter Jessica, he says that Sol first moved to Danville, Illinois, about 147 miles from Chicago. There is no other reference to Danville and I have no idea why or for how long Sol stayed there before reaching his destination in Chicago.

I think Sol chose Chicago because Abraham Grade, his first cousin, had settled there, after leaving Vilna only a few years earlier. A family connection would have been important to Sol. I imagine he and his family knew the Grades well enough in Vilna to discuss Sol's anticipated journey and to arrange for Sol to live with Abraham initially.

While Sol's decision to head for Chicago was almost certainly based on the fact that his cousin had settled there, other immigrants from Vilna also found Chicago to be ideal for their first home in America. By 1870, the first wave of Eastern European Jews had started to arrive in Chicago, with many coming from the poor *shtetls* of Russia. By 1930, there were 275,000 Jews in Chicago. This was roughly 8 percent of Chicago's population at the time. Most are from places like Vilna. Over two-and-one-half million Eastern European Jews emigrated to America between 1881 and 1924.[1]

Chicago is a good choice for Sol. It proves to be fertile ground for the Jewish intellect and imagination, and the raw ambition of those who came hungry and determined. The list is long but, during Sol's time, it includes

---

1. Library of Congress, "From Haven to Home," para. 3.

43

famous Jewish thinkers such as Studs Terkel, Arthur Goldberg, Ephraim Epstein, William Paley, and Penny Pritzker. Saul Bellow will write in *Herzog* of his mixed feelings about Chicago and his academic life there.

The Chicago that Sol saw each day was unlike the cityscape that immigrants encountered in the crowded streets of New York, which were filled with peddlers and pushcarts, and orthodox Jews with their black coats and fur hats. Instead, Sol saw a more diverse neighborhood, with wider streets, no pushcarts, and a mostly merchant class.

It seems likely that Sol moved in with the Grades when he arrived in Chicago in 1913. One of the earliest documents I discover is Sol's Declaration of Intention, dated August 14, 1916, indicating his desire to be an American citizen. He is still named Zelick Kurenitzky then, and as the Declaration states, Anna, "my wife," is still in Russia. Significantly, in his Declaration, Sol says he lives at 1439 N. Rockwell St., Chicago. 1439 Rockwell—a tiny, narrow, two-story brick house, just off Humboldt Park and a few blocks from Hadden—is the home of Abraham Grade and his wife, Clara. Although Anna will not arrive in America until the end of 1916, the ship manifest for her voyage, which is dated close to the time when Sol signs his Declaration of Intention, also identifies 1439 Rockwell as her destination and indicates it is the home of Abraham Grade.

By 1917, Sol and Anna have moved to 2711 W. Haddon, a short walk to Humboldt Park. Assimilated Jews, non-Jews, and Jews in business, rather than the strictly orthodox, have settled in this area. Sol finds work as a tailor shortly after he arrives in Chicago, perhaps with the help of his cousin Abraham. Sol's draft registration card shows that, no later than June 1917, he is working for H. M. Stevenson, which does business at 312 S. Clark St., Chicago, Illinois.[2] This is about five miles to the east of 2711 Haddon Avenue, and would have put Sol close to Lake Michigan, the Art Institute, and Grant Park.

H. M. Stevenson is a well-known union shop that includes journeymen tailors, like Sol, who are just beginning to practice their trade. "Tailors, carpenters, dressmakers and shoemakers made up almost 63 percent of all skilled Jewish immigrants. Overall, the social makeup of Jewish migrants reflected their social profile in the Pale, where the majority of Jews were involved in manufacturing and mechanical occupations."[3] The Jews worked as artisans, laborers in factories, peddlers, and petty merchants. The factory workers were primarily in the clothing sector, as was Sol.

2. See Sol's draft registration card for World War I on Ancestry.com.

3. Balkelis, "Opening Gates," 57.

Sol arrives speaking only Yiddish, but learns English quickly, and likely became an avid reader of the *Sentinel*. The *Sentinel*, founded in 1911, is one of the most important Anglo-Jewish periodicals in Chicago, and is still circulating today. In Sol's early years in America, the paper was published in both English and Yiddish.[4] More than news, of course, the *Sentinel* is filled with ads for the latest goods and services.

In late 1916, Sol may have paused over the many enticing advertisements. He would have been encouraged to let his "dimes soon pile up"[5] in the Corn Exchange National Bank, visit the Palmer House Hotel with the assurance that it was "strictly fireproof,"[6] and send his wash to Family Washing at six cents per pound. He would have learned that he could apply for a first mortgage at 5 percent, or consider buying the Brunswick, with the assurance it was now the world's greatest phonograph and in fact, "plays every American record made."[7] He also could have considered the Art Wig Company for wigs and toupees for men and women both, or perhaps toy with the idea of buying a Chevrolet for $494, this being the "lowest priced, electric started and lighted car in the world."[8]

Sol has not been in America for even a year, when in August 1914, a Bosnian Serb kills the Austrian Archduke, Franz Ferdinand. Germany then declares war against Russia and France. German troops invade Belgium, whose neutrality had been guaranteed by Great Britain, and Britain declares war against Germany. Britain, Russia, and France, the "Allies," each pledge by treaty to reach no separate peace with their enemies.

President Wilson tells Congress in December 1914 that "we have nothing to do" with Europe's war whose "causes cannot touch us." "Our whole duty—for the present, at any rate, is summed up in this motto: 'America First.'"[9] Yet, Wilson fears an attack on an American vessel could lead to an outcry for war. His fears come to pass. On May 7, 1915, off the Irish coast, a German submarine sinks the British transatlantic ship Lusitania, the fastest and most luxurious ocean liner in the world.[10] Of the 1,198 passengers killed,

4. Cutler, *Jews of Chicago*, 137.

5. http://www.idaillinois.org/digital/collection/p16614coll14/id/10683.

6. http://www.idaillinois.org/digital/collection/p16614coll14/id/17038/rec/297.

7. http://www.idaillinois.org/digital/collection/p16614coll14/id/17046/rec/297.

8. http://www.idaillinois.org/digital/collection/p16614coll14/id/17051/rec/297.

9. Beschloss, *Presidents of War*, 303.

10. Beschloss, *Presidents of War*, 303.

128 are Americans. Traveling across the Atlantic now becomes problematic for prospective immigrants like Anna.

Given the onset of World War I, and the chaos in Europe, Sol must have been worried about whether Anna would be able to flee and whether she would ever join him. Although I have not found any letters between Sol and Anna during her years away from him, Sol would have been able to get a glimpse of Anna's life during those years from the stories that appeared in the *Sentinel*, stories that Sol almost certainly read with much apprehension. The *Sentinel* reports that there were 5,000 Jews waiting in line in Vilna for soap and food—and that starvation was rampant:

> I bring you greetings, America, from the Jews of Poland, Lithua-nia, Galicia. I bring you greetings from the Jewish people almost about to die. I bring you greetings from the starving nation, yet from a community that is invincible and full of hope. We know not what is transpiring this night in dark Russia where three millions of our brethren still live. We know but very little of the misery that is overtaking our people in the lovely land of Pales-tine, but we know that where there are now about two and half millions of our people in Poland, Lithuania and Galicia hunger is staring them in the face. In the city of Vilna alone, every day 5,000 people, men, women and children wait for hours in line, with pots under their arms for soap only to be turned away because the supply is exhausted.[11]

New Year's Eve, 1916: Sol reads that the news from Vilna is grim, but that wealthy Jews are trying to provide some assistance. In the December 29, 1916 edition, the *Sentinel* reports on a fundraising event at Carnegie Hall in New York in which 3 million dollars in donations were raised in three minutes after a crowded hall of wealthy Jews heard stories about the thousands of Jews in Poland, Lithuania and Galicia who are gradually dying from sheer starvation.[12] The stories that evening among the 4,000 in atten-dance caused the women to sob aloud as they heard about near relatives, parents, wives, and daughters in these famine-wrecked countries.

Sol has spent three years in America worrying about Anna, and won-dering whether she will be able to come to America. Soon he will know.

11. "$3,000,000 in 30 Minutes," para. 12.
12. "$3,000,000 in 30 Minutes."

CHAPTER 6

Anna's Last Years in Vilna and Her Journey to Siberia (1913–1916)

WITH THE ERUPTION OF World War I in August 1914, Vilna is suddenly full of soldiers and war materials in trains moving through the city. On Yom Kippur, September 17, 1914, German troops enter Vilna, and the Russian forces withdraw from the city.[1] The Germans proclaim they will restore Vilna to the Polish Kingdom. In September 1915, the Germans take Vilna from the hands of the Czar.[2] Now at last, Vilna is no longer Russian, although we never hear Anna say anything about the Germans coming into Vilna, or the end of Vilna as part of Russia.

As 1914 comes to an end, Anna no longer has a choice about whether or not to stay in Vilna. The mass expulsion of the Jews from Lithuania begins on January 25, 1915, in an order issued by the German command. By the end of 1915, half a million Jews have become refugees from Lithuania. "Those who decided to remain were mistreated by German occupation forces near the Polish border. Roving Polish bands assaulted Jews in Vilnius and Suwalk."[3]

Anna decides to take the Pacific route on her journey to America so that, on the way, she can stop in Siberia to visit her father before she crosses the ocean. According to my cousin Jo Ellen, Anna began her journey by

1. "Germans Capture Vilnus and Warsaw," para. 4.
2. "Beginnings of the Vilna Community."
3. Greenbaum, *Jews of Lithuania*, 213.

heading north through ice-bound Siberia via the Trans-Siberian Railway. When I heard this story, I wondered if it was even possible that a young, unaccompanied woman could travel by train, moving east, stop in Siberia, and then make her way to a port in Asia and from there, travel to America. The complexity of it all seemed daunting and beyond reach.

And yet, it was possible. After researching the available train and ship routes, I concluded that Anna's travel was not only possible, but also perhaps common. Her journey is entirely consistent with what I am able to learn about the rail system, then and now. The Trans-Siberian Railway generally originated in Moscow, not Lithuania, so Anna had to first get to Moscow. The journey from Vilna to Moscow is 491 miles, and even today, by car, takes twelve hours.

I suspect that Anna's more affluent family pays the fare for a train from Vilna to Moscow. In Moscow, Anna boards the Trans-Siberian Railway by herself. There are three routes, two of which go through China. One of these Chinese routes goes to Beijing via Harbin, Manchuria, over 5,623 miles of track. The older of the two routes to Beijing was completed in the 1900s and is served by only one train a week. It takes six nights to make the trip, and passengers travel in first- and second-class Russian coaches. Both routes to the Chinese capital require the bogies (the chassis or framework carrying the wheels) under the coaches to be changed at the Russian-Chinese and Mongolian-Chinese borders.

The route to Beijing through Mongolia, is 4,735 miles. The Mongolian route stops in Siberia. I believe Anna took this train and disembarked in Siberia to find her father before she resumed her journey to America.

ANNA IN SIBERIA

Once on the Trans-Siberian Railway, Anna could have stopped in Siberia, and indeed, there is evidence this is exactly what she did. I discover a manila folder in Joe's files marked "Mom's relatives." Inside the folder is a small scrap of paper, no larger than four and a half inches by three and a half inches. On one side of the paper are the words "Alter Rudashevski" and what appears to be an address. *Alter* is Yiddish for "elder." Anna's father? On the other side, there is possibly another name, not quite legible, which seems to say A. Pfgaillesbskise, followed by another address. This address has the initials "C.C.C."

I sent this small paper to a friend of a friend, who can read Russian. The translation that I receive back (of the first side only) states that this small paper "lists a town and region [of Irkutskiy] as being in Russia":

"A Rudamevsky"
Nizhny Udinsk
Irkutskiy rayon (region), Russia

Although not certain, it is likely, that Rudamevsky is a misspelling of Rudashevsky. In that case, the translation of the note suggests that Anna was looking for someone in the Irkutskiy region of Russia—I assume her father.

In fact, there is a Russian region or area named Irkutsk, in Siberia, which was a place where many exiles were sent. It was known, perhaps ironically, as the Paris of Siberia.[4] Many distinguished Russians were sent into exile in Irkutsk for their part in the Decembrist revolt of 1825, and the city became an exile post for the rest of the century. Some of the fine wooden houses still survive, contrasting with the dominant Soviet architecture.

My research shows that the Trans-Siberian Railway does run through Irkutsk,[5] so Anna certainly could have taken the Trans-Siberian Railway to to visit her father. How this small piece of paper found its way into Joe's files decades later remains a mystery.

I don't know for certain whether Anna found her father. But according to the story Jo Ellen tells, Anna supposedly met a younger man who was also an exile with whom she fell in love. This created a conflict: Anna now had to decide whether to stay in Russia with her lover, or go on to an unknown future in America. I am guessing Anna had concern that she and Sol did not have much in common, and that years had passed since she had last seen Sol. Maybe Sol, a simple, humble tailor, without much education, was not what she had hoped for.

But for whatever reason, Anna decided to keep her promise to Sol, to go to America and join her husband. Anna reboarded the train and traveled to Shanghai, China, where she was met by agents from the Hebrew Immigrant Aid Socieity (HIAS), which assisted her with her immigration.

Shanghai was a logical intermediate stop. It had a long history of providing a refuge for Jews fleeing from Europe. Between November 1938 and August 1939, approximately 20,000 Central European refugees, most of them Jews, landed in Shanghai.[6] Indeed, Altman and Eber argue that if more Jews and Jewish organizations had taken advantage of the exit route

4. Jamadi, "Paris of Siberia, According to Checkov."
5. "Trans-Siberian Railway in the World History."
6. Altman and Eber, "Flight to Shanghai," 1.

from Europe through Shanghai, many more lives could have been saved. "The fact that more ships did not sail [from Shanghai] seems to have much to do with the failure to weigh alternatives. The Jewish leadership in Europe and America did not grasp just how significant the opportunity to flee to Shanghai was."[7]

ANNA'S SEA JOURNEY (NOVEMBER 1916)

Anna makes her way from Shanghai to Kobe, Japan, and from there sails to America on the Kamakura Maru Line 13, which departs from Kobe on November 16, 1916, and arrives in Seattle, Washington on December 2, 1916. The ship manifest says Anna is twenty-four years old.[8] It also says she is a tailor, and that her nearest family relation in the country from which she came is "Father, Rudashevskay Nishe, Medaneus, Libin or Lublin." I am not sure what to make of this. Wasn't her father still in Siberia, not in Vilna?

The ship manifest identifies 1439 Rockwell as Anna's destination and indicates it is the home of Abraham Grade. How did Anna know this address, coming out of Siberia? Anna had been on a journey through Moscow, Siberia, and Japan for the better part of a year before she crossed the Pacific. She could not have known where Sol was living unless the Grades were in contact with her in 1916 or she had received a letter from Sol. But how would such a letter have reached her during her travels in Asia? Sol knew even less about where she was during this time. One possible answer is that the Grade family was in contact with Sol's family in Vilna and helped provide this needed information.

Yet, there is one more mystery to solve. On the manifest, Anna lists her last permanent residence as Harbin, Russia. Harbin, however, is in northern China. It turns out that the term "Harbin Russians" refers to several generations of Russians who lived in the city of Harbin, China from 1898 through 1960. By 1913, just before Anna arrived there, Harbin had become an established Russian colony for the construction and maintenance of the China Eastern Railway. Is this why Anna told her son Julius that she had learned some Chinese on her way to America? Did she spend enough time in Harbin with her new lover to learn the language? All unanswered questions. I

---

7. Altman and Eber, "Flight to Shanghai," 32.

8. Jordan Auslander, of Probate & Genealogy Research Associates in New York City, located the ship manifest. The manifest lists as a passenger "Nane Rudashevskay," who is said to be twenty-four years old.

do know, however, that Anna makes her way to Japan, which is her country of departure. Kobe is 886 miles from Harbin.

Joe's version of Anna's journey is mostly consistent, but with a few differences. Joe said his mother had to travel across Siberia to Yokahama, Japan, and from there traveled by ship to either Seattle or Portland. He agrees that she arrived in the United States in 1916. He makes no mention, however, of the mysterious lover in Siberia, nor the intermediate stop in China. Joe also said she went first to Danville, Illinois, and then to Chicago, where Sol was then living.

ANNA ARRIVES IN AMERICA: WAR IS DECLARED

Anna makes her way from Seattle to Chicago, likely arriving there no later than January 1917. She joins Sol, as well as Abrham Grade and his wife, just a few weeks before Woodrow Wilson asks Congress for a declaration of war.

The Germans were already sinking merchant ships and perhaps some ocean liners. On January 22, 1917, Wilson went to the Senate chamber and urged "a peace without victory" in Europe. Illinois Senator Lawrence Sherman, an isolationist Republican, finds the notion ludicrous, saying that Wilson's appeal "would make Don Quixote wish he had not died so soon."[9]

Senator Sherman may have been right. Wilson did not know that, in early January 1917, the Kaiser of Germany had secretly approved "full employment of German submarines against all sea traffic"[10] in the neighborhood of the European war zone. More bizarrely, Wilson did not yet know that Germany had sent agents to Mexico seeking an alliance with Mexico against the United States and promising that, if victorious, Mexico could regain the land in Texas and other southern states it had previously lost.

Wilson's plea for peace without victory did not last long. On April 4, 1917, the Senate passed a declaration of war. The next day, a Thursday, the House passed the resolution. George Norris, a Republican, resisted, claiming that behind the war fever were "munitions makers, stockbrokers and bond dealers." He cautioned, "We are about to do the bidding of wealth's terrible mandate and make millions of our countrymen suffer, and untold generations bear burdens and shed their lifeblood, all because we want to preserve our commercial right to deliver munitions to the belligerents. I feel we are about to put the dollar sign on the American Flag."[11]

9. Beschloss, *Presidents of War*, 309.

10. Beschloss, *Presidents of War*, 293.

11. Beschloss, *Presidents of War*, 317–18.

On May 18, 1917, Congress passes the Selective Service Act of 1917, which authorizes the government to raise a national army. On June 5, 1917, Sol registeres for the draft in Chicago. Anna is now pregnant with their first child. Sol and Abraham Grade go to the draft board together and register on the same day. When they do so, they list the same home address—2711 Haddon Ave, Chicago. Sol's form says he is working as a tailor at H. M. Stevenson located at 312 S. Clark St. The clerk completing the registration form notes that Sol is "tall," of medium build, with brown eyes, not bald, with dark brown hair, and has not lost his arms, legs, or hands, and is not otherwise disabled. Sol signs his name; his first name, Sol, is hard to read, but he is able to write Kuney in a basic script form. Sol has not yet legally changed his name to Kuney, and I wonder how and why he started using this name without any legal authority.

Anna has been in America for less than a year. Her husband, who had left to avoid one draft, has now signed up for another. He has moved in with Abraham Grade, and now, at last, after three years, Anna is with him.

Three years later, Sol will seek US citizenship. On August 26, 1920, when Sol signs his Petition for Naturalization, Abraham and Clara Grade are present, and they both sign an affidavit as witnesses. Clara identifies herself as a housewife and Abraham as a public accountant, both then living at 2542 Wilson Avenue, in Chicago. The form states they have personally known "Zelick" since January 1, 1915, which I believe is actually two years after they first met Sol.

But who was Abraham Grade—and more, what about his half-brother, Chaim Grade? How close were the Kuneys and the Grades, and what were the consequences of the two cousins living together? And then this: Is our family related to the Grades, and why does this matter when I try to understand the Jewish journey of Sol and Anna, Esther and Joe, and now us?

CHAPTER 7

Chasing Chaim Grade

WHO WERE THE GRADES?

ABRAHAM GRADE WAS BORN on June 5, 1887, in Vilna. Abraham's father, Shlomo Mordecai Grade, was a Hebrew teacher and *maskil* (advocate of the Haskalah, the European Jewish Enlightenment).[1] The *maskalim*

> were mainly concerned with modernizing the Jews, by rational-
> izing their religious beliefs and practices, stressing the use of the
> vernacular, and having them acquire non-Jewish culture. They
> wanted to see in Jewish life the adoption of non-Jewish values.
> . . . The *maskalim* invariably regarded the Hasidim as obstruct-
> ing the Jewish emancipation.[2]

Hasidism, in turn, was seen "in all respects [as]a revival of Traditional Judaism, intransigent and determined to defy Westernism and the Gentile world."[3]

There is little doubt about the depth of Shlomo's radical notions. In the foreword to *My Mother's Sabbath Days*, Chaim's wife will later write that Shlomo was "at war" with the Orthodox views then prevalent in Vilna:

> [T]he formidable Rabbi Shlomo Mordecai Grade, *maskil*
> (champion of enlightenment) Hebraist, and early Zionist, who

---

1. Shlomo was the son of Reb Yerucham, another Vilna rabbi.

2. Kaplan, *Greater Judaism in the Making*, 140.

3. Kaplan, *Greater Judaism in the Making*, 139–40.

was well known for challenging rabbinical rulings and was, indeed, at war with almost all Orthodox Vilna. Rabbi Shlomo Mordecai did not defer even to the Hazon Ish, one of the greatest Talmudic authorities of all time, and a true saint who chose young Chaim as his personal disciple.[4]

Shlomo's first wife, Sarah Safer, was Abraham's mother.[5] After Sarah's untimely death, Shlomo married Vella Grade Rosenthal, who was the daughter of Rabbi Rafael Blumenthal.[6]

Abraham emigrated to America on the USS Caledonia, which sailed from Glasgow, Scotland, and arrived at the port of New York on March 5, 1906. Abraham, then in his early twenties, likely took with him much of his father's ideology and radical beliefs. Shortly after his arrival, on October 12, 1907, Abraham married Clara Kabakow, who became Clara Grade. By 1910, Abraham, Clara, and their two children, Joseph and Sarah, were living at 32 Macedonia Street in Chicago. Abraham presumably named his first daughter Sarah, in memory of his then-deceased mother.

Four years after Abraham arrives in America (1906), his half-brother—Chaim Grade—is born in Vilna. Because Chaim is the son of Vella, Shlomo's second wife, he is Abraham's half-brother. Chaim's father is an outspoken advocate of a modern, secular version of Judaism.[7] Chaim is raised in an orthodox-leaning home. He studies for several years with Rabbi Avrohom Karelitz, the Hazon Ish, considered to be "one of the greatest Talmudic authorities of all time."[8] But Chaim must have noticed that his father had no reluctance to reject the Rabbi's traditional views.[9]

Chaim attended the well-known Ramayles Yeshiva with another student, Noah Golinkin, and the two studied Talmud together.[10] Noah and

---

4. Grade, "Foreword," in *My Mother's Sabbath Days*, viii.

5. Jonathan Brent, Executive Director of YIVO, email message to author discussing comments he received from a YIVO archivist: "Chaim's father was Rabbi Shlomo Mordecai Grade and his mother was Vella Grade Rosenthal, but Chaim's brothers were actually half-brothers, as Vella was his father's second wife." When Abraham marries Clara in 1907, the Certificate of Marriage lists his father's name as Solomon Grade, and his mother's "maiden name" as Sarah Safer.

6. https://peoplepill.com/people/chaim-grade/

7. Grade, "Foreword," in *My Mother's Sabbath Days*, viii.

8. Grade, "Foreword," in *My Mother's Sabbath Days*, viii.

9. Grade, "Foreword," in *My Mother's Sabbath Days*, viii. "Rabbi Shlomo Mordecai did not defer even to the Hazon Ish, one of the greatest Talmudic authorities of all time."

10. Golinkin, "The Center of Jewish Scholarship—A Portrait of Yivo in 1939." Introduction to the English Translation by David Golinkin, stating that his father, Noah, studied in the "famous" Ramayles Yeshiva together with Chaim Grade.

Chaim become *hevrutah* study partners, and it seems almost certain that they would have disagreed on most subjects. Noah, who was committed to the traditional view of Judaism, one day would become a rabbi at a synagoague in Arlington, Virginia, where Sol and Joe would become members, and where Noah would seek to restore the study of Hebrew as a mainstay of Jewish education. Chaim, however, no friend of traditional Judaism, and a fervent advocate of a more secular culture, was kicked out of the Yeshiva for writing secular poetry and, presumably, for his leftist leanings.

After Shlomo's death, Vella, his widow, is compelled to sell apples in the marketplace to support her son, Chaim.[11] Later, Chaim flees Vilna when the Nazis invade the city in 1941. He leaves behind his mother and his first wife. Decades later, in his second wife's obituary in the *New York Times*, it was reported that he was under the "common delusion that Germans would persecute only men. Both women perished in the Holocaust and Grade seemed riddled with guilt long after."[12]

Chaim emigrates to the Soviet Union and later to France, where he meets Inna Hecker. Together, they emigrate to New York in 1948, where he settles with Inna in the Bronx. Inna studies literature and receives a master's degree from Columbia. She is a scholar in her own right and will become a force in Chaim's life and legacy.

CHAIM GRADE'S CHALLENGE TO JUDAISM'S FIRST PRINCIPLES

Once in America, Chaim seeks out his half-brother, Abraham; they become close, and write one another with great frequency.[13] On at least one, if not several, of Chaim's trips from New York to Chicago, the two brothers meet

11. Leviant, "Chaim Grade's Centenary."

12. Berger, "Inna H. Grade, Fierce Literary Guardian, Dies at 85," para. 10. See also, Inna Hecker's discussion of this in her foreword to *My Mother's Sabbath Days*, where she writes about the mistaken belief that the Germans were a danger only to able-bodied men, whom they would round up for hard labor. Grade was concerned his wife would be in more danger outside of Vilna—"a decision he later considered the most fateful of his life" (Grade, "Foreword," in *My Mother's Sabbath Days*, xi).

13. Yehuda Zirkind, a scholar who is studying Chaim Grade in Jerusalem, provided me with photocopies of a portion of the large volume of correspondence between Chaim in New York and Abraham and his wife, in Chicago, much of it written in the 1950s.

and spend time together. In his letters, Chaim tells Abraham that he is working on an important new book; in response, Abraham asks for signed copies for himself and his family in Chicago when the work is published. And, in the Yiddish edition of *My Mother's Sabbath Days* ("Der Mames Shabosim"), Chaim dedicates the book "with love to my brothers in Chicago, the sons of our father, Reb Shlomo Mordechai, son of Reb Yerucham."[14]

In 1967, now in America for nineteen years, Chaim publishes one of his most important works. *The Yeshiva* expresses his doubts about observant Judaism in what was then considered a controversial novel. It is written in Yiddish and is not translated into English until 1976 by Curt Leviant. Chaim's wife holds up the translation, waiting with some fanaticism to find a translator who has a literary ear for both English and Yiddish and who can capture the beauty of her husband's writing.

The Yeshiva's protagonist, who some critics suggest voices Chaim's personal views,[15] questions the most fundamental beliefs about traditional Judaism. The introduction to *The Yeshiva* expresses Chaim's doubts: "The first page of *The Yeshiva* states that Tsemakh Atlas, a yeshiva scholar and rabbi, doubts the existence of God and the divinity of the Torah, thus announcing a theme never before attempted in Yiddish literature."[16] The hero is "unlike any other Jewish hero in fiction,"[17] in large measure because he dares to doubt, and to question fundamental Jewish beliefs.

The opening pages of *The Yeshiva* portray Chaim's profound doubts about Judaism. Tsemakh is "racked with doubts about the existence of God."[18] He goes on to question more: "Actually he was grappling with a fundamental principle; he knew that there was a Torah and that without Torah man couldn't find his way—but he didn't know whether the Torah was divinely given."[19] Tsemakh claims he is not sure if he believes in the "First Principle." The First Principle is the existence of God.[20]

---

14. I am indebted to Curt Leviant for this translation and discovery. Chaim's brothers were Abraham and Joe Y. Grade. There is also a reference to another brother in a letter of October 19, 1952, from Abraham to Chaim: "my two other brothers, Joe and Jack" (or Jacob). The family tree on Ancestry.com does not contain any reference to a Jack or Jacob Grade.

15. Leviant, "Chaim Grade's Centenary."

16. Grade, *Yeshiva*, vii.

17. Grade, *Yeshiva*, vii.

18. Grade, *Yeshiva*, 3.

19. Grade, *Yeshiva*, 3–4.

20. In his commentary on the Mishnah (tractate Sanhedrin, chapter 10), Moses Maimonides formulated his "13 principles of faith." These principles summarized what he viewed as the foundational beliefs of Judaism.

Later, Chaim's wife Inna says that these expressions of fundamental doubt were her husband's way of showing the tension between the sacred and the profane, and that it is in the nature of the profane to wage war on the sacred. In her view, "In the end human yearning for the spiritual—the eternal—spiritualizes and redeems even the war of the sacred and the profane."[21]

Yet, Inna's comments may expain away too much. Leviant, who knew Chaim well, said, "I realized that Grade was a secular, non-observant Jew when, early in our relationship, I saw him joyously order and eat *trayf* (non-kosher) meat."[22]

CHAIM GRADE—THE "FAULKNER" OF YIDDISH WRITERS

Chaim Grade died of a heart attack, at age seventy-two, on April 25, 1982. The *New York Times* published a full-page obituary, which quotes Elie Wiesel: "The work of Chaim Grade, by its vision and scope, establishes him at the age of 64 as one of the great—if not the greatest—Yiddish novelists."[23] Chaim was buried in Riverside Cemetery, across the bridge in New Jersey. Inna told almost no one about the funeral, so few attended. Decades later, my wife's parents were buried in this same cemetery. I have been there twice in recent years, unaware, of course, of Chaim's resting place. How odd these crossings of paths.

Following his death, Chaim achieved international recognition as one of the great Yiddish writers. Yet, during his life, Chaim remained relatively obscure. According to the *New York Times*, "Chaim Grade was the other great postwar Yiddish writer, the one few people outside of scholarly circles have ever heard of. And for that, some people blame his widow."[24]

Little wonder that Chaim's fame was slow in coming. As the *Times* would later report: "For more than two decades after his death in 1982, Inna Hecker Grade cantankerously repulsed almost all efforts to translate or publish his work or sift through his papers."[25] From Inna's perspective, Chaim was the greatest Yiddish writer, and he eclipsed the writings of Isaac Bashevis Singer.[26] To Inna, Singer debased the Jewish people and drew characters

---

21. Grade, "Foreword," in *Sacred and the Profane*, vii.

22. Leviant, "Translating and Remembering Chaim Grade," para. 12.

23. Shepard, "Chaim Grade, Yiddish Novelist and Poet of the Holocaust, Dies," B-8.

24. Berger, "In Yiddish Author's Papers, Potential Gold," para. 1.

25. Berger. "In Yiddish Author's Papers, Potential Gold," para. 2.

26. Berger, "Inna H. Grade, Fierce Literary Guardian, Dies at 85."

who were unsavory swindlers, rakes, and wanton men. It was her husband who properly expressed the heart and soul of the Jewish people, and she made it her life mission to ensure that her husband's works were properly translated, and that his place in literary history was preserved.

Inna died on May 2, 2010, without a will and with no survivors.[27] After Inna's death, there was a legal dispute over who was entitled to Chaim's papers and writings. Four major institutions inspected his records and writings and expressed interest: the YIVO Institute for Jewish Research, the New York Public Library, the National Yiddish Book Center in Amherst, Massachusetts, and Haravrd University. Upon learning that Chaim's papers might now be available, one scholar wrote: "This was our thrilling moment in Yiddish literature, this is our Dead Sea Scrolls."[28]

The dispute over Chaim's papers ultimately was heard by the Public Administrator of Bronx County, New York, and the matter was resolved when YIVO acquired the collection in conjunction with the National Library of Israel. YIVO is now the repository and guardian of the papers of Chaim Grade.[29]

Upon acquiring this collection, Johnathan Brent, the YIVO Executive Director, commented that Chaim produced a body of work of "Faulknerian power in its depiction of place and the psychological and moral depths of his characters."[30] YIVO said it hoped that Chaim's writings would be more widely disseminated and his rightful place among the great Yiddish writers even more firmly recognized.

THE GRADES AND THE KUNEYS—A FAMILY CONNECTION

When I first started going through the boxes from Jackson, the role of Abraham and Chaim Grade in Sol and Anna's life, and the question of whether the Grades may have influenced Sol were not in the forefront of my thinking. And yet, the more I researched my family's history and the more I wrote the more I came to see both the connection between the Grades and the Kuneys and the influence of the Grades' views on my family.

There is ample evidence that Sol and Abraham were first cousins. Yet, in writing this, I felt the need to confirm that the use of the word "cousin" on

27. Obituary of Inna H. Grade, *New York Times*, May 12, 2010.

28. Berger, "In Yiddish Author's Papers, Potential Gold," para. 5.

29. "YIVO Institute and the National Library."

30. "YIVO Institute and the National Library," para. 6.

the ship manifest, for example, was not gratuitous or a standard ploy used by immigrants to convince the authorities they would be in good hands in America. Now, after two years of research, I am convinced that Abraham and Sol were first cousins, and that the grandchildren of Sol and Anna, myself included, are the descendants of that branch of the Grade family. As for Chaim, he and I are half-first cousins (twice removed), although genealogical support for this particular designation is not clear.

In addition to the ship manifest for Sol and Anna's journeys, other facts corroborate the Grade/Kuney connection. For example, my cousin Jo Ellen was named after Joe Grade, Abraham's son, who died shortly before she was born.[31]

Jo Ellen also remembers her mother telling her that Scott, Jo Ellen's brother, was named after Shlomo Grade—Abraham's and Chaim's father.

When Julius dies, Scott and Jo Ellen travel to Florida to go through his belongings, and discover that her father kept a copy of Chaim's books, including *The Yeshiva*. Later, Jo Ellen sends me a copy of *Rabbis and Wives*, which is the earlier title and version of Chaim's book, *The Sacred and the Profane*. Inside the front cover, Julius has cut out and left a review of *Rabbis and Wives* from the *New York Times* of November 14, 1982 (translated by Harold Rabinowitz).[32]

There seems little doubt that Julius and Francine were keenly aware of who Chaim Grade was, named their children after his family members, and collected and read his books with interest. It may well be that Julius, like his father Sol, took comfort in the notion of a secular, rationalist form of Judaism, and that the writings of Chaim Grade spoke directly to this sense of his own deep assimilation.

WHY DOES THE CHAIM GRADE CONNECTION MATTER?

By going through the boxes, and with research and reflection, I now see Sol through the lens of Shlomo, Abraham, and Chaim. And, in that sense, I find myself chasing Chaim Grade in order to understand what he and the Grade family might have meant to my family, and what broader meaning they might have for suburban Jews who seem to be discarding every vestige

31. In the fall of 2019, Jo Ellen finds the baby book that her mother, Francine, kept, and there Jo Ellen discovers for the first time that her name was chosen "in honor of Joseph Grade."

32. And, in the boxes I am given, I find a clipping from the *New York Times*, dated July 1, 1982, with Chaim's obituary. Apprently, Joe too has kept his eye on Chaim Grade.

of Judaism, beyond a casual appearance for a sliver of a day or two for the High Holidays, and even this with the hope that it will not drag on too long.

Sol could easily have found the core beliefs of the Grades to fit with his own notions of a less observant, less demanding form of Judaism. The radical secularism of Chaim Grade likely was shared by his brother Abraham, as they both would have received this point of view from their father. And, in turn, Sol probably found comfort that his own secular leanings were fully supported by the Grades. Seeing this now, I understand better why Sol argues with Anna over whether their son Joe needs a Hebrew education or much of anything Jewish at all. First principles pushed aside yet again.

And if indeed Sol is somehow influenced by this radical thinking about Judaism, I find myself wondering how much was lost by this turn to a predominantly secular view of Judaism. Sol and those like him may have been too eager to cast off and turn away from the Jewish texts, and the source of wisdom, comfort, and guidance they provide.

Isn't it possible that, by failing to look deeply into Jewish texts and biblical narrative, they were cut off from the treasures and insights that are so deeply embedded in the Torah, and that, once they had lost those things, they also lost the ability to transmit a meaningful sense of what it means to be Jewish to the next generation? Isn't this the problem that Joe would later have, and why he, too, could never really explain to me why it mattered that we were Jewish after all, other than our survival for over 2,000 years, without a hint about what it was that made us survive and, mostly, what made us worthy of survival?

I have come to believe that because Sol was cut off from Jewish reading and Jewish learning, and because he transmitted a limited view of Judaism to his sons, an entire generation of Jewish families would have to learn how to read the Jewish texts all over again. And because for many of us the task of learning was too hard, it became much easier to simply let it all go. Now, finding it too hard, if not too late, to acquire the knowledge and discipline, I am not at all certain that I can explain why we are Jewish to my children any better than Sol or Joe did.

Is this, then, at least part of the reason why, of my three children, none has joined a synagogue, none attends Shabbat services, and none has pursued any form of Jewish studies as young adults? Yes, time may change all of this. But for now, I find myself—despite having served on the boards of three Jewish institutions, with my daily davening—not at all sure I can explain to my children why we must maintain a distinct voice and role as Jews in a difficult world.

Is this why on each Shabbat I stand alone in *shul*?

CHAPTER 8

Joseph and Esther

Early Years in Chicago (1917–1937)

ON WISHING I WERE A COHEN

In December 1917, Esther and Joe are born one day apart in the same hospital in Cook County, Illinois, one room apart, each baby able to hear the other cry. Esther is born on December 28, Joe on December 29. They are both the first American-born Jews in their families. I do not think Sol is at the hospital for the birth. He may have been at his tailor shop, pressing or mending.

Like Sol before him, there seems some odd confusion about Joe's real name, not to mention his Jewish name—the name that can connect him most deeply with his heritage, and the name that can sometimes change the course of one's life. Joe's birth certificate says his name is "Joe," not Joseph. And there is no middle name. On December 29, 1917, Anna signs an affidavit stating that Joe Kuney is the person known as Joseph H. Kuney. The "H," we are told, stands for Harry, and it is this name that Joe carries with him his entire life, although I have no record showing that he ever changed it from what is shown on his birth certificate.

Of course, Joe's true linkage to his Jewish past is not as "Joe" but as Joseph, the son of Jacob, one of the three great patriarchs of the Jewish Bible. It will take him until 2001, when he is called to the *bema* to read from the Torah, to reclaim his heritage. That is the year he reads from the Torah portion called Vayigash, which describes the moment when Joseph confronts his brothers who have returned to Egypt to buy grain because of the famine in Canaan. He will say to them: "I am Joseph . . . is my father still alive?"

(Bereishis-Vayigash 45:3). Aviva Zornberg says it is in this line that Joseph takes off the mask of his Egyptian role and becomes his true self. This is the moment when his assimilation ends.

So too, then, our Joe, who does not become Joseph for eight decades, does not reveal to himself who he really is, does not complete the journey that Sol started, a journey that took him away from his Jewishness, away from Canaan, and then at long last back to the line of Abraham, when in Arlington he rethinks his need for a bar mitzvah and is called to the *bema* to read from the Torah. So much in a name. It is not good to be careless with birth certificates.

Judaism puts much stock in names. Jewish scholars belive that names reflect one's destiny and are deeply related to spiritual attributes.[1] The story of Exodus, the second of the five books of Moses, tells of the creation of the Jewish people. And this most important of all books begins with this: "And these are the names of the sons of Jacob who came to Egypt" (Shemos 1:1). The commentators note that "a name indicates individuality. The Torah wishes to emphasize that God concluded the covenant not with a nation but with an indvidiual."[2] Indeed, Jewish law requires that the names recorded in the marriage document be written with precision, and that Abraham's spiritual greatness was reflected by his changing his name from Avram to Abraham, that a name reflects one's destiny.

Esther's birth certificate says her mother is Mamie Aronson. Yet she seems to have other names from time to time. She is Mae Cohen, or Mamie, or Mari. By the time I know her, she has forsaken the name on her birth certificate and is Mae, the name she will use for the rest of her life.

Mae comes from a line of Cohens. Joe's handwritten family tree, a document which he saves until the day he dies, confirms that Mae's maiden name is Cohen; her grandfather is David Cohen, and her grandmother is Ida Cohen. So then, when I am born twenty-eight years later, it is possible I am named after my great-grandfather, David Cohen, or my paternal great-grandfather, Fishel David. Or perhaps neither: Who can say?

How could it be, I now wonder, that we were descended from Cohens and no one said anything about this, no one attached any importance to it? But there it is—we are Cohens. A nation of priests. The Cohens are at the

---

1. Lustiger, *Chumash Mesoras Harav*, 2. "Abraham was elevated to spiritual greatness by changing his name. Maimonides says that the name Jacob reflected a certain destiny, while Israel [his new name] reflected a different destiny. The appellation of the book *Shemos* signifies that the Exodus would have taken place even if only one individual had been in Egypt."

2. Lustiger, *Chumash Mesoras Harav*, 2.

very top of the Jewish hierarchy, given the task of preserving Judaism. The priestly class, not expected to work, but to be the spiritual leaders.

I take seriously the notion of Jewish scholars that names and destiny are linked, that the changing of a name can change destiny, that we are assigned names at birth for spiritual reasons that even the parents can only partially understand. There have been times when I had a secret desire to be a Cohen; the notion of the priestly sect appealed to me. It might have been the kind of position I could have handled with some training, perhaps. Of course, the descent is patrilineal, so there is no credit given for the role of the mother, at least according to some.[3] You are Jewish if your mother is Jewish, but you are a Cohen only if your father is a Cohen. Who makes these rules?

But Esther never speaks of this, and never mentions that she comes from a Cohen line. So I am out of luck. Although, when young, I fantasize about changing my difficult last name from Kuney to Cohen. *Not that different*, I think, *and easier to pronounce*. And in truth, some part of me longed for that name. But destiny is what it is, and there is no point in trying to tinker.

THE JEWISH LIFE OF SOL AND ANNA IN CHICAGO

In some sense, if Vilna was the Jerusalem of Lithuania, Chicago was the Vilna of America, or at least the Midwest.

By 1930, Sol and Anna have moved to 2931 Broadway; in 1940, they are at 2945 North Broadway, according to the 1940 census. Irving Cutler, who studies the early Jews of Chicago, writes that the Jews in this area (the Maxwell Street area) created a community with some resemblance to the Old World *shtetl*, with its numerous Jewish institutions.[4] The Maxwell Street area contained Chicago's largest Jewish community when Sol arrived.[5] In 1845, on Yom Kippur day, the first Jewish religious service was held in Chicago. By 1930, when Joe would have his bar mitzvah, there were 275,000 Jews in Chicago.

In this area, Sol could have found some of the same voices of dissent and revolution that he would have heard in Vilna; this was an area of intellectuals and activists who espoused socialism, communism, secularism, and Zionism. Indeed, "Jewish radicals, fairly numerous in the area, frequently

3. M. J. L., "What Are Kohanim, or Jewish 'Priests?'" "Traditionally, only a man can be a kohen, and the status is transmitted from a father to his son" (para. 4).

4. Cutler, *Jews of Chicago*, 66.

5. Cutler, *Jews of Chicago*, 73.

articulated their philosophies from soapboxes on the corners around Humboldt Park."[6] I often heard Sol talk about the Bolsheviks, and although my memory is vague, I think now he was on their side, on the side of social revolution.

There was also ample opportunity for Sol and Anna to find a rich, observant Jewish life if they chose, and a way to provide their two children with a Jewish education. Jewish leaders in Chicago were certainly aware of the Vilna Gaon, and the famous Jewish yeshivas that had been active in Vilna, including the Brisk Yeshiva, which was considered by some the leading yeshiva in all of Europe. When the Russian government closed the doors of the Brisk Yeshiva in 1892, the family of rabbis who had taught there, and their rabbinic descendants, sought to take the same tradition of Torah scholarship and move it to Chicago; and they ultimately founded the Brisk Yeshivas of Chicago in 1974.[7]

Chicago had many synagogues as well. The first synagogues in the West Town were built in the 1890s. Jewish communities and synagogues were all around Sol and Anna. On the West Side, forty synagogues opened.[8] And another twenty synagogues served a Jewish community that had spread to the more affluent neighborhoods west of Humboldt Park. There were also a number of Hebrew schools, including the large Yavneh in the Humboldt Park area, sponsored by four orthodox synagogues in the vicinity.[9]

Yet, despite the richness of Chicago's Jewish life, I believe that Sol veered away from an observant Jewish life. I do not know whether Sol or Anna ever attended a synagogue in Chicago, but they never mentioned having done so. No talk of High Holy Days in Chicago. Work on Shabbat goes forward.

Sol was even resistant to Joe having a bar mitzvah. From stories Joe himself told, we know that he starts Hebrew school when he is approaching thirteen years of age, but is "kicked out" when Sol refuses to pay the tuition. The brief notes that Joe leaves behind indicate that Anna and Sol fight over this, and that Anna arranges for a private tutor to come to the house and teach Joe enough to have a small bar mitzvah ceremony. The tutoring will get him through the ceremony and the reading, but it is hardly a rigorous Jewish education. Within a few years, he will lose even his rudimentary understanding of Hebrew, and remember little. Whatever it is he may like or love about being Jewish remains submerged, beyond the level of easy recognition.

6. Cutler, *Jews of Chicago*, 235.

7. Fishbein, *The Sentinel History of Chicago Jewry*, 192–94.

8. Cutler, *Jews of Chicago*, 74.

9. Cutler, *Jews of Chicago*, 234.

This resistance to a bar mitzvah for Joe reflects Sol's deeper and implacable resistance to even a modest level of Jewish observance. Sol arrives in the New World speaking only Yiddish. He has not been to a Hebrew school nor a yeshiva. And, years later, Sol never speaks to us of Torah, never mentions the weekly *parsha*. Torah to Sol was not something we carry with us everyday.

Yet, who could be judgmental of Sol and Anna if their first priority was getting the job done, the job of survival, with religion a second or more distant priority? One must be careful about elevating religious observance over making a living. The Talmud offers a cautionary note here: "One who benefits from his hard labor is greater than a God-fearing person, i.e., one who is so enthralled by his fear of God that he sits idly by and does not work . . . . By the labor of your hands you will live: you are happy and it is good for you" (Ps 128:2) (Tractate Berachot, 7b).

Sol could well have thought that Judaism was simply too hard, not practical for an immigrant, not for a tailor who had to provide for his family. He must have wondered why Jews had made all of this so hard, needlessly so.

Sol's reluctance to embrace the more observant side of Judaism has strong antecedents that go back centuries. This was not merely an historical mode of thinking that suddenly erupted in the early twentieth century, but a part of the constant tug-of-war that is the permanent fate of religious belief. Christianity itself breaks away from Judaism with similar thoughts: a softer route to salvation; fewer rules; the ability to get work done, after all. Is it not easier for a Christian to maintain one's faith without the constant demands of the *law*, the customs, the traditions, the constant reference to the sacred text? Jesus provided salvation in exchange for *faith*. The hard stuff was off the table. No need for circumcision. No need to worry about the forbidden foods. Sabbath was Sunday. Restrictions were loosened. Access to eternity was less problematic. Jesus announced an end to all the fuss. One could breathe easier; the load was lighter. The chosen people in Chicago have other things on their minds.

I find no fault in what Sol did—assuming I have put this all together correctly. And yet, because of the things I did not see when young, and because of the discussions about Torah and Judaism that I never heard, I learned all too well that life goes on one way or the other, with or without the laws and the observances, and so the secular world acquires its own validity, and as Chaim Grade would later write, the tension between belief and doubt is always with us, even when we walk past the *mezuzah* on our doors and remind ourselves to walk with the Torah each day.

ESTHER AND JOE IN SCHOOL (1925)

If Joe's Jewish education had been lacking, the same cannot be said of his secular education. Joe was able to attend two good public schools, each of which still exists today. Joe attends Nettlehorst Elementary School, built in 1892, a three-story, red-brick building. It is a short, seven-minute walk from North Broadway where Sol and Anna likely live by then. Google Maps says the walk from 2945 to 3252 Broadway, where the school is located, takes eight minutes and is .4 miles.

I took this walk myself around 1952, on a visit to Sol and Anna when I was about seven years old. Esther and Joe had enrolled me at Nettlehorst temporarily while we were there for only two weeks. I attended classes with Richard, and walked from Sol and Anna's apartment to the school. I found the old school and the old buildings of Chicago dreary and intimidating, and wondered why one would want to live in Chicago. The suburban asthetic of blandness had already warped me, and I found no charm in the stately red-brick buildings, nor the vendors selling fresh fruit along the sidewalk.

There is little doubt that Joe was an excellent student, with the mind of a scientist or engineer. The small notebooks he carried later in life have grids, not lines; mine have lines. This is the difference between the father who charts a formula or an algebraic equation and the son who writes prose; no use for graphs.

Joe graduates from Nettlehorst in January 1931. The photograph of his graduating class survives. There are thirty-two girls and fifteen boys. The boys are dressed in white shirts and wide ties. The children do not look like the children of recent immigrants. For some reason, Esther is not in the picture; she either graduated later, in June, or went to a different school.

Esther is thirteen in 1930. She now lives at 4808 Spaulding Avenue with her parents, Martin and "Mamie," both of whom are thirty-four years old.[10] I never learn where she has gone to elementary school. When I ask her brother, Shelley, he reminds me he was born in 1938: Esther was married by 1939, and so he knows little of her youth.

STOCK MARKET COLLAPSE (OCTOBER 29, 1929)

Joe and Esther are eleven years old when the stock market collapses—October 29, 1929. The headline in *The New York Times* the next morning reads:

10. 1930 Census form.

"Stocks Collapse in 16,410,030-Share Day, but Rally at Close Cheers Brokers; Bankers Optimistic, to Continue Aid."

The first paragraph says this:

> Stock prices virtually collapsed yesterday, swept downward with gigantic losses in the most disastrous trading day in the stock market history. Billions of dollars in open market values were wiped out as prices crumbled under the pressure of liquidation of securities which had to be sold at any price. Wall Street was a street of vanished hopes, of curiously silent apprehension and a sort of paralyzed hypnosis yesterday. . . . It was the consensus of bankers and brokers alike that no such scenes ever again will be witnessed by this generation.[11]

Esther and Joe are twelve years old when the Great Depression of 1929 darkens America. The Depression does not seem to put an end to Sol's business, however. By 1930, Sol has acquired his own tailoring business, and the census taker writes "own business" in the column for "where employed." Sol has made the full transition from recent immigrant to modestly successful businessman.

Still, the Depression leaves its unmistakable scars on Sol, Anna, Esther, and Joe. They live in constant anxiety and have vivid memories of scarcity. But, still, no one goes hungry. They do not stand in soup lines, as many others do. And yet, this period will define their views on money and success for the rest of their lives. They now see with great clarity the risk of life: how things can run out, the need for rationing. Life is more fragile than they had thought.

The Depression also marks our lives as suburban children a generation later. When we are elementary school children packing our own lunches in reused brown paper bags, Esther will insist that we not pile on multiple thin slices of inexpensive bologna, on white Wonder Bread. Esther always keeps a watchful eye.

Years later, after they have moved to Rockingham Street and when Joe should be more secure about money, the fear remains. Joe will collect old newspapers, even as an executive at the American Chemical Society, tie and bundle them, put them in his trunk, and drive them to the junk yard in Georgetown just to get a few dollars in return. I remember the drive to the junkyard, located over Key Bridge and on to M Street. The car would be weighed upon arrival, the papers would be emptied and the car weighed again on the way out. A few dollars for a dozen well-tied bundles of newspaper. Nothing thrown out; nothing wasted.

11. "Stocks Collapse," para. 1.

Concern for money and financial stability stays with Joe forever. Later in life, after my older brother Richard takes his own life and his widow Maggie is struggling, Joe will insist that she repay him $10,000 that she and Richard had borrowed only a few months before his death. And when I, too, borrow money from him, he insists on a formal promissory note and interest payments at the going rate. "Just business," he says, but in truth I think it is fear, the fear of loss.

The fear that there will not be enough money, that we can never know if we are safe, passes generation to generation. I get summer jobs, and after-school jobs, and live off a few dollars earned here and there. I do not attend summer camps and do not even imagine joining a country club, at least not for many years. If I have a date, I cut the grass for a neighbor, and hope to make enough money for a movie and a few gallons of gas. One dollar is enough gas for a few days, at twenty-five cents a gallon when I am fifteen.

Much later, the aftermath of the Great Depression leaves us with a palpable sense of scarcity and the need to strive. We are nothing if not insecure about money. We are fully engaged and ambitious because we have not seen or heard of any other way to surivive life. Winston Churchill will remark that the only thing in life he ever feared was running out of money. This from a man for whom hand-to-hand combat caused no anxiety.

LANE TECH (1930–1934)

Joe turns sixteen in December 1933 and attends the Albert G. Lane Technical High School. His annual yearbook for June 1934 survives.[12] Lane Technical High School is a turning point in Joe's life. It is here that he gains his first serious exposure to technical and engineering skills, and then, more importantly, printing. All of these skills will traverse his life.

During the early years of the school's history, it was a manual training school for boys, where students could take advantage of a wide array of technical classes. Freshmen were offered carpentry, cabinet making, and wood turning. Sophomores received training in foundry, forge, welding, core-making, and molding. Juniors could take classes in the machine shop, and by the time they were seniors, students were able to take electric shop,

---

12. Lane Tech today is a large, co-educational seventh-through-twelfth-grade public high school, offering students a college preparatory curriculum, with particular emphasis placed on the technological aspects of a modern education. Lane Tech opened as a manual training school for boys until the 1930s, when its mandate was changed to that of a college preparatory school. The current building, situated on a beautiful thirty-acre campus, was opened in 1934.

which was the most advanced shop course offered at Lane. By the 1930s, Lane had a student population of over 7,000 boys.

Lane Tech has a print shop that changes Joe's life. The print shop is said to be the best-equipped high school print shop in America, with the newest and most advanced equipment of the time. Its print jobs include the four-page *Lane Daily*, the 56-page monthly *Tech Prep*, and the annual 200-page yearbook, plus other out-of-school jobs. Lane offers a course in printing, and it is here that Joe learns the printer's measures, how to read type, and gains practical experience in setting up the daily school newspaper. Later, when he seeks work at the American Chemical Society, his knowledge of printing will prove decisive. For many years, he saves his initials, "JHK" in a solid block of linotype.

Joe's technical skills, his ability to use his hands and build things, should come as no surprise. Joe is Sol's son, a man whose hands are his life: the skill of the tailor; careful measuring, cutting, and fitting. Sol is the quiet worker, standing in the background, distant, at times sullen and even angry, but ultimately deferential to the conflicting demands of his business. Some part of this finds its way into Joe as well.

His high school yearbook confirms his early years in Nettlehorst and that he was the recipient of four scholarships. He is in the Honor Society of 1933 and the winner of an oratorical contest. He apparently dances as well. According to the yearbook, "Kuney was Lane's waltz king." Joe graduates from Lane Tech on June 14, 1934. The graduation ceremonies are held at the Medinah Temple.

Joe buys a small autograph book for his friends to sign toward the end of the school year, and they leave him with their thoughts. There are a few places for his own observations. His favorite sport, oddly, is skating and his favorite subject is tech. Some of his friends say nice things about him. Some saw his future success: "Dear Joe: I hope your future will be a bright and happy one, undiminished by human tears and sorrow. I know you have high ambition in life and will someday climb the steps to success. Your friend Audrey Havelier." I think Audrey had seen in Joe what Esther would see: ambition and drive. It is what we all saw, one way or another.

Others were less kind: "Dear Joe, No matter how fat you get, there's always time to get fatter. Ed Jackson."

Emily has a wish and a request: "Best of luck and success thru high school. Please don't take my hat again."

Others provide sage advice: "Hi Joe. When you get kids, 1, 2, or 3, Name the dumbest one after me."

Some are poetic: "When the golden sun is setting and your mind from care is free, when of others you are thinking, won't you sometimes think of me."

Joe's younger brother, Julius Harry Kuney, was born in Chicago on July 24, 1919. The two brothers are less close and more competitive than Esther's siblings. I am at a loss later to understand why Esther and Joe always seem to whisper about Julius behind his back. I ask, from time to time, about what had happened to cause this rift, but I never get a satisfactory answer. Later, I came to see that one was a scientist and the other an artist. They lived in different worlds.

I found no evidence that Julius goes to Lane, nor would he have been well-suited for a school full of pratical young men, young men who were headed for engineering or science. Unlike Joe, Julius has no instinct for the sciences or chemistry. He will go to the University of Illinois, and receive a bachelor's degree in communications. Unlike his older brother Joe, who is not drafted, Julius serves with the Navy in the Pacific during World War II, where he serves as a communications officer aboard the USS McCalla. Somewhere in our family album is a picture of him in his dress whites. He is strikingly handsome, tall and thin, and has a beautiful speaking and singing voice. Julius will later head to New York and Los Angeles, and make a living in the world of art, theatre, and television.

Esther grew up surrounded by boys, her brothers, and was outgoing and social. She was tall and thin, and her lean body reflected her constant sense of motion and energy. She was a leader, tough-minded, bossy, always taking charge, ambitious, and competitive. She ran track in high school and thought of herself as an athlete. She smoked, drank endless coffee, and played cards with her brothers and sister, sitting around a large dining room table, everyone talking at once, beer and cigarette smoke everywhere: working people, common people. The men wore their white undershirts, saving their dress shirts for workdays. They all had loud voices; someone always calling to "sis," as Esther was known. On visits when we were still very young, we would find a makeshift bed or sofa on the first floor and listen to the chatter, thinking this was normal; that this was how one dressed and talked and acted. They were hardly elegant. This was what Chicago had done to our family.

Esther learned to play cards, to gamble, and became a risk-taker. Later in life, she and Joe would travel often to Las Vegas where she always won at the card tables; Joe always would lose. She could count cards and outsmart the table bosses and dealers. When we went together, she taught me how to play blackjack, and when we later played golf together, she played like a gambler, cunning, smart, and filled with the joy of the game. Joe was risk-adverse. He had no feel for cards or gambling. He was a chemist, a scientist by instinct. He liked math because there was only one right answer; there was no risk involved. He took her to Las Vegas because he would do whatever she wanted.

High school for Esther is mostly sports and stenography. Esther loved sports and was always a great athlete. When I was a child, Esther spoke about running track and jumping hurdles. Much later in life, when she walks with a cane, after surgery for her heart condition, caused by too much smoking, she will refer back to those days, unable to connect the person she once was to what age has done to her. This implacable gulf and inability to hang onto what she most loved rankled her to the end.

Esther graduates from high school, but there is no thought of college for her. She is ready to work and start her life in the business world, and she will be unrelenting in this pursuit. There are a few more years of being at home, but in her heart she knows she is meant for other things. She is lightning-fast on the typewriter and at taking shorthand. I often watched her typing, and remember thinking that her hands were magic; I watched in awe as her fingers raced across the keyboard. Our home will be overflowing with stenography pads filled with the strange encryption of shorthand. She passed on her typing skills to all three of her sons. Our home would always have a typewriter clacking away somewhere. Because of Esther's gift, I would become a faster typist than any secretary in my law office. I waited with great impatience in the early years of the computer, and was grateful when at long last my thoughts could become transposed into text as fast as I could think them.

When Esther finally meets Joe, she will channel her amibition and drive through him, somehow knowing, I now believe, that this is the man who could reflect her own drive and energy, the man who could take her out of Chicago, and away from the tailor shops, the slaughterhouses, and on to a life of something better. Joe may have done fine on his own, but it is Esther who will later provide the guiding force to move them through the years together.

I do not think Esther sets foot in a synagogue in Chicago, and I doubt that she has seen the Sabbath candles lit in her childoood home. Later in life, some of her many brothers and their familes drift off to California and come to embrace Christianity.

But in this early part of her life, when Joe is about to go to college, and she is still single, there is nothing to suggest that she has any particular interest in the Jewish religion or observance.

CHAPTER 9

The Middle Years in Chicago (1932–1946)

JOE'S COLLEGE CAREER WAS the stuff of family myth and mystery—at least until I had a chance to uncover the key documents that laid it all out. Unsurprisingly, it is Esther who plays a key role, both in making college possible for Joe, and later in embedding the myth of how it all happened in our boyish minds. And while I often doubted her, there would come a time when I would realize that she'd done what she set out to do: given us an image of work and grit from which none of us three boys could escape, nor would we want to.

But the myth was simple: Joe was brilliant but could not afford to attend the University of Chicago, even with a scholarship, because the trolley fare was a nickel each way. So, he worked his way through college over eleven years, spending the first six years in a modest technical school as a night student. When he finally did make it to the University of Chicago, we are told he was involved with research on the atomic bomb, although in an indirect, secret way.

Was any of this true? It was certainly the story Esther told us over and over again because she wanted us to know the price Joe had paid for his boys, and for her. And she wanted us to have the drive to do the same if and when life called on us to do more than we might want.

One of the first discoveries I make in going through the boxes is that Joe initially sought admission to the US Naval Academy. On December 9, 1932, when Joe was about to turn fifteen, he wrote to Congressman Fred Britten from the Eighth District of Illinois and requested an appointment to the US Naval Academy. Joe was apparently hoping to find a way to pay for college, knowing that money was scarce and the payment of tuition unlikely. The US military academies are free. The Congressman wrote back, saying "It is quite probable that I can name you as an alternate for admission to the Academy in 1934." Joe then sent Congressmen Britten additional information and endorsements. On September 20, 1933, Congressmen Britten replied: "I am listing your name for appointment to the US Naval Academy in 1934, but I cannot at the present moment state definitely that I will have a vacancy next year. We will see."

As it turned out, Joe was not selected for the Naval Academy. Perhaps it was better that he was not chosen. Joe was hardly the warrior type. Yet, in some ways, Joe may have been a good candidate for the Naval Academy—he certainly had the instincts and knowledge of an engineer, which is one of the key attributes for naval service and command of a ship.

After his rejection from the Academy, Joe began working during the day in a printing shop, and looking for a college that offered night courses—something that was uncommon in the 1930s. Yet, he apparently found the ideal place. Joe's college career is well-documented on forms he submitted many years later to the US Government in order to obtain a security clearance to work at a facility run by NASA. These forms show that, for the first six years, Joe attended technical schools, some of which offered night classes so that working students could attend.

Joe began his college career at the Lewis Institute of Technology in 1934. The Lewis Institute was well-suited for young men like Joe—smart, first-generation Americans who were unable to afford college. The Lewis Institute was founded in 1896 by Allen Cleveland Lewis, who willed his estate to the creation of a school of higher learning open to all men and women, regardless of finances or social standing. All of its programs focused on practical, professional education for both male and female students. It was one of the first colleges to offer night courses.

At the time that Joe enrolled, its student body was made up of over fifty different nationalities, many of whom were first- or second-generation Americans. The 1936 yearbook shows a cover with five students: one woman, one black, one Asian, one Hispanic, and one blond Nordic-looking man. I think Joe found the diversity and the absence of wealthy students to his liking, and he would later tell me that he felt all schools should require uniforms so that one's social standing would not be readily apparent.

The NASA security clearance forms show that he attended the Lewis Institute from October 1934 until June 1935. He then attended college at Northwestern University's McCormick Campus, from October 1935 until June 1936. From October 1936 until June 1940, he lists his college as the

Armour Institute of Technology,[1] which by then had merged with the Lewis Institute. In short, he spent his first six years of college at relatively small technical schools.

Esther and Joe were married in 1939, and with Esther's income, they now had enough money for Joe to transfer to the University of Chicago in the fall of 1940. He graduated with a Bachelor of Science degree in Chemistry in 1945.

So there you have it, Joe's college career—eleven years from 1934 to 1945. We never really believed it when Esther told us that Joe had spent eleven years working toward his college degree. But the boxes from Jackson and the form submitted for his security clearance prove Esther correct.

This story of Joe's eleven-year college career is deeply embedded in our family history. Esther never tires of telling it to us and I see now that she used it to motivate her sons, much as she had her husband. Her endless drive and ambition had made Joe stick it out, for over a decade, and now she was determined that her three boys would understand the price Joe had paid, and be willing to do the same when it was their turn. She was the one who told us we could be whatever we wanted, but she also was the one who made sure we understood the price to be paid.

This story of eleven years working on a college degree defined Esther and Joe and helped me understand their willingness to struggle in order to achieve. In their minds, this is what it took for the son of an immigrant to succeed. I have never doubted that whatever the cost, Esther and Joe would work the hardest, and sacrifice the most, in order to make their way, first through Chicago, and finally to Arlington. For all of their shortcomings, and our endless disagreements and struggles, I never lost my core admiration for their determination and courage, and as a result never knew in my own young adulthood a time to seek comfort and ease. The ceaseless striving was all.

I have never learned when and how Esther and Joe first met. No family member still alive was able to tell me. I am guessing it was shortly before Chamberlain assured the world that he had made a deal with Herr Hitler for peace in our time. Perhaps 1937 or early 1938. Somewhere and somehow, amidst the financial woes of the Great Depression and the German decision to kill all Jews, a young man attending night school at the Armour Institute meets and falls in love with the girl who had been born one day earlier than he had in the same hospital in Cook County, Chicago.

1. These schools are listed on Joe's DOD Form 49, dated July 15, 1980, and was submitted to the DOD for a Top Secret Clearance.

Esther and Joe had much in common, but also differences that could have doomed the relationship. Both had parents from Russia, and both were the first-born American Jews of their families. Both families worked in tailoring or dry cleaning. Neither had money. They were South Side Jews, working class, hard scrabble for sure. Joe with the out-sized intellect and his strong risk aversion, and Esther ambitious and driven, embracing risk, but hardly intellectual in temperament.

Was it love at first sight for these two very different people? Can a man and a woman see one another and, from that very moment, sense a future together? The Jewish narratives in the Bible tell us that love at first sight is both natural and spiritual. Issac—one of the three great partriarchs of the Jewish faith—meets and falls in love with his future wife and the progenitor of the Jewish people with hardly more than a glance.

Isaac has gone out to the field toward evening, to meditate. He is still in mourning for his mother, Sarah, who has only recently passed away. He raises his eyes and suddenly sees camels approaching. His future wife is on a camel, approaching him. "Rebecca raised her eyes and saw Isaac and fell from her camel" (Bereishis, 24:63–64).[2] Rebecca says to her servant, "Who is this man striding in the field coming to meet us? . . . Taking a veil, she covered herself. . . . Issac brought her into the tent of his mother . . . and she became his wife and he loved her" (Bereishis, 24:65–67).[3]

How beautiful a story—falling from the camel, falling in love with barely a look, the overpowering immediacy of the look the two of them exchanged. The Torah reveals its truth with spare language. Between the seeing, the loving, and the marriage, nothing but three brief lines. So much meaning to carry, a kind of wisdom not available from other sources. Rebecca's fall from the camel tells us everything: a moment of revelation when the future is sensed. It is love at first sight, and a love that will create a nation. Somehow they see in each other a destiny. They may not have yet known each other, but even before words, and even before knowledge, love comes into being.

The Torah validates the closeness and eternal love of man and woman: the sacred bond. No wonder Joe defends Esther when I fight with him over some family injustice—of which, to my mind, there were too many.

And so it is with the love between Esther and Joe. Despite their differences, they rarely argue. Years later, their three children see nothing but a seamless love. For all his anger, Joe never says a harsh word to Esther. We see, but are dumbfounded and at times frustrated. Joe accepts Esther for

2. Not all translations agree that Rebecca "fell off." Compare Plaut, *Torah*, 161, suggesting the literal meaning of the Hebrew is "fell off," with the more modern view of Robert Alter that she "alighted" (*Hebrew Bible*, 1:84).

3. Plaut, *Torah*, 161 n.64.

who she is; there is no talking things through to get to the bottom of the issue: the bottom is of no importance. What we see is love and making life safe for the loved one. This most profound of all lessons is what we take into our own adult lives, years later.

ENGAGEMENT (1938)

In December 1938, Esther and Joe become engaged. Esther's parents, Mae and Martin, send out formal announcements that the couple will be at home, Sunday, December 18, to meet guests. The formal, printed announcement seems out of keeping with working-class immigrant families. I am surprised there is enough money for a printed announcement and a mailing to friends and family. The Depression has not taken this away from them. Somehow Joe also has found the money to buy Esther an engagement ring, and she will wear this ring the rest of her life along with a separate wedding band. Later, Joe will embellish it and enlarge it, but for now, he insists that she must have at least this, despite the Depression. Her marriage to Joe is the turning point in Esther's life, and the foundation for every decision she will make from that point forward.

Sol and Anna also send out printed invitations to a bridal shower. "Mrs. S.U. Kuney" invites the guests to a bridal shower in honor of Miss Esther Miriam Aronson, to be held at 2945 Broadway on Friday, June 23 at 8:00 p.m. The wedding will be in September. It is unclear what the "U" stands for in the printed invitation. Perhaps a mistake by the printer who misread "Sol" as "S.U.?" It is apparently not a matter of concern, nor is Anna concerned that the shower is being held on Shabbat. A touch Victorian for this midwestern couple, and certainly not in keeping with more observant Jewish customs, but there you have it.

Esther and Joe are married on July 30, 1939. The wedding takes place on a Sunday evening at 6:00 p.m. in the Ionian Room, Logan Square, Masonic Temple at 2451 North Kedzie Boulevard. Not in a synagogue. The choice of the Masonic Temple suggests that Sol and Anna and Martin and Mae never joined a synagogue in Chicago, and having the wedding in a synagogue was of no importance to the two families.

The Masonic Temple was a famous architectural landmark in Chicago. The building, a massive four-story, steel-framed, brick-and-limestone structure, was built at a cost of $300,000. The mass of red brick is criss-crossed with detailing that gives the building a commanding presence. Towering fluted limestone columns augment the entrance, and a centrally located stone header below the cornice or roofline announces the "Logan Square

Masonic Temple." The building remains today, but it has since become home to the Armitage Baptist Church after it was purchased in 1982.

On their wedding day, Joe and Esther are twenty-two years old. Joe and his groomsmen dress in solid, summer white suits, the bridesmaids in long floral gowns. The Depression has not required a more modest wedding. Everyone is in their finest. Because I discover a marriage contract in Hebrew, it appears the wedding was officiated by a rabbi. The Jewish marriage certificate now hangs in our home; with Esther's and Joe's names written in Hebrew; their pledge to one another. How did Esther know her Hebrew name?

They have no money for a long honeymoon. Joe is still working as a compositor for a newsprint company and is attending the Armour Institute of Technology at night. Following their wedding ceremony, they check into the Hotel Harper-Crest, located in Chicago at 54th and Harper Avenue, and leave the next day, July 31. The rate is $2.50 per day. Joe has saved the receipt. The hotel was a small, popular hotel until 1950, when it was renovated and taken over by a university. Presumably, they leave the next morning for a modest honeymoon. Fifty years later, we celebrate their wedding anniversary at our home in Potomac, Maryland, and make a full-size poster of their wedding day photo.

Their marriage is an unbreakable bond. Beyond reason, they become inseparable for all the days of their lives. There is nothing Joe will not do for Esther. Later in life, he will drive her everywhere, wait for her as she does her errands, buys her the better car. Joe insists all family arguments with Esther end in her favor; no exceptions. We resent this lack of justice, but not until many decades later, when we have forgotten what we were fighting about, do we come to admire it. It becomes clear to us, all three brothers, this is the deep compromise of love that keeps the relationship working and gratifying.

Newly married, with Esther working, Joe can afford to attend the University of Chicago. Joe now begins the first of five years at the university, studying for a degree in chemistry. He and Esther live at 665 Kenmore Avenue. He tells the 1940 census taker he is working full time—which is consistent with his attending the University of Chicago as a night student. The median annual income for a man in 1940 was $956. He is making $940 a year as a compositor in a newspaper print shop.[4]

A compositor is a linotype setter. Joe is the one who puts the metal letters and words together into small units that fit into a single line on a

4. 1940 Census report.

printing press. The skill Joe has learned at Lane Tech now becomes the foundation for his entire working life. It is this job that will ultimately shape his career, when a few years later he learns that the American Chemical Society in Washington, DC is looking for someone with a background in chemistry and some knowledge of printing to head up their business operations. The job is made for Joe.

Esther also is working. She is a stenographer at a shoe factory in Chicago, making $950 a year. Together, they are making $160 per month, or $40 a week. Doughnuts in Chicago were fifteen cents a dozen. Ground beef was fifty-five cents per pound.

Esther has graduated from high school, and that is all the schooling she feels she needs for her career. I never heard her mention any regret about not attending college. Her shorthand skills and typing are excellent. As the years go by, she will fill thousands of the small stenographic notebooks that contain the strange hieroglyphic symbols of shorthand, then known to so many secretaries, but now largely if not completely forgotten. Our home will be filled with these notebooks, and when I find an unused one in the house, I will try to fill it with notes and lists and short stories, all coming to nothing. Just the quiet, endless fascination with words flowing onto paper, shapes forming meaning.

It is during the time when Esther and Joe are about to become engaged, and then married, roughly from late 1938 to 1940, that the war in Europe intensifies and the threat to Jews throughout the world becomes more evident. On November 9 to November 10, 1938, in an incident known as "Kristallnacht," Nazis in Germany torched synagogues, vandalized Jewish homes, schools, and businesses, and killed close to 100 Jews. In the aftermath of Kristallnacht, also called the "Night of Broken Glass," some 30,000 Jews were arrested and sent to Nazi concentration camps.

In 1939, Hitler told Heinrich Himmler to plan for the occupation of Poland and the Soviet Union. On January 30, 1939, Hitler announced to the Reichstag that the result of the anticipated war would be the "annihilation of the Jewish race in Europe."[5] Later, on July 31, 1941, Hermann Göring ordered Reinhard Heydrick, the chief of the Nazi secret police, to prepare a "total solution of the Jewish question."[6] And "22 June 1941 marked the start of Operation Barbarossa, a turning point in Nazi anti-Jewish policy,

5. Engel, *Holocaust*, 36.
6. Engel, *Holocaust*, 60.

resulting in the mass murder of some 1.5 million Jews under Nazi occupation in forests and ravines such as Ponar and Babi Yar."[7]

Esther and Joe have been married for four weeks when, on September 1, 1939, Hitler invades Poland. The *New York Times* headline declares: "German Army Attacks Poland; Cities Bombed, Port Blockaded; Danzig is Accepted Into Reich." Hitler sends a dispatch to his army, making it clear that they are to fight to the death.[8]

Albert Speer, Hitler's architect, explained that the goal was to destroy the Jewish people, not just in Europe, but in America as well. Hitler believed America would remain indifferent to his conquest of both the world and the Jews:

> Hitler was counting on the indecisiveness of the Americans, on their unreadiness to make sacrifices for a national purpose—as Hitler saw it, a degeneracy fostered by their prosperity. He interpreted the Americans' domestic political preoccupations and their "business-is-business" egoism as factors that would keep the American nation from throwing into the scales on time its much greater industrial capacity against a rearming Germany.[9]

By the time Esther and Joe return from their honeymoon, the world has spun into darkness. In the spring of 1940, Hitler's armies have seized Norway and Denmark. By June, the Germans have conquered France, and Italy has declared war against the British and the French. By the middle of 1940, President Roosevelt is assessing the political damage that might occur if he starts a forcible draft of young men for the armed forces, an act that was "unprecedented in peacetime" and would lead his critics to say he was pushing the nation into war.[10]

In July 1940, the Democratic party meets in Chicago to nominate its candidate for president. Roosevelt has to consider whether to seek a third term—an act that no other president has ever done, and that later the states would prohibit by a rare constitutional amendment. The convention is held in Chicago, and Roosevelt is nominated under banners that read "The world needs Roosevelt." The Democratic platform makes clear that America "will not participate in foreign wars . . . except in case of attack."[11]

---

7. Yad Vashem World Holocaust Remembrance Center, "Invasion of the Soviet Union," para. 1.

8. "Albert Speer," A-23.

9. "Albert Speer," A-23.

10. Beschloss, *Presidents of War*, 372.

11. Beschloss, *Presidents of War*, 376.

Joe will turn twenty-three in 1940 and is starting his first semester at the University of Chicago, which he can now afford because both he and Esther are working. The news of the war is all around. Roosevelt is promising to stay out of the war "unless attacked,"[12] but those close to Roosevelt know his true view: no matter what, America must protect England and Europe. And so, in September 1940, Roosevelt calls for a peacetime military draft. Senator Burton Wheeler, an isolationist from Montana, warns that, if Congress passes the draft, it will "slit the throat of the last great democracy still living" and "accord to Hitler his greatest and cheapest victory."[13] But Army Chief of Staff General George Marshall, who later will save Germany in its postwar resurrection, insists there is no conceivable way to ensure our national defense without it. A public poll shows that by June 1940, 86 percent of the country supports passage of a bill to enable the draft.[14]

Assessing the political damage, Roosevelt pushes forward with the draft. Then, on September 16, Congress passes the Selective Training and Service Act of 1940, establishing the first peacetime draft in US history. It requires all men between the ages of 18 to 64 to register with the Selective Service. The Act initially calls for drafting men aged 21 to 35 for a service period of 12 months.[15]

Joe and Julius register together for the draft on October 16, 1940. Joe's registration shows that he is then six feet tall, weighing 230 pounds. He is twenty-two years old, and working at M&L Typesetting Co, at 4001 Ravenwood Avenue in Chicago. He and Esther live at 4602 Kenmore Avenue. Julius registers next, and his draft registration reflects that he is six-foot-one and weighs 204 pounds. The registration also shows he is then a student at the University of Illinois and still living with Sol and Anna at 2945 Broadway.

Because Joe had been married in 1939, he will be deferred from being drafted, at least until 1943 when the draft laws change. His draft card shows he was initially classified as 3-A, which means "deferred for dependency reasons." This classification was abolished in December 1943, but, before that, in 1942, the draft laws were revised to permit all married men deferment from Class 1-A until further notice. "We want the unmarried

12. Beschloss, *Presidents of War*, 376.

13. Beschloss, *President of War*, 374.

14. Beschloss, *Presidents of War*, 374.

15. In early 1942, however, following the Japanese surprise air-raid attack on Pearl Harbor on Sunday, December 7, 1941, and the subsequent declaration of war by the United States against Japan, the service period was extended to last for the duration of the war, plus a six-month service in the Organized Reserves.

men taken first," Democrat Sen. Joshua B. Lee of Oklahoma said. "This is recognizing, in a legislative way, that the family is the fundamental unit of organized society."[16] The purpose of this draft amendment, according to Sen. Lee and other officials, is to make sure that families are "left intact as long as possible."[17] To dispel fears that this new deferment law will cause a personnel shortage in the military, Senators Warren Austin of Vermont and Elbert D. Thomas of Utah state that the "present pools of single men or men without dependents should meet all manpower demands of the fighting forces through this year and well into 1943."[18]

On November 5, 1940, Roosevelt defeats Wendell Wilkie by 54.7 percent to 44.8 percent of the popular vote, with 449 electoral votes to Wilkie's 82.[19] Joseph Kennedy, an isolationist, speaks to the *Boston Globe* shortly after Roosevelt wins the election and says, "Democracy is all but finished in England" and there is "no sense" in getting into the war. He goes on to say that, if America joined the war, "a bureaucracy would take over right off. Everything we hold dear would be done."[20] Roosevelt invites Kennedy to Hyde Park for a "dressing down" and tells Eleanor when Kennedy leaves, "I never want to see that son of a bitch again as long as I live."[21]

Two nights before the end of 1940, Roosevelt takes to the radio: "Never before, since Jamestown and Plymouth Rock, has our American civilization been in such danger as now. . . . The Nazi masters of Germany have made it clear that they intend not only to dominate all life and thought in their own country, but also to enslave the whole of Europe, and then to use the resources of Europe to dominate the rest of the world."[22]

If Esther and Joe and Sol and Anna somehow had hoped, along with others, that the war would not touch them, this would soon give way to the gruesome bloodshed caused by the Nazis, as it played out in Vilna and the rest of Europe. Given the deferment for married men, Esther and Joe may have felt that Joe was not likely to be drafted, although that too would change toward the end of the war. Julius had no such deferment and would later head to the Pacific as a Navy communications officer.

And if Sol and Anna had been wondering what was happening to their family in Vilna, they would soon learn.

16. McIndoe, "Married Men to Get Draft Deferment," para. 4.

17. McIndoe, "Married Men to Get Draft Deferment," para. 5.

18. McIndoe, "Married Men to Get Draft Deferment," para. 7.

19. Beschloss, *Presidents of War,* 376.

20. Beschloss, *Presidents of War,* 377.

21. Beschloss, *Presidents of War,* 377.

22. Beschloss, *Presidents of War,* 378.

CHAPTER 10

The End of Vilna as the
Jerusalem of Lithuania (1941)

IT HAS BEEN SAID that "the German Final Solution and the Holocaust actually began in Lithuania."[1] It was not just the Germans, but the Lithuanians
themselves—those who were now the same age as Sol and Anna, the same
people who might have been their neighbors in Vilna—who attacked the
Jews. After the German army had invaded Lithuania, it was the pro-Ger-
man Lithuanians who arrested any Jew on sight, and often tortured and
killed them, frequently burning them alive in their homes or a synagogue.[2]
In short, "the German Army enjoyed the full support of the Lithuanian
population.[3]

The summer of 1941 appears to be a turning point. In June 1941, there
are about 200,000 Jews who still remain in Lithuania. Then, between June
1941 and December 1941, nearly all of the Jews of Lithuania are massacred
by the Germans and their collaborators. "The Christian majority welcomed
the Germans as liberators and right-wing paramilitary groups began massa-
cring their Jewish neighbors . . . more than 95 percent of Lithuania's Jewish
population were murdered—a more complete destruction than befell any
other Euopean country."[4]

1. Porat, "Holocaust in Lithuania," 159.
2. Greenbaum, Jews of Lithuania, 303.
3. Greenbaum, Jews of Lithuania, 304–5.
4. Brook, "Double Genocide," para. 7.

This would be the "largest loss of life in so short a period of time in the history of Lithuania."[5]

Rabbi Ephraim Oshry, one of the few European rabbis to survive the Holocaust, later writes *The Annililation of Lithuanian Jewry*, in which he tells the story "in horrific detail how the Nazis and their Lithuanian collaborators viciously murdered Jews" but, despite being beaten and starved, the Jews continued to study Torah until their death.[6]

Most Lithuanian Jews were shot during the first months of the Nazi occupation and before the end of 1941. The first recorded action of the Einsatzgruppen, the special task force for the killing of Jews, took place on June 22, 1941, in the border town of Gargzdai, which was the oldest Jewish settlement in the country. On that day, 800 Jews were shot in what is known as the Garsden Massacre. The members of the Einsatzgruppen had trained "for their arduous assignment by murdering mentally ill and handicapped Germans."[7] At first, they chose huge fuel storage depots and tank pits as the site of massacres "of exceptional cruelty and brutality."[8] On December 1, 1941, the German Karl Jaeger sent a secret report from Kaunas stating that "the goal of solving the Jewish problem in Lithuania has been attained. . . . There are no more Jews in Lithunia anymore except those needed for work and their families. . . . I intended to kill off these working Jews too. . . . "[9]

On June 25, 1941, Lithuanian partisans "decapitated the Chief Rabbi of Slobodka, Zalman Ossovsky, and displayed his head in the front window of his house."[10] But Rabbi Oshry reports an even more gruesome version: "The rabbi of Slobodka, Rav Zalman Osovsky, was tied hand and foot to a chair, 'then his head was laid upon an open volume of gemora (volume of the Talmud) and [they] sawed his head off," after which they murdered his wife and son. His head was placed in a window of the residence, bearing a sign: "This is what we'll do to all the Jews."[11]

5. "Holocaust in Lithuania," para. 1.

6. Martin, "Ephraim Oshry, 89, a Scholar During the Holocaust." "Jews were somehow able to part with everything that defined their place in life—home, business, job—but the one thing they could not part with was the Book" (para. 21). See also "Ephraim Oshry," para. 4.

7. Greenbaum, *Jews of Lithuania*, 313.

8. Greenbaum, *Jews of Lithuania*, 313–14.

9. Greenbaum, *Jews of Lithuania*, 326.

10. Greenbaum, *Jews of Lithuania*, 307.

11. "According to Rabbi Oshry, there were Germans present on the bridge to Slobodka, but it was the Lithuanian volunteers who killed the Jews" (Oshry, *Annihilation of Lithuanian Jewry*, 3).

No matter what anyone will say later, the truth is everywhere, for those who read. On August 18, 1941, the *Daily News Bulletin* from the Jewish Telegraphic Agency reports this:

> VICHY, Aug. 17. (JTA)—A decree issued here today sets September 15 as the deadline when all Jews must retire from professions specifically forbidden to them by the anti-Jewish laws. These include such professions as doctor, lawyer, teacher, as well as participation in commercial and industrial vocations.[12]

And then this headline from the Jewish Telegraphic Agency: "Mass Expulsion of Jews from Lublin Reported from Nazi Poland." The story continues:

> A new wave of anti-Jewish terror has been started by the Nazis in Lublin and Zyrardow. . . . The reports describe how Nazi soldiers surrounded the Jewish streets in Lublin and in Zyrardow and ordered thousands of Jewish families to leave their homes. The victims were not permitted to take anything out of their dwellings. They were then crowded into military trucks and brought to the railway stations where they were herded into cattle trains and transported to smaller towns and villages. Their property in their homes was then carried away by military trucks, never to be returned.[13]

When they reached their destination, many died within the first two weeks. "One fifth of the several thousand Jews confined by the Nazis in the incredibly vile Jewish concentration camp in Jaslo, southern Poland, died from exhaustion, hunger and physical mistreatment during the first two weeks of their imprisonment."[14] The description of the Jews' confinement was horrific. "Jews in the Jaslo camp are herded in a small enclosure near the local prison. No food is given to them for days on end. When they do receive some, it is the leavings of other prisoners. As many as ten Jews are locked into stalls in the prison lavatories and forced to remain there even while prisoners use them."[15] The gas chambers will come later.

The news reaches Chicago. The *Sentinel* reports on August 21, 1941, buried on page 31, that the Nazis have burned the Strashun Library in Vilna. The latest Jewish library to be desecrated by the Nazi authorities in Lithuania under their new commissar, Heinrich Loehse, was the Kovno Yiddish

12. "Mass Expulsion of Jews" (*Jewish Telegraphic Agency*), para. 1.
13. "Mass Expulsion of Jews" (*Jewish Telegraphic Agency*), paras. 1–2.
14. "Mass Expulsion of Jews" (*Sentinel*), 22.
15. "Mass Expulsion, of Jews" (*Sentinel*), 22.

Library named after the Hebrew writer, Mapu: "Thousands of books from the beloved institution were dumped into adjoining streets and burned. Accompanying the barbaric rites with typical Nazi ceremony, the participants staged a full-dress celebration attended by high Nazi military and civil dignitaries. A Nazi band played joyful tunes and Nazi soldiers danced in the square."[16]

News of the Warsaw ghetto also reaches Chicago and the rest of America. The issue of the *Sentinel* published the week of August 21, 1941 titles its lead article, "Where the Ghettos Now Stand." One-half of page two contains a black-and-white photograph, with the caption, "Behind the Nazi ghetto walls of Warsaw." The article continues: "[H]itler . . . carried out his plans to make Jews an outcast and derelict people throughout the world. More than 500,000 Jews have been herded together behind an eight foot wall which cuts them off from the rest of the population of the city of Warsaw."[17]

Jews in the Warsaw ghetto receive no bread, and an average of 300 Jews living there die daily from starvation.[18] And then this: "The Nazi authorities in Warsaw have issued an order prohibiting Jews in the ghetto from eating vegetables . . . . Jewish homes are being raided in order to ascertain whether vegetables are consumed."[19] The order amounts to a conscious effort to starve to death the Jews of the Warsaw ghetto. The Nazis are meticulous. No detail is overlooked. The obsession with killing runs deep. The Jews who remain and resist the deportation to concentration camps are systematically killed when Hitler orders the city burned to the ground with tanks and flame throwers.

The reports are the same elsewhere in Europe. The *Sentinel* of August 1941 reports this:

> Hospitals and sanitoriums throughout Hungary are being raided by the police and Jewish patients are being dragged from there for deportation to Nazi-held Galicia. . . . Private reports . . . disclose that it is no longer safe for a Jew to appear in the street. All Jews are stopped by police and asked for citizenship certificates. Those who have no such certificate are immediately arrested. On the other hand, the authorities refuse to issue such certificates to Jews.[20]

16. "Hold Public Bonfire of Books," 31.
17. "Behind the Nazi Ghetto Walls of Warsaw," 2.
18. "300 Jews Die Daily in Warsaw Ghetto," 9.
19. "Nazis Prohibit Jews to Eat Vegetables," 9.
20. "Drag Jews from Hospitals," 31.

Violence also reaches America. The August 1941 *Sentinel* reports that a gang of young pro-Nazis led by a 17-year old German American who had been schooled in Nazi Germany, burned a Nazi cross on the front lawn of a well-known rabbi, Dr. David de Sola Pool. "The gang had been holding frequent meetings, where the members made anti-Semitic speeches and hatched plots against the Jews."[21]

So now I know why Sol and Anna fled Vilna and why the memory of Lithuania seems to have vanished from their memory. The Lithuanians who stood and cheered the Nazis when they burned and killed the Jews were the same people who grew up with Sol and Anna in Vilna. And maybe this is why, when we meet Sol on Broadway, in 1930, he says he is from Russia, and not Lithuania.

ROOSEVELT AND CHURCHILL
PLAN POSTWAR PROGRAM

If America is not yet willing to join the fight, at least it can negotiate what the world might look like after the war.

Roosevelt and Churchill meet in 1941 and sign an eight-point program for reconstructing the world after the war. Despite not having sent a single soldier to the war at this point, Roosevelt wants a vision and plan for the future, an image of the world after the war. Perhaps unlike other future presidents, Roosevelt insists on a clear understanding of what the goals of America should be and how the world should be organized after the war, a lesson later forgotten.

When Churchill and Roosevelt meet on Saturday, August 9, 1941, aboard the USS Augusta, the presidential flagship anchored in Placentia Bay alongside Churchill's The Prince of Wales, their talks produce the Atlantic Charter which lays out the postwar goals of both nations. This was the

first moment the world knew that Roosevelt and Churchill had met, and that they were in total accord about the underlying principles for the world they wanted to build after the extirpation of Nazism. It provided a potent rallying cry for the forces of freedom, so that people could feel they had something inspiring to fight for, and not just something evil to fight against.[22]

This conference is front-page news in Chicago and surely Joe, Julius, Esther, and her brothers read about it. A week later, the *Sentinel* makes this

---

21. "Young Nazis Burn Cross at Noted Rabbi's Home," 30.
22. Roberts, *Churchill*, 676.

its lead headline, next to the article on the Warsaw ghetto: "The Epochal Roosevelt-Churchill Conference."[23] The *Sentinel* provides comfort to Americans but fails to urge sending American soldiers to fight the Nazis: "The understanding reached by the two greatest obstacles to Hitler's conquest of Europe and the rest of the world is properly considered here and elsewhere as marking a definite turning point in the war, the prospects now being bright indeed, for the steady and irresistible advance of the democracies to their goal of defeating and destroying the armed might of the Nazis."[24] The *Sentinel* notes that whether America actually joins the war as an ally would be up to the Axis powers. Many in the United States still insist that the country stay out of the war, beyond sending ships and supplies through Roosevelt's ingenious Lend-Lease program.

The *Sentinel* has little to say about Japan. And yet, toward the back of the August 21 edition is this headline: "Japs Condemn Program as Jewish Plot." "The Japanese press assailed the historical eight-point postwar peace program announced jointly by President Roosevelt and Prime Minister Winston Churchill as a 'Jewish plot' to encircle Japan." The Japanese paper continued, "Jews re-elected Roosevelt for a third term. Jews coaxed Churchill to war against Germany. Jews are conspiring to overthrow the world-ruling powers."[25]

To be Jewish in Chicago was to see daily news of relatives and other Jews in Europe being brutalized, tortured, and killed. Being Jewish now meant harboring the deepest anxieties about survival. Newly married, America not in the war, but with the draft now the law, Esther and Joe, and Esther's brothers, must ask themselves whether they should have children. How many will survive if war comes? Who will be a widow and who will not?

The Jews have been through exile and the destruction of their homeland before. Lamentations describes with equal horror the lives of the Jews who were left alive in Jerusalem after the Babylonians had conquered the City and burned the temple. "Alas, women eat their own fruit/Their newborn babies" (Lam 2:20). How were the Jews to respond to such catastrophe? A biblical prophet, Jeremiah, weighs in on this dilemma. The Jews were exiled from Jerusalem in 597 BCE, after the temple was destroyed by the Babylonians, and they were forced to live in Babylonia. Some say it is only the elite who were exiled and the working man left behind. Jeremiah, in

23. Freedlander, "Epochal Roosevelt-Churchill Conference," 3.

24. Freedlander, "Epochal Roosevelt-Churchill Conference," 3.

25. "Japs Condemn Program as Jewish Plot," 31.

Jerusalem, sends a message to the Jewish leaders and priests in Babylonia. His letter tells them, "Build houses and live in them, plant gardens and eat their fruit. Take wives and beget sons and daughters; and take wives for your sons, and give your daughters to husbands, that they may bear sons and daughters. Multiply there, do not decrease. And seek the welfare of the city to which I have exiled you and pray to the Lord in its behalf; for in its prosperity you shall prosper" (Jer 29:4).

America is not Babylonia, but the new Jewish immigrants, Sol and Anna and the millions like them, are, in some sense, in exile in America. The world they left behind in Europe is being destroyed, and the threat is that Hitler seeks the same destructuion of American Jewry.

But Esther and Joe do what Jeremiah had advised some 2,500 years earlier. In the face of catastrophe, Esther and Joe continue to build for their future and "beget sons and daughters." Richard Philip, their first-born son, arrives in 1941.

So does Japan.

CHAPTER 11

America Goes to War

The Second Generation of Kuneys
in America (1941)

SEPTEMBER 4, 1941: RICHARD
PHILLIP KUNEY IS BORN

ESTHER IS PREGNANT WITH Richard and will give birth tomorrow, September 4, 1941. But for others, today, September 3, is dark. The *Sentinel* reports that, on September 3, 1941, in Auschwitz, Poland, experimental gassing has begun. Six-hundred Soviet prisoners of war and 250 sick prisoners are killed in a gas chamber using Zyklon B (a gas previously used for fumigation). Zyklon B becomes the killing-agent of choice; it is used to gas Jews and others for the rest of the war. At the height of the deportations, up to 6,000 Jews are gassed each day at Auschwitz.[1] Two days later, this: All Jews over age six in German territories are ordered to wear a yellow star, and Jews of Vilna, Poland are confined to their ghetto.

Richard Phillip Kuney is born in the middle of this darkness on Thursday, September 4, 1941, at 6:21 p.m., at the Grant Hospital in Cook County, Illinois. I assume Joe is not in the delivery room. He may be reading the sports news in the waiting room. The Yankees clinch the pennant, the earliest a team has ever done so.

Richard is delivered by Dr. Richard Reich, likely of German descent, and Dr. Short. He weighs 6 pounds, 9.5 ounces at birth, and is 17.5 inches

1. See US Holocaust Memorial Museum, https://encyclopedia.ushmm.org/content/en/article/gassing-operations.

tall. He nurses eagerly, eats well, and after two-and-a-half months is sleeping through the night. By the time he is seven years old, he will be four feet tall.

Esther starts to fill in the pages of "Our Baby's First Seven Years." She and Joe have signed the page on the date of Richard's birth. It is not a simple scrap book; it is, as explained between the covers, "A Baby Record Book including scientific charts which prove of practical service to the Mother and growing child." It is prepared with the aid of Dr. and Mrs. Horner and Dr. and Mrs. Calvin for "The Mother's Aid of the Chicago Lying-in Hospital." Produced in 1928, the foreword speaks to Esther:

> A baby's book should contain a great deal more than a mere record of worldly events affecting the new candidate for citizenship. It should have all the delicate and lovely sentiment attached to the birth and beginnings of life of the new individual, but it should include more than this. It should be a record showing the gradual physical and spiritual development of the body and soul. . . . The writer would therefore urge upon all mothers to fill out carefully this book as the child develops. Not alone will she have great pleasure in recalling the memory of these childhood days, but she will be in a position to render the grown child and adult, and even to his children, a distinct service. Indeed, she will thus make her contribution to society.[2]

Esther follows the doctor's advice, save perhaps for any mention of "worldly events." Given the nature of such events, who would want them in a baby book? Still, for years, she dutifully fills in the various pages in her neat and professional handwriting. She will take the baby book with her later when she and Joe leave Chicago and will save it for the rest of her life. There is no baby book for me or my younger brother, Steve. Perhaps by then the thrill or need had worn off?

She writes that Richard is named after "his two great grandfathers." But, who are they? There is no written record of their names in the boxes. Does she know the name of Sol's father, one of Richard's great-grandfathers? Anna's father is Fishel. Turning to Esther's family gives no clues. Mae's father is David Cohen and I do not know the father of Martin, Esther's father. There is not a single reference to the derivation of Richard's name in any of the boxes or any other document I have seen. Whoever these ancestors were is now lost to us. Like so much else, the boxes only tell a small part of the story of this immigrant family and those who did not make it to America.

Cards flood in. A card is signed by Mr. and Mrs. Ed. N. Apfelbaum. Ed is a forty-three-year-old personnel clerk at the post office whose daughter,

2. Nusbaum, *Our Baby's First Seven Years*, foreword.

Francine Apfelbaum, then eighteen, will later marry Joe's brother, my uncle Julius. Another card is "From a proud Uncle Julius." The scrapbook contains a list of gifts, and who gave them. "Granny"—Anna—has given Richard a baby buggy and Uncle Julius the baby book. Julius may not have noticed that the baby book reflects a strong Christian bias and focuses a fair amount on church matters.

Eight days after his birth, Richard may have had the traditional Jewish *brit mila,* the covenant of circumcision. Dr. Horner's babybook advises new mothers to track spiritual development, but there is no mention of this ceremony in Esther's baby book, which otherwise tracks virtually every significant event of my older brother's early life. I am certain Anna would have insisted on a *bris.* But if she did, we have no record of it. Of course, he could always have had the surgical procedure performed in the hospital, a circumcision without the religious ceremony.

Circumcision is the symbol of the covenant that God made with Abraham (Gen 17). *Brit mila* transforms an essentially surgical procedure into something with transcendent meaning; the outcome is the same, but the meaning is not. Still, *brit mila* does not make an infant boy Jewish. From a traditional point of view, if the birth mother is Jewish, an infant boy is Jewish at birth. Deborah Dash Moore writes, "The decision to circumcise a son is often the first difficult decision a parent must make. It initiates parents into demanding responsibilities of Jewish parenthood."[3]

Perhaps Esther and Joe were not seeking that kind of initiation; perhaps they were distracted. Anna may have urged it but ultimately lost what would have been the first of many similar arguments about making things Jewish. Things were being said in public, even in America, that made Jews feel uneasy and insecure. On September 11, 1941, Charles Lindbergh makes a speech on behalf of the America First Committee in Des Moines, Iowa, which included remarks that would be instantly controversial: "The three most important groups who have been pressing this country toward war are the British, the Jewish and the Roosevelt administration."[4] Lindbergh said he admired the British and Jewish races, but claimed that the Jews' "greatest danger to this country lies in their large ownership and influence in our motion pictures, our press, our radio and our government."[5]

The next day, White House Press Secretary Stephen Early said there was a "striking similarity" between Nazi propaganda and Charles Lindbergh's comments in Des Moines. Lindbergh's remarks were widely criticized in

---

3. Teutsch, *Guide to Jewish Practice,* 27.
4. "Charles Lindbergh Makes 'Un-American' Speech," para. 3.
5. "Lindbergh Accuses Jews of Pushing U.S. to War," para. 27.

the American press, even among pro-isolationist newspapers such as the *Chicago Tribune* and the Hearst media empire.

Richard, however, is free from political concern. So is Esther, it seems. According to Esther, Richard is an active and happy baby, a little commando. "At age of four months talks constantly. All day long laughs out loud. Really hollers when it gets near feeding time." The details! By thirteen months, he is walking alone and "dances to radio. Very good walker." By two, he is playing catch with a ball. ("You should see him throw snowballs.") By thirty-two months, Esther has learned to be cautious about what she says in front of him: "There isn't a thing he can't say now. Must be very careful when talking in his presence as to language." He is easily toilet-trained.

Richard is a "kangaroo." By three, he is jumping up and down. ("Never stops much to neighbor's regret.") By four, he is skipping and balancing on one foot. ("Our poor neighbors.") "Have to get Richie used to playing with smaller children. Our little commando is plenty tough." But Esther liked him tough. It was part of her own essential self. And so he remained the same active and aggressive person throughout his too-short life. That he was once a happy and secure baby fills me with sadness when I think how his life turned out later. Where did all the joy go, the eagerness on his young face? So hard to keep our children safe.

Richard has been home for one month and is doing doing well, when on October 9, 1941, a news dispatch picked up by the *Sentinel* from Geneva reports what has happened to Vilna, the "jewel of Lithuanian Jews": "The city is almost dead, with all Jewish shops closed, little food available, and few Jews seen in the streets . . . life seems to be at a standstill. . . . Once the course of the waters of learning, of piety—it is a ghost city mourning its past."[6]

It is probably best that Esther leaves out of the baby book the news of worldly events. She has other things to attend to. The rest of the city is nervous. On November 2, 1941, the then well-known Maurice Samuel is scheduled to make his first Chicago appearance at K.A.M. Temple. The *Sentinel* reports, "Appropriately, his lecture-sermon was titled, 'If we live through this.'"[7]

For Richard's first Thanksgiving, in November 1941, Anna would have made a large dinner. Despite her Jewish beliefs, she readily adopts the American holidays, at least where food is concerned. It was a good day to put the *Sentinel* aside. "As Thanksgiving Day was about to be celebrated

6. Fishbein, *Sentinel*, 41.

7. "Maurice Samuel Makes First Chicago Appearance at K.A.M. Temple," para. 1.

the overseas news mounted in intensity of tragedy and sorrow. Goebbels enunciated his 'Creed of Anti-Semitism' . . . . If one wears the Jewish Star of David he thereby is marked as the people's enemy. . . . Jews are the enemies' emissaries among us. The Jews have no right to pose among us as equals."[8]

On December 4, 1941, the *Sentinel*, on its main editorial page, addresses "The New Nazi Deportation Atrocities," and summarizes what it calls the unbearable agony of Nazi captives: "News of Nazi atrocities fill the *Sentinel* pages during the early 1940s. Bleak stories arouse a helpless world that writhes in frustration, as the world powers turn their backs on the plight of the Jews in Hitler's Europe."[9]

JAPAN ATTACKS PEARL HARBOR

Then, the ability to turn one's back comes to an end, as does the hand-wringing over whether to enter the war. Japan makes the decision for President Roosevelt. On the morning of December 9, 1941, Sol, Anna, Joe and Esther open the *Chicago Tribune* to the following headline: "US and JAPS AT WAR. Bomb Hawaii, Philippines, Guam, Singapore."[10]

On the night of Sunday, December 7, 1941, after hearing the news, Americans stand vigil in front of the White House. The American death toll at Pearl Harbor is 2,403. Eleanor Roosevelt gives a radio address to America: "You cannot escape a clutch of fear at your heart."[11] Despite some evidence of warnings and advance knowledge that Tokyo's foreign ministry had sent urgent instructions to its diplomatic posts to destroy most of their codes and important documents, this being a clear signal that the Japanese were on the verge of war, American military and political leaders claim to be surprised.

But it was hardly a surprise. On November 27, 1941, General George Marshall wired Walter Short in Honolulu that "negotiations with Japanese appear to be terminated." And Admiral Stark warned General Kimmel, who was in charge of Pearl Harbor, saying "[a]n aggressive move by Japan is expected in the next few days." On November 30, 1941, the *Honolulu Advertiser* warned, "Japanese May Strike Over Weekend." Admiral Kimmel, however, did not move the destroyers but kept them tightly together, making destruction easier; the planes were grouped together as well. Later, Henry Morgenthau, Jr., Secretary of the Treasury, told his wife, "We have

8. Fishbein, *Sentinel,* 41.

9. Fishbein, *Sentinel,* 41.

10. "US and Japs at War," 1.

11. Rothman, "This Is What Eleanor Roosevelt Said," para. 8.

always been led to believe that the Navy was our first line of defense and Hawaii was impregnable. . . . The whole fleet was in this little Pearl Harbor base. The whole fleet was there! . . . They will never be able to explain it."[12] The Roberts Commission later decided that the primary blame belonged to Admiral Kimmel and General Short. A court martial was considered. Admiral Kimmel was reduced to two stars and quit the Navy, living in "suspended disgrace."[13] When he died in 1968, he was interred at the Naval Academy, under a gravestone emblazoned with four stars, as insisted by his family despite the claim by others that he was at fault for the loss at Pearl Harbor.

How long can one argue over history? Over mistakes made? The mistakes we make never seem to go away. Time passes, but history clings to us; we cannot shake it. Kimmel's grandson now devotes his life to proving his grandfather blameless. We want to tell him it is okay now; it is past.

But maybe nothing is really past. Time's movement is partially an illusion. History is with us always. Our lives are lived on multiple planes. Even as late as 2016, Kimmel's grandson was appearing at conferences with slide shows and arguing for his grandfather's innocence.

Thomas Kimmel, the grandson, is well credentialed. He attended the Naval Academy, saw active duty in Vietnam, then went to law school, joined the FBI, and began an intensive study of Pearl Harbor. According to his presentation, Admiral Nimitz had gone to Pearl Harbor two days after the attack, and one week later submitted a report to President Roosevelt stating that neither Admiral Kimmel nor General Short had been alerted to the impending attack, despite the information Washington had. Roosevelt supposedly made them change the report to read that neither of them was "alert."[14] Or so Kimmel says. Is he being straight with us, or revising history?

Come early 1942, Jewish refugees are fleeing from the war in Europe. Escaping is risky, deadly. On February 24, the MV Struma had been trying to take nearly 800 Jewish refugees from Axis-allied Romania to Mandatory Palestine. The *Sentinel* reports that "the big story of the year (1942) is the horror-packed explosion of the Struma." "750 dead in Struma Explosion" reads the *Sentinel* headline. The story continues: "A ghost ship full of Rumanian refugees seeking shelter was refused permission to land in Turkey. Unseaworthy and overcrowded, it was almost lost in a storm. Two of its

12. Beschloss, *Presidents of War*, 382–85.
13. Beschloss, *Presidents of War*, 388.
14. Kimmel, "Interview of Tom Kimmel."

passengers went insane even before reaching Turkey. Five miles north of the Bosphorus it was blown to bits."[15] Still fresh in the minds of the *Sentinel* and its readers is the tragedy of the SS Patria, which sank in Haifa Harbor after the refusal of the Palestine administration to let the passengers disembark.

A few weeks later, on April 27, 1942, Sol who is then forty-nine, reports to his draft board at 2723 North Clark Street in Chicago. He states that he is a tailor, living at 2945 Broadway, and working at 2931 Broadway. He reports his birthdate as July 21, 1893. He weighs 219 pounds and is five feet eleven inches tall. He has gained a lot of weight since 1920, when he was naturalized as a citizen. Anna feeds him well. Plus what he eats when she is not looking, things she must never know.

Sometime in early 1943, Joe, who had earlier been turned down by the Naval Academy, now applies for appointment to the United States Naval Reserve. But, on August 14, 1942, he is turned down because he is "overweight by 73 pounds, flat feet with 3rd degree calloses and varicose veins of the left leg."

Julius has better luck with the Navy. Julius had registered for the draft on October 16, 1940, when he was twenty-one years old and attending the University of Illinois at Urbana. For some reason, his draft registration shows his name as Julius Udell Kuney. But almost all of his later records, including his voter registration, identify him as Julius H. Kuney. He was later commissioned as a Lieutenant, Junior Grade on May 1, 1944, and served as the communications officer on the USS McCalla. The McCalla was active in the Pacific and was involved in war duties during 1944, including antisubmarine duties in the South Pacific.[16] We still have photos of Julius in his Navy whites and blues, a strikingly handsome man.

NOAH GOLINKIN'S EFFORTS TO
SAVE JEWS IN EUROPE

News of the concentration camps is becoming more prevalent. Later, many will say they did not know, but the evidence is to the contrary. Even when Roosevelt knows the time has come to bomb the railway lines to Auschwitz, the American Air Force argues that it would require risky daylight bombing, and refuses to undertake it. Churchill is incensed. Hitler will insist on killing Jews long after the war effort is lost, devoting critically needed German soldiers to the killing of Jews, and ironically, diverting German troops from the Allied invasion of France on D-Day.

15. Fishbein, *Sentinel*, 42.
16. "McCalla II (DD-488)."

Others in America and elsewhere are trying to help get Jews out of Europe alive; among them is one young rabbinical student named Noah Golinkin, who, with a group of other rabbinical students, decides that American Jews must do more to alert the world to what is happening to the Jews in Europe. In December 1942, Golinkin and rabbinical students from the Reform and Orthodox seminaries take part in a delegation that meets with Dr. Stephen Wise, the most prominent American Jewish leader of that era.[17]

Golinkin and his colleagues meet at Dr. Wise's office, anxious to share their ideas for confronting the European crisis. But Golinkin is disappointed with what he hears. Dr. Wise rejects their proposal to call for increased Jewish immigration to the United States, fearing that such calls would provoke anti-Semitism. Hence he shows no interest in their offer to publicize the plight of European Jewry on college campuses. So, in early 1943, it is Golinkin, together with his Reform and Orthodox colleagues, who organize Jewish-Christian interseminary conferences and rallies to bring the plight of European Jews to the attention of Americans.[18]

It will be only a few years before Golinkin will move to Arlington, Virginia, as will Esther and Joe, followed later by Sol and Anna. And then, all of these lives will intersect—Sol and Anna, Noah and Chaim, Esther and Joe.

SEPTEMBER 1942: RICHARD IS ONE

Of course, there is still everyday life, which must go on. Esther's baby book records Richard's lovely first birthday party; by now she is calling him "Richie," and later I will call him "Dichie." There are references to gifts from Grandfather Kuney yet, oddly, no reference to Esther's parents. Sol and Anna have a dog named Whitie, and Richie loves him.

Esther records carefully all who come to the party and what they give. There is a sweater from the Apfelbaums—the parents of Francine—now Julius's wife. And then this: a shirt from great-grandparents Cohen. Where have the Cohens been all this time? Where are these children of the ancient high priests, and how is it that they do not work their way into my family memory, or become a spoken part of our heritage?

Perhaps it is best the Cohens, if they are priests in any sense, are not around to see our life in Chicago. Saturday afternoons are for baseball or time in the park. Not *shul*. Esther and Joe would go to one of the nearby

<hr />

17. Medoff and Golinkin, *Student Struggle against the Holocaust*, 32–33.

18. Golinkin, "Wonderful Life." Eulogy delivered by Rabbi Golinkin's son on March 2, 2003. Rabbi David Golinkin, Noah's son, is now the President of the Schecter Institute of Jewish Studies in Jerusalem.

parks with Richard. Joe would take his 16-mm movie camera; we still have the movies. These movies show Esther as an attractive woman in her late twenties, playing and laughing with her young son; she wears a lightweight summer dress, her hair is still dark brown, and she has a wide smile, filled with joy and energy. Richard and Esther play; they are natural and easy with one another. There is no sign of things to come. When did the rending start, I now wonder?

There seems to be little in the early years of Esther and Joe's marriage that reveals any sense of their being Jewish. There are no Jewish books, at least none that remain; no synagogue membership. Joe is much like Sol in this regard. He is focused on his work and on getting his degree, and he has little need or time for anything Jewish. And one might ask, why would he? Why interrupt the flow of life? There are complications enough.

Anna may have had other thoughts, but until Richard is born, it probably was not a pressing concern. She may notice the absence of regular religious services, but holds her tongue. They are doing fine. Who needs more? Anna and Sol live nearby and they see Esther and Joe and their grandson often. They visit for meals. They are close and, even if Sol is somewhat remote and at times sullen, it is all Esther and Joe need or want for now. Who can tell what will come later? No one is pushing them to be more observant; they have not even thought about Richard's Jewish education.

Yet, even if nothing is said, both Esther and Joe surely see the Jewish life Anna has brought with her from Vilna. They see the festival meals, the kosher food, the three sets of dishes, and without a word being said, something is passed on to Esther and Joe. It is not, after all, the words that do the heavy lifting of transmission, but the acts. Because Esther sees a devoted Jewish grandmother, she will, many years later, begin to light Shabbat candles in her own home, cover her head with a cloth napkin, as Anna did, and say the prayers in her version of Hebrew because, like it or not, Anna has embedded this Jewish part of her soul in another generation. Memory will do its thing—no use in kicking and screaming.

THE RELIGION OF BASEBALL

Of course, there are other places to go besides *shul* if you are seeking to nourish your soul. If you wanted to find Joe on a summer's day in Chicago, before he and Esther were married, and long before Arlington, a softball or baseball field was more likely than *shul*. There was something about sports for both Esther and Joe. But isn't there always *something* about most things? Nothing just is. Everything has its own subtext, its own metaphor, a larger meaning lurking around the edges. The Romans learned that the first structure they had to build in any newly conquered city was a colosseum. We cannot live well without a steady diet of metaphor and drama. How else to make sense of the universe?

Joe is just twelve years old, and already he is spending much of his free time at the Chicago Cubs' Wrigley Field. Sixty years later, he writes about this in a letter dated January 3, 1992, addressed to the baseball lover and ABC newscaster, George Will:

> A group of us used to go to Wrigley Field after school, where they would let us into the bleachers for free to see the last two or three innings. What a thrill to watch the likes of Hack Wilson, Kiki Cuyler, Charley Grimm and the many others of those great teams of the late twenties. It took about ten years before I could bring myself to see a Redskins game because of my long and continuing affection for the Bears. But my first and continuing love is the Cubs.

Before Esther and Joe are married, sometime around 1936, Joe becomes a part-time umpire in an adult softball league. The surviving photographs of this period show Joe in the dark black suit of the umpire, then the fashion, despite the summer heat, and the heavy padded chest protector; the players are in full uniform on a professionally lined field. He later will bring with him to Rockingham Street the small plastic, handheld counter for balls and strikes, the rotating dials that count strikes to three and balls to four, lest the umpire forget where things had left off. When I discover it much later in his drawer, sneaking around their bedroom when they are not home to see what they keep tucked away, I take it out and play with it and turn the dials. I try to find a new use for it, but cannot.

Baseball is serious business to Joe. In 1936, he applies for a position as an umpire for the Olympic Baseball game to be played in Berlin. Sadly, on July 25, 1936, he is notified by letter that his request has been denied because of the few positions and larger number of applicants. In 1939, Joe becomes a member of the local union for umpires—the Umpires Protective Association of Chicago. In 1941, he is still carrying with him his membership card for the International Federation of Amateur Softball Association of Umpires.

When Joe becomes a father in 1941, he turns again to baseball. It is how he spends much of his time with his young son, Richie. Richie loves it as well, and at twenty months, "Daddy bought him 'ball and bat' at Cubs baseball game. It is his favorite toy," writes Esther in her baby book. Esther and Joe live close to Wrigley Park, where the Cubs play baseball for many years without night lighting, so all the games are played in the daytime.

Joe's love of baseball never ends. Most of the pictures taken of him later in life, when he is well into his 70s and early 80s, show him with baseball hat and glove, playing in a seniors' league. There, in those pictures, I see the large smile, still a bit forced, with the overly large artificial teeth he had acquired late in life. But the new teeth do not really do the job. Joe never learned to smile naturally; the pain is always there—even with his new white teeth. Not until I study the pictures he saved do I realize how harsh his father, Sol, must have been with him—how else to explain the inability to smile naturally?

Joe, like George Will, saw the patterns in baseball that seemed to mirror his notions of how life worked, or was supposed to work. Even if Joe cannot talk to his own children about his Jewishness, at least not early in our lives, he is able to talk at length about baseball. The sports world anchors his philosophy. Is this what an assimilated, first-generation Jew does? The sports world fills a vacuum. He has learned his own lessons on grit and hustle and on bearing the unbearable. Both Esther and Joe urge upon us three boys the notion of "sucking it up and going on gut." Joe's favorite song was a then popular title—"I Didn't Promise You a Rose Garden."

Baseball becomes the key metaphor in his awkward attempt to transmit his philosophical underpinnings to us. Joe talks endlessly about success and failure and the thin line between the two. He will tell me that you only need to hit .300 to be considered one of the best—at anything, not just baseball. To survive. You don't have to succeed all the time, and not even most of the time. But you have to be in the game, on the field; you cannot excuse yourself, nor can you sit it out. In business, he tells me, just be right fifty-one percent of the time and you will do fine. Where, I wonder, does he get this from? Joe is trying to harden us to the inevitable failures, trying to make sure we don't get too distracted by failure and the sure-to-come rejections.

The overarching philosophy that seemed to find voice in Joe is the notion of the arena: the man of action. In a letter to Congressman Jack Kemp, dated November 4, 1977, Joe expresses his admiration for a speech that Kemp gave, in which he quoted Teddy Roosevelt. Kemp writes back, quoting Rudyard Kipling:

> It is not the critic who counts; nor the man who points out how the strong man stumbled, or where the doer of deeds could have done them better. The credit belongs to the man who is actually in the arena, whose face is marred by dust and sweat and blood; who strives again and again; who errs and comes up short; who knows the great enthusiasms, the great devotions; who spends himself in a worthy cause; who, at the best, knows in the end of the triumph of high achievement, and who, at the worst, if he

fails, at least fails while daring greatly, so that his place shall never be with those timid souls who know neither victory nor defeat.

Maybe this was the lesson Joe was trying to teach us over the years. To stay in the *arena*. Whatever that arena might be, whatever struggle it might be. Joe wanted us off the sidelines, and he certainly wanted us to think long and hard before we decided that whatever needed to be done, in whatever sphere, could be done by someone else. A simple creed.

The arena was where the "war" was fought or played out. The daily question Joe asked me, and from which I silently flinched, was this: "How goes the war?" *What war?* I wanted to ask. Did he mean the personal war, the one we fight against ourselves and those around us? Was this part of his message on grit, on the quality one had to have if one was in fact to step into the arena? Was he warning me that the arena was where one belonged, but that it could be devastating to one's sense of self-worth? The measure of life is not how often you fall down but how often you get back up.

I never liked Joe's constant reference to life as a war; I felt there had to be a different sense of things—not always a struggle, not always a contest. Something quieter, some sense of peace. *Shalom*, the Jewish word for peace, became central to me later. I wonder now if Joe had been fighting his own war all those years, and that in part, this was his unfortunate heritage from Sol and Sol's life in Vilna, where brutality had too much visibility.

But maybe I was having trouble with being committed and fully engaged. Where was the middle ground that made the strenuous effort less ill-fitting for someone like me, someone not suited for combat?

Years later, I learned to reframe these admonitions as a call to perseverance. It took me many years to see in Joe's words something akin, at least in a small way, to what Jewish scholars have to say on this notion of struggle and, if you insist, on life as war or staying in the arena. We are not necessarily obligated to complete the task, but neither are we permitted to cease trying. Try to finish the task, no matter what. *Making the effort* is the obligation. I only saw much later that the temptation to lay down the pencil, or give up too soon, was fatal. I was sometimes tempted to do so. But as Joe knew, there are nine innings, and each is of equal importance. We all grow weary and want to stop. But that's exactly what you cannot do. "Heart," the song about Shoeless Joe from *Damn Yankees*, makes the same point: heart in the midst of what seems like failure is what is needed. No wonder Joe's smile was always trying to emerge.

So there it is. Joe's philosophy reduced to a few baseball analogies, a Broadway song, a few additions of his own—perhaps lacking the intellectual veneer and the religious trappings of Torah or Talmud, but not so far off the mark. Baseball is certainly easier than Jewish ritual and, God knows, more entertaining than Shabbat services. Less confusion and uncertainty. The most fundamental craving that holds things together, played out not in the real world but on a baseball diamond, a game of such regularity that if we play by the rules the outcome will be what we expect. And here, I agree with Joe on at least this—we both valued in our different ways that the comfort and rhythm of life could emerge from small tasks completed each day without fanfare, like the quiet modesty of the tailor from Vilna who practiced his craft each and every day, and started all of this for our family. Just stay in the arena.

ESTHER'S SPORTS WORLD

Esther's sports world was much the same as Joe's, and she, too, would come to look at sports as the source of wisdom, the basis for a life philosophy of accepting what was hard: achievement and struggle at the forefront. "Suck it up and go on gut." In high school, she had been a track star, and later, when she took up golf to spend more time with Joe, she would excel and become highly competitive, always on the course. Always the "war." She was a feminist, although she never used that word and may never have heard it. She had helped her own parents run a household of six siblings, mostly boys. She organized and managed the family and never expected to do anything other than that as an adult. She would always work and never saw herself as a stay-at-home mother, even though she never quite framed it that way.

Shortly after Esther and Joe move to Arlington, and before they can even think about playing golf at a country club, they join a bowling league in Rosslyn, Virginia. They each buy their own personal bowling ball and bag, and years later, on Rockingham Street, we find the fancy balls and bags in the unfinished walk-up attic, among a few reminders of what they did when they first began their life in the suburbs. The bowling gear perfectly captured their hard-scrabble, working-class background, a world in which they felt entirely comfortable.

But golf later becomes their consuming passion. As a young boy, Joe had caddied at a nearby golf club, and he fell in love with the game. Joe is poor, and those who play are rich. He is an outsider. So he keeps his thoughts to himself. Yet, like many caddies, he learns from watching and talking to the wealthy players, and in short order, becomes a very talented golfer. The "waltz king" from Lane Tech apparently can readily master the rhythm of the golf swing, a move I could never replicate.

When they move to Arlington, Esther and Joe are not well-off enough in the early years to join a country club, so Joe will go to the driving range and hit a bucket of balls, while we watch, more than a little bored, but not yet ready to try it ourselves. Much later, they will surprise us. When I am seventeen years old, they will join Westwood Country Club in Vienna, Virginia, but which was then called Westbriar. And years later, they will even buy a new condominium near the Club, which will become the center of their life. This was where Esther and Joe spent their Saturdays, and after they retired, most every day.

Football is another love. They bought season tickets to the Washington Redskins and never missed a game. That Esther would never give up her passion for the game plays out many years later, after Joe has passed away. I saw this myself, just after Joe Gibbs, the once-famous football coach of the Washington Redskins, had been hired back by the team, having retired years earlier. It was September 2004 and it was Coach Gibbs's first game back at FedEx Stadium in Maryland. I asked Esther if she would like to go, and then I called a special agent and purchased two tickets at a cost of $1,000 so that we could sit in the elegant private booths where waitresses serve you and there are television sets and fancy wood paneling. During the game, I see that Esther has something on her mind. I ask her how she liked our seats. She looked to the lower part of the stadium, to the exact spot where she and Joe had sat for over twenty years, among people whom she had gotten to know, and who could never afford the seats we were in now. "I liked it there," she said, pointing to the seats that were once hers and Joe's.

Those seats, on the thirty-yard line, and back about twenty rows, were where she sat with Joe and her working-class friends who, like them, had purchased season tickets for years, where she sat with her memories of Chicago and her brothers. That was her world, not the world of wood paneling at a football game, not the fancy boxes or seats where waiters bring you drinks and food. She was still from Chicago, after all these years.

But even their religion of baseball, football, or golf was not so far off the mark from what Jewish scholars have said about the Torah and its teachings. "It is not in heaven . . . nor is it beyond the sea" (Deut 30:12–13). The "it," the spiritual, is found here on earth, right before our eyes, in all the small and daily tasks. The simple things; even the games. They were connecting to a community, even if not quite yet the Jewish community—although that too would come later—because Esther, for all of her lack of things Jewish, would figure out how to connect herself to the life of a synagogue in a way that few others had done. And this too, along with the baseball, and the football, would find its way into our memories and guide our life. There is simply no way around it: we believe what we see. What else can we truly rely on?

DECEMBER 1942: WORK ON THE BOMB

It is 1942, and Joe has not been drafted. And for most of the war, it appears
he will not be. Instead, along with other chemistry majors, Joe is doing lab
work or possibly research at the University of Chicago, where the leading
scientists are working on the top-secret atomic bomb. We grow up thinking
his work related to the bomb but are never able to confirm this. Presumably, all of that is still classified. Yet, it is a race to build the bomb before
Hitler does, and to end the war. Then, while Joe is there, the world is forever
transformed, and the Atomic Age begins. At exactly 3:25 p.m. on December
2, 1942—almost one year after Pearl Harbor, quietly, in secrecy, on a squash
court under the west stands of old Stagg Field at the University of Chicago,
at the corner of Ellis Avenue and 57th Street, Enrico Fermi and his colleagues engineer the first controlled, self-sustaining nuclear chain reaction.
It is this moment when they know, with near certainty, that they can build
and deliver an atomic bomb that can destroy a city, end a war, and destroy
life on this planet.

Joe's brother Julius is more directly involved in the war. The war in
the Pacific is still being fought in 1943, with no end yet in sight. Although
the defeat of Hitler has now begun to feel more likely, the same is not true
of Japan. Julius is in the Navy and stationed in the Pacific. He sends home
photographs of himself on an unnamed Pacific island, wearing his combat
metal helmet, his jungle utilities, and a submachine gun held tightly to his
chest, pretending, like we all did, that we were warriors. We Kuneys are
many things, but surely not that. But still, we wanted the picture—I did
the same in Vietnam where we wanted to capture the image and so posed
with anything we could find, be it a helicopter or a tank. Odd that we see
ourselves as performers, not the real thing, when we were actually there and
the war was real.

Joe and Esther must still be worried about the draft in 1943. On December 28, Joe receives a notice of classification, now indicating he is classified as 1-A. This means he is available for military service. Then, on February
8, 1944, he receives another notice of classification, classifying him as 2-A,
which provides a temporary deferral because of his dependents ("dependency"). A third notice, dated July 11, 1944, also has Joe classified as 2-A.

Surely, the invasion of Normandy would mean the end of the war in Europe.
It would just be a matter of time before the Allies could march across France
and into Berlin.

While it appeared that D-Day would soon end the war, and that Joe would not be drafted, circumstances changed in December 1944. When the Battle of the Bulge occurred, Joe felt for the first time that he might be called for active duty. By December, the Allied armies had started to move inland from Normandy and were fast approaching Berlin. It must have been clear to the German people and to Hitler that the war was all but over. Yet, in one last desperate effort, Hitler orders his army, which now includes children, to fight to the death.

On December 16, 1944, three German armies (more than a quarter-million troops) launched the deadliest and most desperate battle of the war in the west in the densely forested and difficult to traverse Ardennes region of France. The once-quiet region became bedlam as American units were surprised and fought desperate battles to stem the German advance. As the German armies drove deeper into the Ardennes in an attempt to secure vital bridgeheads west of the River Meuse, the line defining the Allied front took on the appearance of a large protrusion or bulge, the name by which the battle would forever be known.

A crucial German shortage of fuel in the frozen forests of the Ardennes proved fatal to Hitler's ambition to snatch, if not victory, at least a draw with the Allies in the west. Lieutenant General George S. Patton thwarted the German counteroffensive. The Battle of the Bulge was the costliest action ever fought by the US Army, which suffered over 100,000 casualties. Joe will tell us later it was this offensive that caused him the most concern about the draft, despite his flat feet and the extra weight he carried.

THE BEAST IS DEAD

Joe's worries about the draft would soon end. By April 1945, Berlin was all but captured, although mostly by the Russian army, as Eisenhower had agreed to let the Russians take the lead in the liberation of Berlin.

On January 16, 1945, with the Allied forces and Russians advancing toward Berlin, Hitler had retreated to a below-ground bunker with a few of his closest advisors—the *Fuhrerbunker* in Berlin.

Hitler had given the command to his army generals to fight to the death. But on April 11, 1945, some 325,000 soldiers of Germany's Army Group B were surrounded and surrendered, leaving the path to Berlin wide open. By April 19, the Germans were in full retreat, and Berlin was bombarded by Soviet artillery for the first time on April 20. By the evening of April 21, Red Army tanks had reached the outskirts of Berlin.

The *Sentinel* reports in the last week of April 1945, "Berlin Has Fallen."

According to some, Hitler had suffered a total nervous collapse on April 22, when he was informed that the orders he had issued for SS General Felix Steiner's Army Detachment to move to the rescue of Berlin had been ignored. Later that day, Hitler asked the SS physician who shared the bunker what was the most reliable form of suicide and was informed that the "pistol-and-poison method" was best—that is, combining a dose of cyanide with a gunshot to the head. On April 30, 1945, Hitler killed himself by gunshot. His wife of one day, Eva Braun, committed suicide by taking cyanide. Goebbels and his wife also killed themselves and their six children with cyanide.

Before his death, Hitler orders that his body be burned so that the Russians cannot display his corpse in public. In this sense, then, Hitler is never seen again except as charred remains. When the Russians discover his body in the underground bunker, they have to do a dental examination of his teeth to make sure the badly charred remains are his. No photographs are taken. He has disappeared. Evil beyond all comprehension; then gone.

The *Sentinel* reports the news. "The lair of the Beast has been stormed and captured . . . soon a new world will arise from amidst the dust and dirt of his ashes—a great new world that will be fit for men to live in."[19] The editorial page of the *Sentinel* proclaims, "The Beast is Dead." "After twelve long, terrible years, the beast that was Nazism lies humbled in the dust. . . . The worst is now behind us. We have come out of the valley of death into green pastures. Before us lies the hope of a great new world. We must make sure that we meet its challenge."[20] The long night had ended. It was the dawn.

Years later, Hitler's bunker is covered over with asphalt and it now sits below a parking lot next to an ordinary apartment building. There is no sign, no marker. The Germans have refused to give the site any sense of historical importance. But, of course, the memory of all that happened hangs over us every day, and our sense of what it means to be Jewish somehow always includes thoughts of what occurred during those dark years.

19. Fishbein, *Sentinel*, 45.
20. Fishbein, *Sentinel*, 486.

CHAPTER 12

The Closing Days of Life in Chicago (1945–1947)

JOE CONTINUED TO HEAR from his draft board following the capture of Berlin and the suicide of Hitler. On January 23, 1945, Joe was again classified as 2-A—perhaps because he was still entitled to a deferral on account of having a child. But then, on June 5, 1945, with the European war mostly over, but the war with Japan still active, Joe was reclassified as 1-A. On June 27, 1945, he received an Order to Report for Physical Examination on July 12. He apparently did not pass the physical exam and was reclassified as 4-F, on July 24, 1945; this meant Joe had been rejected for military service. The last draft card I discover shows he was again reclassified, this time as 4-A on September 25, 1945. This classification was a deferral for men who were over age twenty-six. Joe is twenty-seven, and would be twenty-eight shortly.

In June 1945, Joe graduates from the University of Chicago with a Bachelor of Science in Chemistry. He has managed to stay out of the war—whether he wanted to or not.

I am born only a few weeks after Hitler killed himself. On August 2, 1945, I come into the world in the same hospital Esther and Joe were born in some twenty-eight years earlier. The proximity of my birth to the war frames history for me. Hitler was not a person from the distant past; he was someone who only too recently had walked on the earth. The nearness in time of

Hitler to my life will stay with me always. Had I been born in Germany on the same day, and had Hitler lived a few more months, I would have been sent to the concentration camps. To the furnaces.

For reasons that are never explained to me, and that take seven decades for me to more fully understand, I am named David R Kuney: no middle name, just an initial. Nor am I given any explanation, over the years, of who or why Esther and Joe chose "David." My birth certificate lists Joe as a linotype operator working for a typesetting company. Joe has just learned he will not be drafted, which is good news, since Japan is still weeks away from surrendering.

Years later, I learn the possible source of my name. It is in 2019, when I return one morning to see what has become of the former Arlington-Fairfax Jewish Center, and ask to see the Memorial Board with the names of the deceased on engraved name plates. The Memorial Board used to adorn one of the large cinder block walls that ran the entire length of the main sanctuary, but for some reason they have been taken down and moved into a smaller library—really nothing more than an office. *So, who will ever see the names?* I wonder that day, as I find my way to the new, less honorific location. Those who enter the large sanctuary will look in vain for the past members who built the Center—including Esther and Joe.

I want to see again the names of my parents and grandparents, and others I may have known who have passed away. It is then that I notice for the first time that the name plate for Esther is missing, so I take a photograph to remind myself later to order a plaque for her. But, by the time I get around to it, it seems as if Etz Hayim ("tree of life"), the synagogue's new name, is considering closing its doors—like many other synagogues. I wonder what will become of this Memorial Board, with hundreds of names engraved on metal?

I also notice on the morning of my visit that Anna's name plate says, in Hebrew, she is the daughter of Fishel David; there is no last name shown. I only learn Fishel's last name in 2019 when I find a picture of him in the boxes from Jackson. I note how religious and scholarly he looks, and see Joe has written on the back of the picture: "Mom's dad: Rudashefsky." The boxes keep revealing.

Was I named after my great-grandfather, a man whose name I never knew until I went through the boxes? It is possible. Fishel David Rudashefsky would have been eighty-three when I was born, give or take, but under Jewish custom, a child is not named after a living relative, so I assume he passed away before I was born in 1945. Esther and Joe also may have choen my middle initial "R" for Rudashefsky. The "R" would certainly be easier to live with than "Rudashefsky." A small favor now, I see.

The forgetting of names seems to be a regular occurrence in our family: discarding identity, along with the history it carries, all the mystical possibilities of tradition and memory. Had none of them studied the second of the five books of Moses, *Shemot* (the Hebrew word for "names"), which tells of the naming of the children of Israel and how the names fix our destiny, instilling dignity?

Under Jewish custom, I should have been circumcised eight days after my birth and thus initiated into the Jewish religion the same as Abraham was, 5,000 years earlier. Abraham performs the ceremony himself, alone, when he is ninety years old. It takes him days to recover. I do not have a written record of my circumcision and do not know whether it was performed as part of a religious ceremony or in the hospital by a doctor as a matter of course.

Today, the procedure seems commonplace—regardless of religion—for most. Yet, it was not always so. In 198 BCE, circumcision was performed primarily in the Jewish community and may have gone unnoticed were it not for the fact that Greek men typically exercised in the nude. Assimilation and hellenization were all the rage.[1] Jewish males who joined them would expose their circumcision, "a condition that Greco-Roman culture regarded with both derision and horror."[2] So desperate were Jews to assimilate that young Jewish men committed to Hellenization "made foreskins" through the cosmetic surgical procedure of epispasm. "To surgically undo circumcision, in the eyes of the author of 1 Maccabees, was to undo being a Jew."[3]

Esther and Joe do not have assimilation or Hellenization on their mind, and I can only guess now that they made the decision in August 1945 based on the customs of the day, and not with reference to the historic and spiritual significance of circumcision. Besides there were other things to worry about. It was still baseball season in Chicago. *Were the Cubs playing at home?* Joe wonders.

TRUMAN'S DECISION TO USE NUCLEAR WEAPONS

In the days leading up to my birth, Japan has yet to show any sign of ending the war in the Pacific, and there is talk that it may take one million American troops to storm Japan through beach assaults and ground troops in order to end the war.

1. Fredriksen, *When Christians Were Jews*, 10–11.
2. Fredriksen, *When Christians Were Jews*, 10.
3. Fredriksen, *When Christians Were Jews*, 10–11.

President Roosevelt dies on April 12, 1945, and former vice-president Harry Truman has been president for only a few weeks when he is confronted with an historic choice: whether to continue to wage war with soldiers on the ground or try to force a surrender through with the use of the atomic bomb. The bomb had never been used before, and its reliability and its effects were still largely unknown.

Truman gives the order to launch the atomic bomb.

Esther has been home from the hospital after my birth for a day, maybe two, when on August 6, 1945, at 7:15 p.m. Washington time, the United States drops the atomic bomb on Hiroshima, instantly killing over 100,000 people. That morning, President Truman had been aboard the Augusta, along with some press personnel. Shortly before noon, near Newfoundland, Truman was having lunch when he was handed a note advising him that Hiroshima had been bombed four hours earlier.[4] The message read: "Results clear-cut successful in all respects. Visible effects greater than in any test." Truman grabbed a crew member and said, "This is the greatest thing in history."[5]

If a radio had been nearby, Esther and Joe could have heard President Truman's message to the American people, delivered the next day at 11:00 a.m. Washington time:

> Sixteen hours ago an American airplane dropped one bomb on Hiroshima. . . . It is an atomic bomb. It is a harnessing of the basic power of the universe. . . . We are now prepared to obliterate more rapidly and completely every productive enterprise the Japanese have above ground in any city. We shall destroy their docks, their factories, and their communications. Let there be no mistake; we shall completely destroy Japan's power to make war. . . . If they do not now accept our terms they may expect a rain of ruin from the air, the like of which has never been seen on Earth.[6]

David McCullough tells of the great joy of American servicemen in the Pacific and Europe who were preparing to be shipped to Japan for a land invasion had the bomb not been used or been successful. One such soldier, Paul Fussell, a twenty-one-year-old soldier who had suffered wounds in the leg and back, remembers a sense of elation: "we would not be obliged to run up the beaches near Tokyo assault firing while being mortared and shelled,

---

4. McCullough, *Truman*, 454.
5. McCullough, *Truman*, 454.
6. McCullough, *Truman*, 455.

for all the fake manliness of our facades we cried with relief and joy. We were going to live. We were going to grow up to adulthood after all."[7]

There is, however, no word from Japan and no sign of surrender, so Truman orders a second bomb. Three days later, another atomic bomb is dropped on Nagasaki, killing 40,000 people.

Just before the bombing, a meeting is held in Japan's Supreme Council for the Direction of the War. The meeting was deadlocked, with three powerful military commanders arguing "fervently against surrender." One of the three said "It was time now to "lure" the Americans ashore . . . for one last great battle on Japanese soil—as demanded by the national honor, as demanded by the honor of the living and the dead. Would it not be wonderous for this whole nation to be destroyed like a beautiful flower?"[8]

But when news of Nagasaki was brought to the participants, the meeting was adjourned and within twenty-four hours, Emperor Hirohito decided to surrender, provided that he could remain sovereign. Churchill told the House of Commons that the only alternative would have been to "sacrifice a million American, and a quarter of a million British lives" to finally force the Japanese to surrender.[9]

On September 2, 1945, Japan formally surrendered.

Two days later, Richard turns four. Esther picks up the baby book and writes, without any mention of the bomb: "Had cake, cookies, candy, fruit jello and fruit. Richie enjoyed the singing of Happy Birthday better than anything else. Guests arrived at 2:30 and left at 5:30."

So it is—one new baby a month old, anther having cake and cookies for his fourth birthday, and life ending in Japan for at least 140,000 people. There is no accounting for this; the constant killing as life goes on. But how could it be any different? For what could Esther and Joe have done to change the events that had just occurred, or those that might be coming?

1947: LEAVING CHICAGO—JOE AND JULIUS GO THEIR SEPARATE WAYS

As the war was coming to an end, Joe's brother Julius and his wife moved to the West Coast, where Francine continued her career in dance. Julius and Francine moved to 3236 Velma Drive in Los Angeles, although it is possible Francine moved there first, waiting for Julius to return from his tour of duty in the Pacific. A West Coast home would have made sense for wives

7. McCullough, *Truman*, 456.
8. McCullough, *Truman*, 459.
9. McCullough, *Truman*, 459.

whose husbands were serving in the Pacific. According to voter registration records, they later moved to 6666 ½ Whitley Terrace, Los Angeles.

Francine had become a dancer, and had appeared in a few movies. As part of her career, she posed for a publicity photo showing her in a moody and slightly suggestive costume. She signs it, "To Mamma and Papa Kuney: The swellest 'extra set' of folks a girl ever had. Love Francine. 1943."

Francine joined the Screen Actors Guild on August 1, 1944 and signed a contract to serve as an extra-dancer with Republic Productions at a salary of $66.75 per week. On October 4, 1945, she landed a contract with Columbia Pictures as a dancer, with a clause that prohibited Columbia from using her as an extra. The term was for six months starting on October 4, and she was to be paid $100 per week.

Julius and Joe and their families will never again live in the same city, nor will they form a close bond as brothers. When I get to know Julius in the 1950s, I see him as the artistic, bohemian side of our family. At times, I wish Joe were more like him—more easy-going and affable—hardly the qualities that Joe possessed.

In looking back and trying to assess whether Sol influenced both of his sons to move away from an observant form of Judaism, I see now that in his own way, Julius expressed a continuing interest in things Jewish—more so than I had thought when we were younger. He produced an award-winning television program for many years, *Look Up and Live,* which aired on CBS from January 1954 to January 1979, and although nondemoninatonal, it was intended to reach young people with inspirational messages. And, Julius, more so than Esther and Joe, seemed to stay in touch with the Grades, collected Chaim Grade's books, and named his children after the Grade family.

Julius and Francine never returned to Chicago, nor did they ever grow closer to Esther and Joe. They had lost interest in Chicago, with its slaughterhouses and heavy industry.

Esther and Joe are also on the verge of leaving Chicago for good. On January 26, 1947, Joe receives his "honorable withdrawal card" from the International Typographical Union. Presumably, he requests this card because he knows he will soon be leaving Chicago, and hopes to be moving out of the labor force and into a management position. If he has his way, Joe's days as a printer will soon be coming to an end. So, too, will our family's days in Chicago.

Joe learns of a job opening at the American Chemical Society in Washington, DC. They need someone with a degree in chemistry and a knowledge of printing. He and Esther talk it over before he applies, realizing that if he gets the job, they likely will have to move to one of the close-in suburbs surrounding Washington—possibly Arlington, Virginia.

Esther wonders, as does Joe: *What is Arlington?* They have never set foot in a southern state. What kind of life might they be headed for.

CHAPTER 13

General Robert E. Lee's Arlington

Geography is destiny.[1]

—ABRAHAM VERGHESE, *CUTTING FOR STONE*

JOE GOES TO ARLINGTON for the first time in 1947, when he travels to Washington for his initial interview with the American Chemical Society. I assume he flew into what was then the small terminal at National Airport, and then took a cab for the short ride to the ACS. His new office will be near 15th and K Street in Washington. If he is offered a job, as is almost certain, he will need to look for a new home for his family.

Who told him whether to head north to Maryland or south to Virginia to find a home? Most Jewish families will later head north, to the suburbs in Montgomery County, including Bethesda and Potomac. By the 1960s there is a dense Jewish community and many Orthodox Jews in places such as Baltimore and Pikesville, Maryland.

Joe, however, heads to Arlington, although within just a few years it will be apparent that Virginia and Maryland may as well have been separate countries as far as Jewish familes were concerned. Arlington, after a hundred years of growth, and long after Sol and Anna had emigrated to America, would never have more than a few Orthodox Jews. A keen observer, a first-generation American Jew, whose parents were from Europe, and who was

1. "Abraham Verghese," 3:01–3:03.

trying to find a place to raise a Jewish family, would have done well to select Washington or Maryland. But never Arlington. The only synagogue in 1947 is in a shoe store on Wilson Boulevard; there is no Hebrew school or *cheder* for the children.

Assuming Joe has rented a car, he may have taken the relatively short drive down K street, crossed over Key Bridge, and then to Arlington. The Francis Scott Key Bridge was the first major bridge between Washington and Arlington. When it is proposed, the Georgetown merchants object to it, and construction does not begin until 1917, the same year that Sol registers for the draft. When Sol arrives in America in 1913, the passage over the Potomac is made on an old wooden roadway built over a dilapidated aqueduct bridge used by the Union Army, which is camped across the river in a small area called Clarendon—the same place where, years later, the first Jewish synagogue in Arlington will begin to hold services in a shoe store.

Crossing Key Bridge, Joe finds himself in what was then known as Clarendon. George Mason, one of the founding fathers, and his son John owned much of lower Clarendon until 1830. Later, George Mason University would be built there on Wilson Boulevard. Clarendon was mostly farmland until 1900, and cows belonging to the Arlington Dairy Company were still grazing at Whalen's Field as late as 1950. Today, the skyline is filled with high-rise office buildings, but that was not the view Joe saw when he crossed over Key Bridge for the first time.

Clarendon was largely car dealers and a Sears—the very same Sears that would later become central to our life in Arlington. It was where we bought everything we needed to build the basement of our home on Rockingham Street, and it was where we bought our bikes and where, on the sixth or seventh day of Passover, we finally gave up eating unleavened matzah, and began to eat bread and congratulated ourselves on having gotten this far, no one there to remind us of our obligation to hold fast to the tradition for a full eight days. Surely, we were just shaving a little off here and there, and who would notice, after all?

But Joe bypasses Wilson Boulevard for now, and turns slightly right, traveling up what is Lorcom Lane, avoiding Wilson Boulevard and Clarendon. He might have liked what he saw. Driving north on Lorcom Lane, the country is filled with parkland and is heavily wooded, and with the view of the Potomac on the right it might remind you of the scenic drives in upstate New York. There is not much topography in the flat Piedmont lands of Virginia to move a soul, but the drive along the Potomac is uniquely lush, wooded and graceful with twists and turns in the road, rising around the river's edge. This is where some of the wealthier and more influential Jewish families lived. Dr. Julius Siegel, a chiropractor, built a large home on

Military Drive, and his son, Danny Siegel, would later become a nationally recognized Jewish educator and rabbi.

But this neighborhood is well beyond Joe's means. Driving further up Lorcom Lane, which then curves onto Lee Highway, he will come, after only a few minutes, to the intersection of Glebe Road and Lee Highway, and he will not venture further. Here, the Potomac River falls out of view, and one is greeted instead by the new commercial development, strip malls, and billboards.

Just one short block east of the intersection is where Joe will find his first home in Arlington—for his wife, for Richard, and for his eighteen-month-old son, David. The Glebe Theatre is almost in the back yard. It is a modest home; two bedrooms and one bathroom for four and then later for five.

Arlington, at least in the 1950s, was not the ideal place for Jews. It was the home of Babbitt, the home of Republicans: the people who Sinclair Lewis wrote about in 1922, who were renamed "Rabbit" by John Updike in his novels, and who had, in their views of life and success, an avaricious vacuity. In Lewis's imaginary town of Zenith, the chief virtue is conformity and the religion is described as "boosterism."[2]

Blandness is what I saw; that is, when I was finally old enough to see Arlington as something distinct, as a place that had context and contour. I saw mostly a stifling conformity. Eisenhower had run for president in 1952 and became known as the "Corn Flakes candidate," signifying the introduction of advertising men into political campaigns, but also adeptly describing the drab ordinariness of life. Whether that was fair or not is another matter. But the Babbitts and Rabbits were certainly there in Arlington, and they acted out their roles mostly as portrayed in the literature. These were people whose daughters went to ballroom dancing classes and later to cotillions; the same parents sent their children to segregated public schools and belonged to country clubs with written rules that prohibited Jews. Wives were still at home, and few thought much, if anything, about careers in business or elsewhere. Whether they had drinks in the afternoon, as often portrayed in the literature of the moment, I do not know.

No need to even mention Blacks. After the US Supreme Court called for the end of school segregation in 1954 in *Brown v. Board of Education,* Virginia lawmakers passed a series of "Massive Resistance" laws, which were

2. Taylor, "Our Damaged Nobel Laureate," para. 1, describing Sinclair Lewis's use of the term "boosterism" as meaning a kind of smug provincialism.

designed to delay or limit the scope of integration. It was not until February 2, 1959, when the Arlington County Police, dressed in riot gear, would guard the first Black students who sought to attend Stratford Junior High School, the first school in Arlington to be integrated. No one asked, when we were young, *Where did the Black students go to school?*

What was this place called Arlington, a place did that did not exist in the early years of our country? What turned it into a gentile, Republican enclave of sheer blandness in the 1950s, the embodiment of the Eisenhower era, where no one ever protested anything? And then, what made Esther and Joe and a small handful of other young Jewish families settle in Arlington, and then on Rockingham Street, it, too, being a newly created street where none had existed before?

When the country was still putting itself together, there was no notion of Arlington County. But the new federal government, with George Washington as president, needed a place to locate its capital. So, with the passage of the Residence Act of 1790, Congress approved a new permanent capital to be located on the Potomac River. Part of the land needed came from Virginia and under the Organic Act of 1801, Congress placed the cities of Washington, Georgetown, and Alexandria (the piece that came from Virginia) under the exclusive control of Congress. But, when the citizens of Alexandria learned that, as part of the new federal capital, they no longer would have the right to vote, they petitioned Congress to transfer the land back to Virginia. This happened on July 9, 1846, when President James Polk signed the legislation that permitted the "retrocession." And so, what was briefly part of Washington, D.C., later became Arlington, Virginia.

Arlington was one of those southern places where the memory of the civil war still lingered—although to be fair, there would come a time when "Northern Virginia" was seen as too liberal to be part of the otherwise very southern Commonwealth of Virginia. When Joe first arrives in Arlington, and for much of his adult life, he will drive up and down Lee Highway—Route 29 which runs north and south, including through Charlottesville, Virginia. What does Joe know of the "Lee" for whom this highway is named, not to mention Lee's history and impact on the South, on Arlington, on the schools that we attended and the way we talked about the Civil War, about segregation, about most everything?

He should know because General Robert E. Lee is still everywhere in Arlington, and even more so when we first arrived in the late 1940s. His home, the Curtis-Lee Mansion, is perhaps the most visible landmark as one drives over Memorial Bridge, leaving Washington and heading into Arlington. Yet, even the home itself has its own history. Lee's mansion was taken over by the US Government, and made into a burial lot for the Union soldiers killed in the Civil War: 600,000 dead union and confederate men, more than all the wars in US history combined. That the Civil War lasted so long and cost so much in the lives of the nation's youth is Lee's fault. A graduate of West Point, he chose to defend Virginia from his own country. A lesser general than Lee might well have surrendered years earlier, but Lee, like Grant, is gifted and tenacious and so the war drags on until nearly a quarter of the male population under thirty is dead on both sides. Lee could well have been tried as a traitor; hung. But no. Grant wants healing, so Lee is free and unrepentant following the surrender of the South at Appamatox.

This burial site for the dead Union soliders was placed on what was once Lee's private property—a beautiful home situated on a slope overlooking the Potomac River, and with a view of what would later become Memorial Bridge and, more ironically, with its perfect view of the Lincoln Memorial, although all of this is still decades away. This was one way of punishing Lee, who despite having led the only rebellion against the United States is never tried for treason, and is otherwise left free following the surrender of himself and his then-starving army.[3]

Lee's family, however, never forgives the United States, and his sons later sue the government, contending its family home was confiscated without due process. And indeed it was. Lee's son prevails in the lawsuit before the Supreme Court, but in 1883, Congress purchases the property from Lee and turns it into a military reservation. Later it will be renamed Arlington Cemetery, and it will seem as if this was what it was always meant to be. But everything has its history, and its mystery.

So, by the time Joe is looking for his first home in Arlington, driving up Lee Highway, deeper into the South, he has lost sight of what exactly it was that Lee was trying to do, not too long before the fatal battle of Gettysburg. It had always been Lee's dream to one day invade Washington and hold the capital hostage until the Northern armies, the armies of the United States, were forced to surrender. He had hoped to place Washington under siege, and to starve the army and its residents until they sought an end to the

---

3. Although not widely known, Lee is facing indictment, and it will be almost 100 years before the US government finally drops the issue of his guilt. Reeves, *Lost Indictment of Robert E. Lee.*

war: a recognition of the South as a separate nation, as well as its inhuman institution of slavery.

One might dismiss the Civil War as having no bearing on immigrants from Vilna and their son and the other first-generation Jews who moved to Arlington. But I see it differently, and I felt it growing up in Arlington. The Confederate armies had camped and marched and made plans to invade and destroy Washington not more than a short walk from our homes, first in Glebewood, and later on Rockingham Street. I was never sure I didn't see their ghosts marching down what was later named Lee Highway, and I know for certain Esther and Joe never quite knew who Lee was, nor that he had been a traitor to his country and was later indicted (but never tried) on charges of treason. Memory is faulty and incomplete. But one cannot grow up in the South, even in the 1950s, without those gray ghosts and thoughts of the Confederacy still fresh and alive. It will be seven decades before the world demands that the statues of the South's fallen heroes be removed and the Southern flag taken down. But not then; back then it was still veneration.

Indeed, some of the clashes between the Union soldiers and the rebellious South occur at a place known as Hall's Hill, just a half mile from where Esther and Joe would find their first home in Arlington and just a few yards from the first McDonald's where I would work in high school to earn some extra money. Despite their efforts, however, Confederate forces are never able to capture present-day Arlington. I sold fifteen-cent hamburgers on old battlegrounds and slave quarters. History, too, leaves its footprints in the soil, reminders that time past is still with us.

Lee, dreaming of invading Washington from the North, makes the fatal mistake of starting his campaign against Washington from even further north, in Gettysburg. But General George Mead, also a graduate of West Point, is unrelenting and Lee makes his most famous misstep: the charge by General Pickett. Today, you can stand in the still-naked, upward-sloping field where Pickett stood just moments before his final charge, facing hundreds of cannons and thousands of rifles, and you would know to a moral certainty that when the air was filled with lethal lead, coming at all angles, and covering every available inch of space, the Confederacy would be destroyed. Even a child could see such an outcome. Lee will never forgive himself for this. And with good reason.

Do Joe and Esther not know they are considering moving into the South—the Confederacy? It had only been eighty years, give or take, since the last war dead had been buried in Lee's front yard. Esther and Joe were still fresh from the fear of the Holocaust and the Battle of the Bulge. To them, I guess, the Civil War was in another lifetime. Joe might have told you that by the time he started thinking about leaving Chicago, the war was long over and no longer mattered. But there was no separating the Civil War and the politics of the South, even in the mid-1950s. That this southern state would give rise to a staunchly Republican political party and an absence of Jews was not as unrelated as Joe might have thought. Had Joe done what we did—grow up in Arlington and attend its public schools—he might have changed his mind.

And so, on Rockingham Street, an entire generation of Jews, we who had fathers who were the first American-born Jews in their families, had to first discover that we were Jewish, and then had to define it against the backdrop of a heavily gentile environment, without the help of a generation or two of Jewish settlers from the Old Country. We had to map this out for ourselves, with little guidance. We would ultimately learn more about Virginia history than the history of Vilna, more about Jefferson than the Gaon of Vilna, the great rabbi of the eighteenth century. Little wonder we wound up hanging by a thread to a version of Judaism that asked so little, was so forgiving of forgetting that one could not be certain it was worth the candle.

Where things happen matters. An event here will not be the same if done there. Time and space are not indifferent. Unless you walk the land, you will never understand it.

CHAPTER 14

The Second Migration
Chicago to Glebewood (1946–1952)

Go forth from your land and from your birthplace and
from your father's house, to the land that I will show you.

—GEN 12:1

JOE'S SEARCH FOR A first home for his young family has taken him to the
intersection of Lee Highway and Glebe Road, in the center of Arlington
County. Here, he finds a small row house, located at 4766 N. 21st Road,
a street of connected modest homes located near the bus line and within
throwing distance of the Glebe movie theatre. He will have to convince Esther that this makes sense, but move he must; it is in our Jewish blood, and
the move seems to fix our destiny: "My father was a wandering Aramean,
and he went down into Egypt with a few people and lived there and became
a great nation, powerful and numerous" (Deut 26:5).

The neighborhood is known as Glebewood, in deference to the old
Glebe movie theater, which is less than thirty yards behind the row houses,
along with its large parking lot for our view from the rear window. Lee Highway is on the main bus line so that Joe can easily take the bus to work, down
Lee Highway, across Key Bridge, left on 16th Street. About twenty minutes
in traffic, less on Saturdays. The archives in the Arlington County real property records show Esther and Joe as the owners, but it has no purchase date.
They sell the home in 1952 to Ed and Nelie Graves for $11,750. The year that

121

Eisenhower was elected president, running against Adlai Stevenson. What had they paid? Ten thousand dollars, give or take.

The house was built in 1937 and when Joe finds it, it is ten years old and at the very edge of development from DC. There was little residential development as one went south, down Lee Highway. None of the schools that I would later attend, other than John Marshall Elementary School, were yet built: no Tuckahoe or Williamsburg or Yorktown. Just pastures. There is no beltway linking Maryland and Virginia, and there are no shopping malls, no synagogues.

Our home consists of two bedrooms, one bath, a small basement area—a total of 1,200 square feet. The front of the house measures about twenty-five feet from side to side: room for the front door, two small windows, and a small brick façade. When you open the front door, the stairs leading to the second floor are in front of you, only a few feet away. Upstairs are two bedrooms and one bathroom. Room for the four of us, at first, but, then in 1948, there will be five when Steven Ross arrives.

Esther and Joe were the first of their families to be born in America, and for them, having their first small home was still a wonder—something they might not have imagined had Joe not gone to Lane Tech, learned both chemistry and printing, and then, through some act of providence, found himself newly employed by the American Chemical Society.

Richard and I share a room and possibly a large bed. Later, I seem to recall a crib for Steve. When we were in bed, and talked too loudly and refused to sleep, Joe would threaten to come up the stairs with a rolled up newspaper. When he tried to smack us with the paper, we would roll up against the wall and hope he could not reach us.

A black-and-white photograph found in the boxes from Jackson and labeled in pen on the back says "1947," and it shows our new Glebewood home. There is an old 1940 black four-door sedan parked on the street, its make and model now lost to me, and there, barely visible behind the wheel of the parked car, a young boy, probably Richard, who could by then reach the steering wheel. It is summer and a young girl sits across the street playing with her dolls and watching her baby sibling in a crib, which has been brought onto the grass, what there is of it, patchy and unattractive. An older man, hands in his pockets, dress hat, walks down the street, head drooping, wearing an expression of dullness. Not in the photo, but still vivid in my mind, are the two elderly ladies, unmarried, who live next door, and who, from time to time, smile at us, but beyond that, there is not much to recall.

Around the corner, and slightly up Lee Highway is a supermarket. Once or twice Esther sends me on shopping trips, with no more than a quarter or two, to buy some milk, or a loaf of Wonder White Bread, but I am not yet six and I am not always certain what things cost and how much to pay. Across Glebe Road is a three-story retail building, still standing, where a new dentist named Dr. Mostek has his practice. He apparently is not well-trained, and later Joe will claim he did as much damage as good to our young teeth.

Our old house is still there, looking much the same, although almost seventy years have come and gone.

Of course, when Joe is offered the job at the American Chemical Society, Esther knows she will have to leave her large family and her brothers and move from Chicago. It was never an issue. Like Ruth, Esther pledges her life to Joe, willing to go where he goes, repeating what Ruth says to her husband's mother, Naomi: "Where you will go, I will go, and where you will live, I will live; your people will be my people, and your God will be my God. Where you will die, I will die, and there I will be buried. Because only death will be between me and between you" (Ruth 1:16). So it was with Esther and her Joe.

Esther follows Joe to Glebewood having never seen Virginia before, or even known Arlington existed. Esther's job was to be with Joe, to be by his side, and to provide support. And he, in return, would protect her, at all costs, right or wrong. She would provide the extra energy and determination that made their life work. She had rolled up her sleeves to do the work of the eldest sister in a large family of six brothers and sisters, and she did not unroll her sleeves until the very end, when she would finally bury Joe, not able to live much longer or well once he was gone. As gifted as Joe was, as bright and educated, without her, I am sure he would have gotten off-track, wandered into something less meaningful, made compromises and never made it to Arlington and his life's work. This would prove to be the silent script that kept playing in our heads, no matter what. This was what marriage meant to us, exactly as we had seen the two of them make it work.

Esther took great pride in what Joe had accomplished, and she was conscious that it set her apart from her younger sister and brothers, who had not married spouses with Joe's education, and who would stay in working-class Chicago, or wander even further afield, moving to Los Angeles. It was Joe, however, who had graduated from the University of Chicago, a place filled with the world's leading intellectuals and scientists. Later, when Joe had to travel to annual conventions for the American Chemical Society, Esther would go with him and run the information booth, and with her energy, drive, and outgoing personality, soon gained a certain notoriety, a modest star of sorts—what she was striving for.

Esther's ambition was always at the ready; I never saw her lay it to one side, never saw her fail to make a decision that required work and focus. I think now she had always been looking for her Joe, even "Big Joe," as he was sometimes known, now over 210 pounds at almost six feet tall. She had the ambition and courage to move away; she left her four brothers, her sister, and her parents, behind, and when she returned to visit, she felt triumphant; she had done what none of them could do. Joe was too talented and Esther too ambitious to consider staying in Chicago. He had spent eleven years getting his degree and working at night for a printer. He had talent and drive. Something else was waiting for him. His middle name became "Hustle"; Joseph Harry Kuney or Joseph "Hustle" Kuney.

Barely settled in Glebewood, Esther loses no time in taking charge. She puts her two younger boys, Steve and me, in a stroller, and walks the neighborhood to introduce herself to each of the neighbors. It was how she approached life. Light a cigarette, drink an extra cup of coffee, roll up your sleeves, meet people: outgoing, tough, determined. Later, when she and Joe would take their many trips to Las Vegas, she could outcount and outsmart the dealers who manned the gambling tables.

Bucky Mason lived up the street. He was my age, with short blondish hair and a tough veneer. Bucky's parents owned a television set and we would watch *The Howdy Doody Show* with Buffalo Bob Smith and Clarabelle on NBC, a TV show that had just started in 1947. In the early 1950s, Bucky's parents got one of the first color television sets in the neighborhood. We would wait years before Joe would feel financially secure enough to spend the money for ours.

What kind of name is Bucky? I might have wondered, if it had occurred to me to think about what was missing from Glebewood. There were no Jews in sight. For all of her toughness and cordiality, Esther could not and did not meet a single Jew living in Glebewood.

The few Jews who had settled in Arlington, North Arlington that is, had moved even closer to Washington, and lived off Glebe Road near Arlington Boulevard in a development known as Buckingham, right across from the old Buckingham movie theater. If you proceeded further down Glebe Road, crossing over Route 50, then onto Arlington Boulevard, you were soon in South Arlington, a somewhat less affluent section, and not one where the wealthy Republicans lived. Once you crossed Route 50, you were outside the border of the Republican stronghold.

THE BROYHILL PLANTATION

That there were no Jewish families in Glebewood should not have been a surprise, at least if Joe had known more about his new neighborhood. If you were the son of a Vilna immigrant, and had wanted to replicate a densely Jewish life, you would not have picked Arlington, still part of the American South. There are segregated schools and restrictive covenants in housing, with many major law firms closing their doors to Jews or announcing quotas. Sheldon Cohen, who would later become the head of the Internal Revenue Service, describes life in Washington, DC in the 1950s thusly: "I was first in my George Washington University Law School graduating class in 1950. I was accepted at a leading firm. 'We don't mind hiring Jews,' they told me. 'But would you mind changing your name?'"[1]

Ida Jervis tells a similar story about her early years in Arlington: "We signed a paper for a house and the man suddenly remembered to ask us what our religion was and even though my husband was in the United States Army that just wasn't good enough for him. He ripped the [contract] thing up."[2]

Arlington also attracts the Nazi Party. In the late 1950s, George Lincoln Rockwell, founder of the American Nazi Party, moves its headquarters to Arlington. Later, Rockwell will move just a few blocks from our house on Rockingham Street, up Williamsburg Boulevard, next to the bank and barber shop where we get our hair cut. The police are around Rockwell's house most days, and we go up to his front door to dare Rockwell to come out. One day, we venture too close and he does come out, running and shouting at us to get off his property. I recall him taking out a small pistol. We stayed away after that. Rockwell later will move closer to Washington & Lee High School, which Richard attends. We never hear more about him, but I later learn he was murdered in Arlington by a lone gunman.

The Jewish families near Washington are mostly in Montgomery County, Maryland, but Esther and Joe have no way to know this. The major Jewish real estate developers were almost entirely located in downtown Washington or Bethesda, Maryland. Among the most prominent were Samuel Eig, Charles E. Smith, Morton Luchs, Morris Cafritz, Albert Small, Bernard and Carl Gewirz, Carl Freeman, and Abraham Kay.[3]

What should we call this place in Arlington other than Glebewood? Where we once lived deserves a better name, something more than Glebewood, something more than a movie theatre. If Vilna was the Jerusalem of Lithuania, what, then, was Arlington?

---

1. Apelbaum and Turman, *Jewish Washington,* 40.

2. *L'Dor v' Dor in Arlington County,* 4.

3. Years later, many of these builders would become clients of Melrod, Redman and Gartlan, where I was an associate from 1976 to 1978.

I think of it now as the Broyhill Plantation. Here was a place where the resurrection might be believed; would have currency. Unless you were our family, of course.

Broyhill is everywhere, and only a stone's throw from our modest home in Glebewood. Driving up Lee Highway, toward Washington, up a steep rise, to Old Dominion Bank, we see signs for M.T. Broyhill & Sons, Corp. Broyhill defines Arlington. Here was the great icon of whiteness, of Republican country-club life, of privilege and correct manners, of ease and confidence—all qualities I could see but never achieve. Even if we were the chosen people, it was not for this.

I see it now as the Broyhill Plantation, perhaps only recently emancipated, if at all. The descendants of former slaves in Arlington have moved but a few short blocks south on Lee Highway, to a place called Hall's Hill. This was where most of the African Americans lived when we were new to Arlington. The children should have gone to Stratford Junior High, the nearby junior high school, but when we were young they were not allowed to go there. Stratford would only be integrated when a federal court ordered it, and when the Arlington County riot police were there to escort them into the building. We thought nothing about this. This was what it meant to be living in the South, the Broyhill South, the Republican South: well-mannered racism; signs everywhere. Broyhill for Congress. Broyhill homes for sale. Our father, our king.

Broyhill was our Robert Moses. He owned and then developed and built much of Arlington, and later McLean, Virginia. He and his friends and his large family lived in Country Club Hills, down Lorcom Lane and off limits to us Jews. Land titles and deeds in the 1950s in both Washington and Northern Virginia frequently prevented selling one's home to Jews or Blacks.[4] No one said we weren't welcome visitors, but neither did they invite us into their homes in Country Club Hills. I went to school later with Broyhill's daughters and cousins, and all of them, all the look-alikes, had their plaid skirts and matching blouses, Ladybug, Villager, color-coordinated, all perfect, all untouchable. Not that we ever knew where or what to touch. We were the inept generation, clueless in the early fifties until the sixties turned this all around, so that no one now can even recognize what life in the fifties looked like—plain vanilla.

---

4. Ober, "How Racial Covenants Shaped D.C. Neighborhoods." Valerie Schneider, an assistant law professor at Howard University School of Law and director of the school's Fair Housing Clinic, explains: "They usually restricted a sale of property to whites, so sometimes they excluded particular groups of people—blacks, Jews, religious minorities. They ran with the land so they were intended to last in perpetuity" (para. 7).

Broyhill was a master builder. His company was considered by some to be one of the largest homebuilders in the world. Construction began on his first subdivision in 1957. Following World War II, Broyhill and his two sons developed dozens of subdivisions in Arlington and Fairfax, and at one time they were building up to 1,500 homes a year. They developed almost everything you still see: Broyhill Crest, Broyhill Park, Broyhill-Langley Estates, Broyhill Forest, Broyhill Hills in Arlington, and Sterling Park. Perhaps somewhere Temple Broyhill.

So there he was. Broyhill. Arch-Republican. Towering Christian. Broyhill's smiling face, there on every other billboard. No mention is made of his staunch opposition to every form of integration. In 1955, he was one of eighty-one US Representatives who vowed to oppose by "every lawful means"[5] the US Supreme Court holding in *Brown v. Board of Education,* which had outlawed segregation. He and Richard Harding Poff of Virginia were the only two Republicans to sign the Southern Manifesto, seeking to oppose integration. As a longtime member of the committee overseeing the District of Columbia, he, along with three other members of Congress, insisted that schools in the District reinstitute segregation.

He was an unrelenting and outspoken opponent of home rule for the District, arguing that the US Constitution placed ultimate responsibility for the nation's capital on Congress, and he battled for years against measures to increase the authority of city residents to manage DC affairs.

So here we were, in Glebewood, just starting out, trying to make a go of things on the plantation, not yet concerned with much of anything that was Jewish.

DAILY LIFE IN GLEBEWOOD

On August 28, 1947, Richard is vaccinated by Dr. Benjamin Stein. He will be our family doctor for the next two decades and we will see him long after we are in our late teens, and long after he has moved from his offices in Washington to Bethesda, Maryland on Bradley Boulevard. Now living in Potomac, Maryland, we pass his former house daily, with the entrance for patients next to the paved driveway. His office frightened me as a child, when we had to get the shots he dispensed, with the old, thicker needles that made us scream.

Richard turns six on September 4, 1947. Esther's baby book recalls the party "down in the basement" in Arlington. "Played games. Had gift bag for all of the children and ran movies for an hour. All had grand time." Pants,

5. Hevesi, "Joel T. Broyhill," para. 4.

books, and games make up the gifts. Richie did well that day. Those in attendance are duly recorded "David, Mother & Daddy, Eileen Sumpter, Bunny Axtree, Barbara Heiper," and others.

Because Richard was born on September 4, he was not eligible to attend first grade in Arlington, since a child must be six by September 1. Esther and Joe enroll him in a private school in Washington, DC, where he has some difficulty. He takes the public bus by himself. No one then thinks that children cannot manage such journeys alone. Such was the grit of Southside Chicagoans.

I find other photos as I go through the boxes, although only a few are from our days in Glebewood. Esther has written "December 28, 1947," on the back of several. The first is Joe in the small backyard, not more than ten by twenty feet, his arm around Richard and me as he crouches down. There is a white picket fence in the backyard between the connected row houses, and an electric meter on the brick exterior wall. I see the unfinished basement through a small window, partially above ground so that some daylight might have gotten in, if only for a few minutes each day. It is warm for December, and none of us is wearing a coat.

Joe will try to teach Richard to ride a bike. But, instead of buying him a small twenty-four-inch bike, the one with training wheels, he is convinced Richard can handle the larger twenty-six-inch bike without the training wheels. Joe will train him in the back, near the Glebe Theater, which is at the bottom of a slight decline from our home. I think here the "hustle" gets out of hand; Joe pushes too hard and the bike is out of control, as is Richard, and both bike and Richard crash into the outer wall of the Glebe Theater. I do not think the bike survived. Richard did, in a sense, but this may well have been his first introduction to what Joe wanted us to be: the effort, the pain, the need to push beyond what we were ready to do. Hustle has its downside.

Joe takes a separate picture of Esther that same day, as she, too, stands in the backyard next to the white picket fence, in a dress with short sleeves, the fashion of the 1940s, looking as if she were an extra in a Hollywood movie of that time. But instead she is the one who is there with us, who lived those years, and dressed in this fashion. She is so young. How do I not remember this? Our parents were once in their thirties, struggling with new homes and young children. Why do we insist on seeing only as they were when they are old and have long since given up their careers, their commutes, their dreams? I have put this picture of her on a counter that I walk past each day. *Was this who you always wanted to be?* I wonder. I feel this is the first time I have met my mother. I see her now as she wanted to be seen and not as she became later, after time and disease had taken their toll, collected their due.

JOE AT THE OFFICE: THE AMERICAN CHEMICAL SOCIETY

Joe has just turned thirty. No more Southside Chicago. Joe joins the American Chemical Society in 1946.[6] His office is in downtown Washington, DC. It is located at 1155 16th St. NW, about two blocks off K street. The ACS will move temporarily for renovations, but today still occupies the same 16th Street address, although in a newer structure that looks strikingly contemporary.

Joe's career at the ACS is a success, and we three young boys, as we watch from a distance, are certain that whatever he does at work is important—and that he does it every day without complaint. In our mind, this is what a man does, what a person does. You get dressed each day, go to the office, sit behind a desk in downtown Washington and then go home for a family dinner. The world is orderly; the work is done. The normal life. We will do the same. These simple acts are what define manhood, fatherhood, reliability. A job held long, with an office in Washington. Whatever he actually did, the details of the work, we could not guess, but we knew it was done each day without fail, and that became the only way we too could understand our future adult lives, and how we would measure our lives: our own version of Sol's thimble and thread.

Joe is perfectly suited for his job at the ACS and ultimately will become the Director of Business Operations. His own biographical sketches claim that "while there [I] pioneered innovative microfilm approaches and the application of photocomposition, including the first production operation of a computer-assisted program." But we never really know what this means. He is a chemist and a publisher and something of a scientist and engineer, and yet we three boys have very little of this skill set, least of all me.

In 1942, the ACS is headed by Harrison E. Howe, who edited its leading publication, *Chemical Industries*. But in 1942, Howe is succeeded by Walter J. Murphy, who served until 1959, and I am guessing it is Murphy who interviews and hires Joe. At the dinner table each night, where we ate as a family without fail, Joe would talk about Murphy and Esther would listen, at least until she needed to interrupt with a story about her own day. I still can hear Murphy this, and Murphy that, so that I become certain it is Murphy who is running Joe's universe.

Murphy apparently earned his position, and under him, the role and publication list of the ACS grows dramatically. It is under Murphy's leadership that the ACS begins to publish its national weekly newsmagazine,

6. Oddly, at least two draft "biographic sketch" documents claim he started work there in 1936, but he was still in technical school in Chicago then, so this seems unlikely.

Chemical and Engineering News. This is the magazine that arrives weekly in our mailbox and I see it for most of my childhood. I look through it from time to time, but it soon becomes clear to me that whatever this field is all about, it is not for me. The diagrams of complex chains of chemicals and the algebraic formulas make little sense to me or my two brothers, and none of us pursue a scientific or engineering career.

The American Chemical Society has a significance that none of us brothers fully grasp. The ACS is the leading institution in America for chemists, including academics. Under the leadership of Richard Kenyon, the ACS expanded its publications in the late 1950s and 1960s to include seventeen periodicals, and was devoted to providing a primary chemical information system necessary for scientists to be kept well informed of developments in their field.

Initially, in the early 1940s, ACS publications are printed at Mack Printing, located at 20th and Northampton Street in Easton, Pennsylvania. Mack Printing also becomes a part of our life. Joe will take us there for visits, and it is where he will fly frequently to inspect the printing operations. It is old-fashioned: hot lead characters pressed against paper; linotype operators who set the keys and letters. Nothing digital back then—all done by hand, the skill Joe had learned at Lane Tech, and similar to the work he had done in Chicago.

This part of Joe, however, does attract me, and deeply so. The world of print and journalism is where I find comfort. Later, I feel a lingering affection for all things printed, and, in high school, I am strongly attracted to journalism, the world of print, and publishing stories. Part of me wants to be a journalist, a writer, one who observes and tries to make sense of things. I will later write feature stories for the Yorktown High School newspaper, the *Patriot,* and will serve as its business manager. So here I was, after all, following Joe.

By 1959, and maybe earlier, Joe's name is on the masthead of *Chemical and Engineering News,* where he is listed as the Assistant to the Director of Publications. The Director of Publications, the senior person, is C. B. Larabee, and, just as with "the rabbi," we hear about Larabee during our early years on Rockingham Street, where dinner discussions alternate between the two.[7] No detail was too small, and Esther and Joe would review their workday world with each other, while the three of us mostly ate in silence.

7. Larabee retired in 1962, and was succeeded by Richard L. Kenyon, who was then named Director, Staff Division of Public, Professional and International Communication. Kenyon died suddenly and unexpectedly on March 30, 1976 of a heart attack. The headquarters staff of the ACS was reorganized in 1971, and I now wonder whether Joe's departure in January 1973 was somehow related to this.

Joe will later become the Director of Business Operations. His career and contributions are larger than we are able to see from Glebewood and even later, from Rockingham Street.

Joe is also a writer. His biographical sketch notes that he has "published extensively in several areas of study and investigation dealing with the publication of journals. Under his direction, ACS produced the first computer-aided composition for journals on a production schedule." At some point, Joe writes articles for *Encyclopedia Britannica*, and each year we receive several free volumes, which we collect on a bookshelf kept in Richard's room, the room facing Rockingham Street, and the room which I yearned for while Richard still lived with our family.

Joe attends annual board meetings and conferences. Celebrities attend the ACS's annual conferences, including Linus Pauling, Ted Kennedy, and Isaac Asimov, a leading science fiction writer. Joe tells us his field is called "information retrieval." He tells me one night, "If you can't retrieve information, then what good is it?" Little did I know that he was so deeply immersed in the early stages of the digital age, and the same logic by which we, as lawyers, live or die as we now search through millions of cases for text and language that serves as precedent in our cases. But we knew none of this as children and I made no connection between what he was doing and what I would spend my life doing. The nose on our face, as they say, is invisible.

THE REBIRTH OF ISRAEL

It is 1948, and the Jewish world is about to change, and perhaps to change forever. It has been almost 2,000 years since the destruction of the Second Jewish Temple (70 CE), and since the loss of the Jewish homeland in Israel.

On May 14, 1948, at midnight in Jerusalem, David Ben-Gurion proclaims the independence of Israel. Eleven minutes later, at 6:11 p.m. in Washington, DC, President Truman announces that the United States has recognized the Jewish state, an act that helps guarantee a Jewish home. Within hours, the Arab states declare war on Israel and attack it from all sides.

The call to make Palestine a Jewish homeland had been rekindled in the late nineteenth century, and was championed by Supreme Court Justice Louis Brandeis. In 1917, during World War I, the British had seized Palestine from the Turks, and in that same year had announced what became known as the Balfour Declaration, in which the British Government formally endorsed the idea of a future Jewish home in Palestine, which comprised no more than 10,000 square miles.

The mandate, however, remains only a promise at that time. During World War II, in 1947, the Attlee government of Britain announces it will withdraw from Palestine and turn the issue of a Jewish homeland over to the United Nations.

And so it is that Truman finds himself confronted with the issue of a Jewish homeland. The creation of a Jewish state is seen by some as a risk of war. Europe is dependent on the Arab states for 80 percent of its oil, and the creation of a Jewish state could be disastrous. George Kennan, part of Truman's administration, considers the Palestine situation insoluble for the time being.[8]

Then, on November 29, 1947, over the Thanksgiving weekend, the United Nations votes for partition by a narrow margin, thus creating the state of Israel. The Arab delegation walks out. Zionists in the audience declare, "This is the day the Lord hath made."

It is Truman who helps make Israel possible. His wife, Margaret, will later write that the most difficult issue confronting Truman was what to do about Palestine.[9] It may be fortunate that, by this time, Roosevelt had died and Truman had become president. David K. Niles, who was Truman's special assistant for minority affairs, later wrote that he sensed in Truman a fundamental and deep sympathy for the plight of the Jews and that he never sensed the same with Roosevelt. "Had Roosevelt lived," Niles said later, "things [for the Jews and Israel] might not have turned out as they did."[10]

I cannot say whether the birth of Israel changed how Esther and Joe felt about being Jewish, nor their commitment to becoming actively involved in Jewish organizations and later joining a synagogue. Surely, nothing altered overnight, but now looking back, I wonder if this monumental event was a factor in the still slowly emerging Jewish consciousness in each of them.

1951: FIRST GRADE—A JEWISH
CHRISTMAS IN GLEBEWOOD

Come September 1951, I am six and Esther has taken my hand and is walking me down Glebe Road for about a mile to John Marshall Elementary School. Who is watching Steve? I do not remember our other walks, Esther and I, hand in hand, but for some reason I remember this one. It is likely my first day at public school, and Esther, still not a working mom, decides to take me. I assume she continued to do so most every day.

8. McCullough, *Truman*, 601.

9. McCullough, *Truman*, 595.

10. McCullough, *Truman*, 596.

Esther is thirty-two years old, a young woman and quite beautiful. We have pictures of her standing in the back yard of Glebewood, smiling and wearing a fashionable dress. Her hair is dark and long, and she has the sleek look of a woman of ambition and skill. One day, standing just inside the door of our Glebewood home, I look up and see this pretty young woman. I tell her I want to marry her when I grow up, but she tells me she is already married to Joe. I am not happy to hear this. I wish I could have remembered her this way—this was the image of herself that she must have carried through her entire life, not that of the older Esther who colored her hair blond to cover the grey.

John Marshall Elementary still stands today, almost exactly as it was in 1952, at 2501 N. Glebe Road, between 25th and 26th streets. But it is no longer a school. Today, it is the John Marshall Building and houses medical offices. It was an old school even in the 1950s, several stories high with red brick, a design that will soon vanish in Arlington as the new sleek, cinder-block, one-level schools start sprouting up everywhere. I will never again go to a school that is not brand new: Tuckahoe, Williamsburg, Yorktown—the first class in each school. This is antiseptic Arlington; the clean life. Later, I cannot understand how anyone could bear the old brick schools of Chicago and New York. I had not yet internalized any sense of charm or age or permanence. Arlington was about "new." Chicago and New York seem old, dirty—places that can't be trusted at least until someone cleans them up.

When we arrive in Arlington, in 1948, there are only 11,492 students enrolled in all of its public schools.[11] By 1955-56, when the World War II baby boomers begin to show up, the school population has doubled to 23,000.[12]

It is hard to recall much of first grade. What I do recall are the over-sized crayons we were given and the cloth bags we each used in order to collect them. I did not understand, however, that to me, many of the colors looked the same. It would not be until sixth grade, when I fail my first color-blindness test, that I learned one could be color-blind. Now I understand why all the parked cars along the street in Glebewood seemed to be a non-descript grey; but then, so did all of Glebewood.

11. "Yorktown High '68," contains the history of elementary schools that fed into Yorktown high school for forty years or more.

12. "Yorktown High '68," para. 4.

BEING JEWISH IN GLEBEWOOD

I do not believe there were any Jews in Glebewood. I do not believe I understood what it meant to be Jewish, although there is a record of my attending a Jewish Sunday school. There is no discussion in our home about the recent birth of Israel, no blue and white flags with the Jewish star. At John Marshall Elementary School, each morning, first thing, we say the daily prayer from the New Testament and the pledge of allegiance to the flag: One Nation under God. No one thinks we are being forced to say Christian prayers. And had you asked me then, I would not have known the difference.

On Saturdays in Glebewood, we sometimes went to the double features at the Glebe Theater, never Shabbat services. As I recall, the double features cost a quarter each. Esther and Joe would usually let us walk to the theater, the three brothers together, a team of sorts. *Annie Get Your Gun* and *Cinderella* are released around 1950. *Tarzan* is popular.

Although I have no recollection of our family ever attending Shabbat services while we lived in Glebewood, the boxes from Jackson did disclose that Esther and Joe had enrolled me in 1950 in the Kindergarten program then being offered by the Center.

Even if Israel and Shabbat are not discussed, Christmas makes a splash in my memory of those years. It is Christmastime in first grade, and we are talking about the birth of Jesus. We have a Christmas tree in our house. I find photos of Steve and me, both dressed as Roy Rogers in cowboy hats with toy pistols and holsters—our Christmas presents. Another picture shows Richard on the lap of a well-dressed Santa Claus, presumably asking for his Christmas wish list.

I loved the Christmas tree, which we put up for several years at Glebewood and at least one year on Rockingham Street. I remember with great fondness our trips to pick out the tree at the large lot on Lorcom Lane and Glebe Road, with the wonderful winter smell of the forest of freshly cut pine trees on the newly fallen snow. It was magic. Esther and Joe could not let go of the sheer beauty of Christmas.

Right before the Christmas break, my first-grade teacher gives us some items to take home and share; one is a large color picture of Jesus. It is attractive and I am excited to share it with my parents. Jesus has a large, golden halo and, to my six-year-old eyes, he is impressive, startling, something to show one's parents.

Anna, whom we call Granny, is visiting us from Chicago, and is sitting in the living room in our Glebewood home. I excitedly run up to her and show her the gift from school, the picture of Jesus. After looking at the picture for a moment or two, she turns to me and says, "We are Jewish and we don't believe in Jesus."

When were Esther and Joe going to reveal this secret? Whatever it was I was supposed to be learning at Sunday school obviously had not made much of an impression. Certainly not compared to the smell of Christmas trees and the glow from Jesus's golden halo. So now the secret is out. I am not like my classmates. I believe in some other God. Our God does not include Christmas. How can that be? Granny—Anna—doesn't tell me about the tree and why we shouldn't have one.

I don't fully believe Anna. My friend from up the street, Bucky Mason, and I still argue over whether there is or isn't a Santa Claus. We hang on to the belief for a little while longer. We are still getting money under our pillow, as well, from the tooth fairy.

I am guessing Anna talks to Joe. Perhaps she says she is worried about whether her grandchildren are getting a Jewish education. Perhaps seeing Jesus and the tree may have made Anna wonder if she and Sol should move to Arlington.

I don't know for certain what Anna told Joe, nor what Joe said in this conversation. But I do know that, not too long after this, Sol and Anna would indeed move to Arlington, that they would live a block away, and that shortly after, we no longer would guess about our Jewishness.

The time for Christmas trees was coming to an end.

CHAPTER 15

Rockingham Street

Vilna Again? (1952)

IN JULY, 1952, SHORTLY after my conversation with Anna about the picture of Jesus, we are packing up and moving somewhere, leaving Glebewood. I do not recall seeing a moving van, but there may have been. This is the last time I will see the inside of our Glebewood home. We are moving about 1.5 miles up Lee Highway. Right turn on Quantico, left turn on 26th St., left onto Rockingham. 2445 N. Rockingham Street to be exact. This will be home for the next nineteen years, until 1973, when Esther and Joe move to White Plains, New York, when Joe's days at the American Chemical Society come to an end—a move I still see as a sad mistake.

There isn't much to Rockingham Street, not at first. I have no recollection of ever seeing it before the move. I do not recall Esther and Joe driving up and down the street, walking the street, none of the things that one might do before buying a home.

Why are we moving? Steve's birth in 1948 means we are now three brothers; Glebewood is too small. But I think the Anna conversation provides a truer rationale. Anna had seen our Christmas tree and heard me talk about Jesus and our daily prayers at school. We were moving to a new neighborhood where, in short order, there would be other Jewish families and a possible new home for Sol and Anna, who could leave Chicago and move closer to Esther and Joe. Close enough, perhaps, to keep an eye on their three grandchildren and make sure that my early interest in Jesus was just an accident of sorts. But even if I am right, and Anna wanted something more for us, something more Jewish, could she really make it happen? She had fought with Sol over Joe's Hebrew school in Chicago. Could she do any better with Joe's children—the three of us?

Esther and Joe sign a contract to buy their new Rockingham home on June 18, 1952, but it's not a direct sale. There is a contract of sale dated October 19, 1951, shortly after I start first grade at John Marshall, between Sigmund Goldblatt, as purchaser, and Bernard Steinberg, as seller. The Goldblatts then execute an assignment of their rights under the contract to Esther and Joe on June 18, 1952. The deed is dated July 1952. Esther and Joe close on the sale shortly before the Fourth of July.

How could Esther and Joe afford their new home? The modest house costs $18,950 at a time when Joe's salary as en editor is $7,750, according to the loan application. Joe's files, still preserved, show much of the loan history. I see again how Esther and Joe handled their money. They need to be careful, prudent, not overstep, and they keep detailed records of every penny. The Depression must seem like yesterday to them. Joe also has not forgotten the eleven years he spent struggling financially to get through college. Later, when Joe lends money to us—Steve, me, and Richard—we all have to sign promissory notes and pay interest. It leaves me with a permanent fear of running out of money, and I think now my later decision to specialize in bankruptcy law must have had its roots in this fear.

The boxes from Jackson contain a number of loan documents from the summer of 1952. The loan application from the Prudential Insurance Company of America is for a loan in the amount of $11,500. The monthly loan payments are $72.80 for principal and interest. Esther and Joe are both thirty-four years old. Esther records in pen and ink, in a small book, each payment. The down payment for the house is $6,707.61, and it appears that Esther and Joe borrowed $4,000 of this amount from the American Chemical Society to make up the shortfall from their savings. They sign a separate note to the ACS agreeing to pay interest of 4 percent and monthly payments of $50.

In 1964, Esther and Joe refinance the mortgage and increase the loan to $16,500, now with American Security Corporation. Esther and Joe become long-term customers of American Security Bank, for which I will later do legal work when I become a law partner at Aronoff, David, Harvey, Hagner & Kuney. Life comes full circle. It's good to know history.

The house is brand new, barely finished. The asphalt street has just been poured, and is barely wide enough to park cars along the curb, and still have room for cars to drive up and down the street at the same time. There is no driveway, only a dirt path next to the house that we one day will cover with concrete. There is no garage. The cars lived outside, coated with ice in winter and untouchably hot in summer. There is no room for a second car.

Some of our luckier neighbors had a carport that kept the sun and snow off their cars. One of them is Lieutenant Cadle, a member of the Arlington County Police who parks his motorcycle under the carport. I hope one day we can afford a carport.

The house is a one-story rambler, with a basement and a walk-up attic: three bedrooms and one bathroom. We would compete for the bathroom and had no choice but to be patient, no matter the agony. We had one telephone and it was a party-line at that, shared with someone else. When you picked up the receiver you could hear the other conversation and would have to wait until it was over. It was a blessing when we could finally afford our own private line.

We had no air conditioning, nor did I know anyone who did, at least not in the early years on Rockingham Street. Years later, Joe will install an attic fan and claim this makes the house cool enough. It does not, of course, but at least we grow up well acclimated to the ceaseless heat and humidity of Washington. No one ever told us we were supposed to be comfortable. Richard will get the room facing the front; Steve and I will share the slightly larger room facing the rear of the house, and the two of us share a closet. No one says the house is too small; no one says the summer is too hot.

Only in going through the boxes do I learn that, on March 19, 1965, Joe had contracted for the installation of an air conditioning unit. I was now at the University of Virginia and have no recollection that this work was ever done. Had I moved out too soon?

The lot on which our new house sits is fairly large. The plan shows that the home is only thirty feet off of Rockingham Street, and a mere twelve feet from our neighbor to the left. But the lot has a total of 10,628 square feet or almost exactly one-quarter of an acre. There is a large creek in the backyard, which years later the county will fill in with pipe and new sod. The backyard is large enough for Esther to erect a clothesline about twenty yards long, where she hangs our clothes to dry, long before we finally buy one of the new dryers they sell at Sears. There is a wonderful smell to the fresh clothes hanging on the line. I still can see Esther hanging the clothes or taking them off the line, and folding them neatly into the wicker laundry basket before bringing them inside. Esther was not alone. In 1955, the cost of a dryer was still too expensive for the average homeowner.[1]

The backyard is wide enough so that we three boys can make a mini football field, and it is deep enough so that if we stand on the future patio and hit a Wiffle Ball as far as it can go, it will just barely clear the chain-link fence our neighbor will later erect. This will give us the thrill of trying to

---

1. "Appliances," para. 1.

leap over the fence and make catches that would leave the fans astounded, at least those who are there in our imaginations. Cars and baseball become our primary loves, such typical and bland suburban children, with nothing on our minds but sports and games and driving. This was the quiet period, or so it seems, before the disruption of girls and our burning desire to be free of our parents and their control.

I remember the small kitchen table in the equally small kitchen. When Joe sits at the head of the table, he is within easy reach of the refrigerator, so it is no trouble to reach in and grab more food for our meals. There is never wine or alcohol. Milk and meat are mixed; there is one set of dishes. We never discuss, and perhaps never hear, the word "kosher" for many years. We eat as a family, always, five of us squeezed around a laminated kitchen table from Sears, as physically close as a family can be.

But there is a TV in the living room, and from the head of the kitchen table, Joe can see it. On Sundays, he will watch professional golf on our 12-inch black-and-white TV. None of us three brothers had the least interest in golf: on the small set, one can see only a body swinging a club, but the ball is invisible, and the reason for the game is beyond our grasp. There is not much else to watch, only four channels—NBC, CBS and ABC, plus one local channel, WTTG—and a rotary dial to change the channels.

Joe is constantly improving and enlarging the house. It both amazes us and frightens us; at times, it makes me want to escape from the endless chores, although in the end, Joe does transform the house into a much better home.

Some of the changes are small, but they add incrementally to our life. Joe buys a door from the lumber yard in Rosslyn, adds four legs, and it is here, on this wonderful six-foot surface, that Steve and I will spend hours playing year after year. We build our forts of Lincoln logs and buy tin soldiers who man the walls and prepare for combat. We roll the dice and decide who lives and dies. Later, we play Tactics II, a complex board game created by Avalon Hill that you can still find on Amazon, though it has long since gone out of production.

Joe builds far more than a desk. Somehow, he is able to teach himself how to design and build an entire finished basement. He starts to add framing, flooring, ceiling, plumbing, electrical. In order to install the wood framing, he has to drill holes into the solid concrete floor in order to insert the metal bolts that will hold the framing. But Joe does not own the kind of drill that would do this job easily. So, Richard and I are tasked with using hammer and chisel to make the holes, and we have to hit the hammer hard enough to make two-inch holes through the concrete. It takes hours for each hole. I am desperate to get away from this.

On October 28, 1954, Joe writes to the Prudential Insurance Company asking for a new mortgage on our home, noting that he has already added one bathroom and one bedroom in the basement, and his plans include completion of the basement recreation area, a terrace, and a porch, most of which he builds by himself. In 1961, he buys concrete from the Virginia Concrete Company and manages to install a driveway with little or no professional help.

On June 16, 1961, he obtains a building permit from Arlington County to act as his own contractor and build a wooden deck that will be nine feet by twelve feet, on wood posts, supported by concrete footings and a floor. How can he possibly do this? Yet, the deck is erected, and on summer nights, Esther and Joe sit on the deck, read the Sunday newspaper and watch their boys play whatever sport is in season in our large backyard.

The other jobs we helped with were no easier: holding wall board above my head, on a ladder, while Joe nailed it to the floor joists above us; laying two-inch squares of tile over a sticky, smelly black tar on which the ugly square tiles would be laid for the flooring. All this with no training, no background. Where did such skills come from? Was this the very same skill that had made Sol such an expert tailor? The spatial sense, the ability to measure things; to cut them carefully and precisely—these are the skills I see in Joe over the years, and yet these skills pass me by. I seem to have trouble sharpening pencils correctly, and one day ruin a new set of colored pencils, as Joe looks at me with amazement and disappointment.

And then it was done, and suddenly we had a different home: a basement with a pine-paneled bedroom where I would spend my teenage years; a private bathroom; a bar; a ping-pong table; a laundry room. How had Joe done all this? He had never built any part of a house, never lived in a house, never been to a lumber yard, never owned a single tool, and yet he had somehow studied and learned to erect frames and walls and ceilings and floors. Was this the enduring gift from his years at Lane Tech? It was a skill I would never be able to re-create, but it was what made our house at Rockingham Street bearable. It was the place where Richard, at nineteen, would bring home his new pregnant bride, Maggie, after he had dropped out of college. The basement became the scene of so much joy and heartbreak. Like any home, I guess.

TUCKAHOE: "GIVE US THIS DAY OUR DAILY BREAD"

It is September 1952. I have just turned seven, and it is time to start second grade. Tuckahoe Elementary School is under construction, about half a mile from our home. It is almost finished, but not quite. So, for second grade, we march another half mile to an older school called Stewart. Tuckahoe opens in 1953, but it is still not quite finished. For a short period of time, we take a bus to Nottingham Elementary. Richard, then something of a leader and very serious, is a safety patrol, and I can see him now with his patrol badge and white straps making sure we are safely on and off the bus. Then, when Tuckahoe opens a few months into the school year, we younger children move to the new school. Richard and the older students stay at Nottingham.

Richard is remote in my seven-year-old eyes; he knows what he is doing, who is in charge. He is an eagle scout. I will at times be known only as Richard's younger brother. We are never close, not truly, and I have no recollection that we ever really talked as brothers, shared secrets, or had any special moments together. We were four years apart—just too much of a gap, I guess. He was orderly and disciplined, and at the time I was not. He could please Esther and Joe, while I was not doing well on that front. I argued and tested the limits, pushing against them until they lost their patience. Steve saw what I was doing, and how poorly it was working out, and learned from me what not to do. Well, so be it. I miss Richard now, but at the time, he was yet another obstacle to my doing what I wanted.

I was comforted by Tuckahoe's cleanness, its newness, its pristine, secular quality. Not at all like the Jewish day schools that would soon appear across the Potomac River in Maryland. They would have sayings from the Torah, the Midrash, the Talmud above the black boards; we would have Christmas trees; Easter eggs; the pilgrims and the Capitol.

But there is religion at Tuckahoe. Well, someone's religion. We pray at Tuckahoe. We begin our day with the pledge of allegiance to the flag, followed by a daily prayer. I remember liking both. Our prayer asks God "to give us this day, our daily bread," and I find no problem with such a modest request. It is not clear which God, but it seems doubtful it is the God of Sinai and Moses. It seems good to start the day with a prayer, even in secular, colonial Virginia. I still remember the exact words; how could I not? We said this every day for the first six years of my education in Arlington:

> Our Father who art in heaven, hallowed be thy name. Thy kingdom come. Thy will be done, on earth as it is in heaven. Give us this day our daily bread; and forgive us our trespasses, as we forgive those who trespass against us; and lead us not into temptation, but deliver us from evil.

This prayer comes from Matthew and Luke, a prayer from the Christian Bible. No one mentions that there is a Jewish Bible. Was the "daily bread" the body of Christ? It never comes up. No one mentions that we are praying to the Savior, to Christ. But why should they? In Arlington, everyone seems to have the same beliefs, or so we think. No one points out the differences. We make nothing of it. It is just school life in a new building, with new lockers and a new cafeteria, and a multi-purpose room with a large stage for shows and a curtain that moves electronically. Isn't this what the immigrants had come to America for?

Yet, something is starting to happen on Rockingham Street. For reasons that no one explains, many of our new neighbors are Jewish. Ricky Okin lives down the street. His parents, Julius and Jeannette, are very liberal parents who never make Ric do anything he doesn't want to do and let him drop out of Hebrew school. He is a grade ahead of me. He has the kind of freedom with his parents I crave but never achieve.

Kenny Karb, a year younger than I am, lived directly across from us on Rockingham Street. His father was Max Karb. Max's wife was Betty Cafritz, part of the Cafritz family, well-known Jewish real estate developers in Washington, DC. Conrad Cafritz would later become one of my law clients, although we had a very difficult relationship at best. As big as it is, Washington is a small town.

Down the street were Bobby and Ken Frank, the children of liberal intellectuals. I have no recollection later of ever seeing them at the Arlington Jewish Center. Perhaps they went elsewhere? Helen and Haskell Jacobs live at the corner of 26th Street and Rockingham; their older daughter attends Oberlin; Judy is their younger daughter, but we rarely see them. Richard Perlstein lives a block away. Larry Lapidus is just around the corner. Joan Suskind is also nearby on 26th Street. So many Jews within a block or two. Was all of this a mere coincidence?

Elizabeth Cornell, known as Bibber in our youth, is not Jewish, but I never notice. Her sister is Pruney, and if you were old enough, you probably would know that these are not the names of Jewish children. Across the street is Bill Blackburn, and his father, Colonel Blackburn, fresh from a tour of duty in Japan. Marie Dornin, a Catholic, moves in between Bill's house and Bibber's house.

Next door to us is a Marine major, Skip Carpenter. That he seems casual and something of a regular guy fools me into thinking this is true of all Marines, which I learn, much to my surprise when I become one, is far from true. On the other side of our house, is a very strange old man whose basement window is near the property line. We sneak over and secretly spy on him at night. He seems to be tinkering with clocks. His age scares us. We are not used to anything old, not here in Arlington, where everything is being unwrapped from its cellophane.

We are very careful with money. A meal ticket for a full meal at school is forty cents a day, but only four cents a day for a milk card. The milk card is blue, the meal ticket pink. I longed for the pink, but Esther decided we would pack our own lunches, almost always peanut butter and jelly, and spend the four cents for the small half pint of white milk from Thompson's Dairy, located in Washington. Chocolate milk cost the same. No one thought of soft drinks.

Even if Esther and Joe had wanted to send us to a Jewish day school, they could not have done so. The Charles E. Smith Jewish Day School would not be founded until 1965, and then, across the river in Maryland. The Berman Hebrew Academy in Washington, DC had opened in 1944, but it was for modern Orthodox Jews. I recall no mention of this secret place where young Jews could study together and where the walls had posters of Jewish holidays and festivals, and meaningful quotes and thoughts from Torah, and where pork would not be served, unlike our schools where hot dog day was special, and I would eat as many as they would serve me, usually ending up sick. I never heard the word *yeshiva* growing up, which proves deeply embarrassing some 50 years later when I confess this lack of basic knowledge to other board members at the Pardes Institute of Jewish Studies. They must wonder if I converted late in life. And maybe in a sense I did—although born Jewish, officially at least.

As children, we believe what we see more than what we are told. We see Jesus, Broyhill, and Cadillacs. That is fine; that is how things were in Virginia, in the South. Later, a decade or two, the effort to see my youth as sharing something in common with the Jewish experience in Brooklyn, or Chicago, is unreachable. I remember instead clean lockers, a nice gym, and the friendly lady behind the cafeteria counter who would give us a second slice of bread and butter if we could present our trays with our lunch fully eaten, vegetables included. No blessing over the food required here. No washing of the hands. But still, clean and new. This is what we had come from Europe for.

THE CATHOLIC EMPIRE: OUR FRIENDS
AT D.J. O'CONNELL HIGH SCHOOL

Across the street from Tuckahoe is a large open field, an entire block, acres of tall grass and weeds. But not for long. On September 9, 1957, Bishop Denis J. O'Connell High School opens its doors as a college preparatory school, admitting 360 ninth-graders from the six founding parishes: St. James, St. Thomas More, St. Ann, St. Charles, St. Agnes, and St. John. Greeting the class of 1961 were Brothers of Christian Schools and Sisters, Servants of the Immaculate Heart of Mary (IHM), who would guide the students' education.

D. J. O'Connell was the forbidden land of the rich Catholics. We at Tuckahoe had modest softball fields, with moderately nice diamonds, one facing another, and almost large enough for two games to be played at once, as long as hitters from each side did not hit deep balls to center field. But D. J. O'Connell had large, immaculate fields of lush green, and its own football stadium, and rumored basketball gyms inside that none of the Jewish kids on Rockingham Street would ever see. After all, we would never dare walk across the street and ask to see what miracles might be on deck for that day, there in the land of the immaculate mother, or father, or sister, or saint of one kind or another. We were just the hardscrabble kids; we had used baseballs that turned brown and had the seams coming apart. Nothing immaculate here. Our basketball nets were metal and the courts too short for a full-court game.

Where was our D. J. O'Connell? The Catholics were training their young people with a rigor and energy that the Jews never seemed to muster in the early days of Arlington. Maybe later across the river, in Maryland but not here, not in Arlington. They had the pope and vast sums of money. We had nothing but a young rabbi from Vilna. They had a chapel in their school that vaulted three stories, with stained glass, and a large crucifix. We were using the second floor of a shoe store in Rosslyn—one that sold Buster Brown shoes—for a synagogue. They had saints and angels. We had saddle shoes and white buck shoes. How could we compete with all this gore and glory? Their God was still bleeding on the cross each Sunday, and ours spoke Hebrew and remained mysterious and unknowable.

And how was I to know, still so young, and walking past this great monolithic high school near my more modest elementary school, that this was where they taught the children of the largest, most organized religious group on the face of the earth? The words of James Carroll, writing in *The Atlantic*, captures the enormity of the Catholic institution and the relative smallness of me and my Jewish colleagues when he writes about the "Trappings of Empire":

> The virtues of the Catholic faith have been obvious to me my whole life. The world is better for those virtues, and I cherish the countless men and women who bring the faith alive. The Catholic Church is a worldwide community of well over 1 billion people. North and South, rich and poor, intellectual and illiterate—it is the only institution that crosses all such borders on anything like this scale. As James Joyce wrote in *Finnegan's Wake*, Catholic means, "here Comes Everybody." . . . The world

needs the Church of these legions to be rational, historically minded, pluralistic, committed to peace, a champion of the equality of women, and a tribute to justice.[2]

So, then, we Jews clearly were not "everybody." We were without an empire, without a D. J. O'Connell, we needed to make our way through the world, trying to hold on to something, trying to be the partner of God, trying not to be hated, and yet we were hanging by a thread, the same thimble and thread that Sol carried with him in his suitcase from Vilna in 1913. But our temple had been burnt to the ground, and our families in Europe murdered, so how were we ever going to compete? Unless, of course, as it would turn out, it would be both Jews and Catholics who would move decidedly toward a secular life, so that there would come a time when you could hardly tell us apart.

Later, when I am older, I, too, have to confront the question: What does it all matter? Just be healthy and happy, the Jewish parents say to the newly inter-married young children. So much forgetting; the same process started when Sol left Vilna, when I marched off to John Marshall Elementary School, hand in hand with my young mother, to say the daily prayer, when Moses came down from Sinai to confront the failure of his nation to hold firm. Did they really think the golden calf had freed them from Egypt? Hoping for the best is a dangerous game.

SOL AND ANNA MOVE TO ARLINGTON: THE END OF CHRISTMAS FOR THE KUNEYS

I start third grade in 1953. Sol and Anna move around the corner from our new home on Rockingham Street to the land of the Broyhill Plantation, a land filled with car dealerships and temples for the Babbitts. Sol and Anna have never been inside a car dealership. They have never seen a suburb. I think now that they might have come to save us. After all, we still had a Christmas tree that first year on Rockingham Street. Anna soon put an end to that. Even if Sol had every intention of moving away from his Judaism, when we saw the two of them, standing side by side, slightly bent with age and hardship, we could not help but see the survivors from the Old Country, with its still unfathomable Jewishness. Like it or not, we could not become untethered. Even just the few words of Yiddish, spoken over and over again, kept reminding us of who we were, or at least, who we were supposed to be.

---

2. Carroll, "Abolish the Priesthood," 78.

Their house is a one-level home at 2600 N. Roosevelt Street: no basement, one bathroom, two bedrooms, a living room, a kitchen, and a workroom. Nothing else. All of life in a few modest rooms and a small work area leading to the outside where they set up their sewing machine and where we spent hours getting our clothes mended and fitted. "Go to Granny and Dad"—the words that we heard so many times from Esther and Joe when something needed to be fixed; when a dinner needed to be picked up and carried to our home, still hot and in the metal pans. That was our life. How did we ever live without them?

I do not know who paid for Sol and Anna's house. But it may matter. Had Sol and Anna been frugal and saved enough so that they could afford the move? Had they wanted badly enough to be with Esther and Joe? Or had Joe decided it was his duty to bring Sol and Anna closer to their children and grandchildren? Joe was like that; a strange combination of moral insistence, and yet also remote, stern, and at times angry. So then, we were always pushing against him, never toward him, even though we still admired him. But I never achieved the full embrace, and we never found peace in one another.

I think now that no small part of the move was Anna's decision. In a word, Anna was coming to put an end to Christmas for the Kuneys. She had fought with Sol enough over being observant, put up with his refusals to let her boys attend Hebrew school and his seeming indifference to their bar mitzvahs. When she saw that we were ignoring our Judaism, that we were celebrating Christmas, saying prayers in school that referred to our "savior," she may have insisted that she and Sol move to Arlington, to do what could be done to save some small part of our Jewishness. She would bring three sets of dishes from Chicago and change them each Passover, although I am sure we never paid much attention to which were for milk and which for meat. Anna still lit Shabbat candles, covering her head with a napkin, hands over her eyes, saying the blessing in a language we did not understand. Eyes closed, her thoughts perhaps returned to Vilna, or to parents who had long since vanished from her life, or to something else: the young man she loved for a short time in Siberia, and then had to leave behind.

Every Jewish holiday meant dinner with Sol and Anna, and a great feast, food beyond reason. Food was, for us, the great transmitter of tradition and culture, but not quite enough; not Torah, but perhaps threads of Torah in the warm and succulent meals she labored over to share with us here, in Arlington, around this small table, seven of us clustered. Anna was the cook and baker that Esther never was and, I suspect, never wanted to be. Esther was absorbed in helping Joe, and dinner was nothing more than a task to get done. Food was how Anna spoke to us about things that have no words.

Anna is an artist with the oven. In America, she spends endless hours baking cakes, pies, and breads, and the rolling pin and flour, on waxed paper, are constantly on the red formica kitchen table. She is rolling dough, kneading dough, making and baking, and we are forever taking food from her home to nourish us back at our house. She speaks the language of food. Her love for us was mixed with the warm, sweet smell of freshly baked apple pies filling her small kitchen, with freshness from the "ice box" and the white flour sprinkled over the waxed paper on the red kitchen table, her hands covered in white. *Ess mein kind*! Yiddish, the Old Country. How often we heard this. Eat! This is my love for you.

Sol and Anna are both gifted tailors; gifted with the sewing machine and can make or fix any item of clothing. They mend things. In Arlington, a black 1930s Singer sewing machine sits inside the small workroom in their tiny two-bedroom house, just inside the back screen door where we always find one of them, fixing, sewing, piddling. They work the foot pedals and the hand wheel, and the sewing needle moves up and down gracefully and miraculously, tying together stray strands of fabric into a garment, a pair of pants, a shirt, something one of us three brothers has torn in our play, our wild running, our youth, our carelessness when someone is always there to fix things for us. No matter if we fall and rip a new shirt. Anything. Like my father later, they can make things with their hands, a gift from the angels. But the gift is not given in perpetuity. It is soon gone, used up perhaps. My hands hold a pencil, paper, keyboard, and nothing more.

If Sol wanted to make a vest, he would labor carefully over each small and seemingly insignificant stitch, each part of the slow, methodical, laborious process. I wish now I had asked him how he did this. I would try to grab the pieces and force them too quickly together, would become impatient with their separateness, and would be unwilling to stay patient through the process, to see it through; it would make me anxious, and then, at times, self-destructive of my own goals, rushing, too intent on being done, too focused on the end and not on the process. Was this not the root cause of leaving things undone: a lack of patience, that saintly gift so central to one's well-being, always out of reach for me?

Sol, in the backroom of a men's clothing store in Parkington, the first mall in Arlington, is altering the suits of customers, making small talk as he pins their cuffs. He asks them to look in the mirror, agrees to get it done in a rush, never mind the coming of Shabbat. Was his mind wandering back to some memory, to Vilna? To pogroms?

GIMP SUMMER

The Catholic girls at D. J. O'Connell had summer camp too. God knows where. They were gone for the summer with their rich boyfriends to do things that we never dreamed of: paddling canoes, swimming in lakes, horseback riding, archery. To my knowledge, only Ricky Okin went to camp, and I seem to recall learning about how one went from camper to counselor-in-training and then to even greater levels of supervision. For us, though, it was a time to get jobs cutting grass for the neighbors. The very best job paid four dollars for each cut, enough for gas, two movie tickets and popcorn. Perfect.

Because most of us on Rockingham Street could not even think of summer camp, we spent our summer at home, with most of our day at the nearby elementary school, where the county hired older teenagers to provide modest recreation—softball, archery, checkers, and the like.

I have come to think of these days as our gimp summers. "Gimp" consists of long strands of colored, pliable plastic, capable of taking any shape, which we made into lanyards to hold keys. Still, this was the perfect symbol of Arlington in the 1950s, something that at once could be anything or nothing, make of it what you will; just be polite, white, and wear the correct clothes.

Steve and I would walk over to the softball field most summer days, looking for a softball game. Other days, we would stay home and hit the Wiffle Ball as far as we could, which was usually about twenty yards, and pretend we were in center field in Yankee Stadium, that we were Mickey Mantle or Hank Robinson, chasing down a high fly ball hit well over our heads, running full speed toward the fences, or the parked cars in the narrow street. We would make the impossible catch, over and over, until we were exhausted. Had we been asked, we might have admitted that we were glad no one was making us go to *shul*; that instead, we could play baseball as long as we wanted, pretending to make catches in front of thousands of fans.

This was our youth, and I was content. I don't know what they were doing at the *yeshivas*. I never knew the weekly Torah portion. I was fine with just my bat and ball. At night, the Senators' baseball game was on the radio. The part of me that wished I was a Cohen, or that Fishel David, my great-grandfather, had been a rabbi, was lying dormant.

SHABBAT ON ROCKINGHAM STREET

If Vilna on Friday night looked like the Holy Land, then Rockingham Street in the early 1950s was the opposite: the un-Holy Land. Not a quiet day of peace and rest, but instead a day of work; mostly a workday around the house—dreaded. Joe would put on his old khaki pants and a sweatshirt, and Esther would dress in her oldest shirt, sometimes even one of Richard's old t-shirts. To an eight-year-old, it was ugly and hard to look at, and I wished for those days when Esther and Joe would have a meeting or some event and would leave us to ourselves. On mornings when I saw they were in nice clothes, I was happy because I knew they were going out and we would be spared the work routine.

Still, they were determined to make this home fit us. We would vacuum and dust and wash the walls, clean the bathroom, weed the garden, cut the grass. Endless. *Why can't I get away from this?*, I remember thinking.

Then errands. To the lumber yard. To Sears. Are Jews somewhere saying Kaddish? The morning Shaharit service? Listening to a sermon? We sit quietly in the old 1949 Pontiac with whitewall tires and look mindlessly out the window; down Lee Highway, down Wilson Boulevard. Clarendon. Maybe a quick stop at Old Dominion Bank where we each opened savings accounts with just a few dollars.

Shabbat did not mean Torah, or Torah study—not for us in the early 1950s. I never heard the word *parsha* (the weekly reading) and my view of the Jewish Bible had come mostly from Classic Comic Books, the ones that cost fifteen cents instead of a nickel, but which included stories of Moses crossing the Red Sea and Daniel in the lions' den. I recall Samson bringing down the pillars in some ancient temple, having first been sheared of his hair.

On some Saturdays, Joe takes me to his office on 16th Street, just off K Street. We are a family for whom K Street is the commuting route, which I will replicate most of my adult life. On Saturdays, Joe sits behind a desk that looks, to my childish eyes, as large as a truck. Papers are stacked; the office is glorious. I know immediately that this is what I want to do one day: whatever it is that Joe does.

I walk down the hall of his office and discover the supply closet. There are pens and pads, paper clips, rubber bands, staples—all without limit. I am filled with joy. Yellow wooden pencils make me happy. The pads need to be filled with words. What can I write? Anything will do. Later in life, I will recreate my own supply cabinet at home, filled with an ample supply of pads and a variety of pens and folders.

At some point, I discover that, if I fold a sheet of paper in half, and turn it sideways, I have a book—an empty book. So I line it with a ruler, and now

I have a book with lines. I start to write words, any words. They just come to me. I cannot stop them. Whether good or not, I cannot tell. I walk to school and compose limericks and rhymes and lyrics for songs. It is not good, but it just keeps coming. I am awash in words.

PASSOVER AT SEARS & ROEBUCK

I don't recall exactly when we attend our first Yom Kippur or Rosh Hashanah service. It must be shortly after we move onto Rockingham Street. The Arlington Jewish Center is in its small original building, not yet the three-story structure it would become and still is today. What is now the social hall in the lower level was then the main sanctuary. We had folding chairs for seats and a makeshift stage for a pulpit. Rabbi Golinkin led the services, and a cantor was hired for the holidays only.

We managed to fast on Yom Kippur, but it was painful, and my most vivid memory is that I am seven years old, and asking Joe if Steve and I can go outside and wait for services to be over. The service is too hard for us, and we have no idea what it is all about. Esther complains mostly about not being able to smoke and have coffee, and we all have headaches. It is not a good time for any of us, and we are always glad to see it end. If the holiday was intended to be a time of renewal, we seem to miss the point.

Sukkot came next and some other nameless holidays, but these we managed to skip. We never built a *sukkah* in our backyard. Once Rosh Hashanah and Yom Kippur were over, we were done with the Jewish holidays. We were on our own until Passover, and that was months away.

Our life centered around Sears. We bought everything there. We may have failed to attend *shul*, but we certainly did not miss the weekly trip to Sears; it had hardware for building things, and the Rosslyn lumber yard was nearby. Joe would go to the lumber yard, and have the framing freshly cut and sawed and then tied securely to the top of our car or protruding out of the trunk.

So it was no surprise when we would find ourselves at Sears, in the basement, on the fifth or sixth day of Passover, and before the eight-day holiday was over. We were not supposed to eat bread for eight full days, but we were hungry and it was lunch time, and in our family, mealtime was key. Sears' basement had a stand where you could get hot dogs and a Coke, and where you could sit at a small table. We would do our best to wait the full eight days, but being at Sears on a Saturday was too tempting. We gave in and ate the bread. Of course, the hot dogs were not kosher, and for all I know they were made mostly from pork.

Joe never told us that Passover had other layers of meaning. No one mentioned to us that the Hebrew word for Egypt, *Mizrayim* also means "the narrow places," and from that, of course, the exodus out of Egypt is the eternal quest for our own exodus out of our own self-made narrowness and slavery. The issue of the biblical exodus was not whether it was historically accurate, but whether it mirrored and explained in some way our own exile and exodus each day.[3]

Nor did Joe point out that there were two versions of the Ten Commandments, and that it was only the second version that references the coming out of Egypt, and this because, so say the scholars, there are two creation stories: first the creation of the world and then, the creation of the Jewish people.[4] From here, he might have speculated on why it matters that we were created, as a people, and whether we had to safeguard that creation.

It would not have been wrong if Joe had talked about escaping our narrowness and the sacred obligation to stay connected to our people, to our history. But like many Jews here in exile, in suburban Virginia, such words may have been hard to come by, and even harder because we had not read our own texts, and thus had never truly had the ability to explain what it is, exactly, we are all about, what we are even doing here.

But yet, for better or worse, this was how we lived our Jewish life—on Rockingham Street, just a stone's throw away from the Catholic empire.

---

3. Berlin and Brettler, *Jewish Study Bible*, 1397. "The exodus and its aftermath is celebrated [in Psalm 114] not only as the liberation of Israel, but as an event through which all of nature came to see the power of God. The exodus is a cosmic theophany that alters the course of nature."

4. In Exodus 20:8, God commands the Jewish people to remember the sabbath day because "in six days the Lord made heaven and earth and sea." Yet, in Deuteronomy, 5:15, we are told "Observe the Sabbath day. . . . Remember that you were a slave in the land of Egypt, and the Lord your God freed you from there with a mighty hand and an outstreached arm." Thus one commandment refers to creation of the world, the other to the creation of the Jewish people.

CHAPTER 16

Arlington-Fairfax Jewish Center (1950)

ARLINGTON-FAIRFAX JEWISH CENTER: THE EARLY YEARS

ARLINGTON JEWISH CENTER BEGAN in a shoe store.

If Arlington was the Broyhill Plantation, and the comfortable home of the gentiles, how did it happen that its first synagogue emerged, and one which would change the course of our family's Jewish development? We need a short look back in time to see how this came about, and more, how Esther and Joe became involved in synagogue life after having never set foot in a synagogue before their arrival in Glebewood.

In the summer of 1940, five men came together to form what would later become the Arlington Jewish Center.[1] In 1942, this small group of Jewish families met for the High Holy Days as Ohev Shalom in a room above a shoe store, known as the Jones Building on Wilson Boulevard, located across from several car dealerships and hardware stores.[2] The store was

1. *L'Dor v' Dor in Arlington County.* The history of Etz Hayim, the current name of the Arlington-Fairfax Jewish Center, is now stored on a video, and a transcript is available. The founders were Sholom Friedman's father, Herman Schwartzman, Harry Austin, Michael Hornick, and Frank Kahn. The first holiday services were held at Ashton Heights Women's Club with Rabbi Goldman. The evening services were held at Abe Bayda's house.

2. According to Jerry Jacobs,who was president of the synagogue in 1975, and now the informal archivist, the new shul was founded in 1940. Its first president was

owned by S. H. "Doc" Friedman and was located in the heart of Clarendon, home of lumber yards, as well as the bowling alley where Esther and Joe often would go.

By sheer luck, the Center found its first wealthy member who would later provide the critical financial support. Jerome Dick, who was later to become the influential president and a wealthy donor of the Arlington Jewish Center, recalls his first involvement: "I was sitting with my wife outside a shoe store on Wilson Boulevard. We heard singing and we looked at each other and I said, 'I'm sure that's Hebrew.' And sure enough, over the shoe store was a synagogue. So we joined right away."[3]

In 1947, when Esther and Joe are thinking about moving to Arlington, the synagogue still has no building. But, in 1944, the congregation had acquired the land that the synagogue sits on today. In 1947, at about the same time as Esther and Joe move from Chicago to Glebewood, ground is broken for the future synagogue on Arlington Boulevard. Initially, it is one story, with a flat concrete roof. This first section is completed on February 22, 1948. Later, in 1955, the second level will be built, which includes the main sanctuary where I will be bar mitzvahed.

So, just when Esther and Joe arrive in Glebewood, the Arlington Jewish Center is beginning its first move out of the Clarendon Shoe Store, and on to its future location on the main thoroughfare of Arlington Boulevard.

RABBI NOAH GOLINKIN COMES TO ARLINGTON: FOLLOWING THE SERVICE WITH ONE'S FINGER

By February 1948, the Center has completed construction of its first floor, so it turns to finding a permanent rabbi. That search ultimately leads to Noah Golinkin, who will change the Jewish life of our family and many others.

Noah Golinkin was born in Zhitomir, Ukraine, which was then part of Imperial Russia, but he spent much of his early life in Vilna, perhaps not far from where Sol and Anna had grown up. He was the son and grandson of rabbis. Golinkin witnessed first-hand the pogroms of Vilna and other cities in Eastern Europe. What he saw was not so different from the brutality that Sol and Anna had escaped. According to his son, David, when his father was

---

Herman Schwarzman, followed by Aaron Lewittes (1941–1942); Harold Wilkinfeld (1942–1944); Dr. Frank Feldman (1944–1946); Harry H. Goldstein (1946–1948); and Albert J. Kramer (1948–1949).

3. Apelbaum and Turman, *Jewish Washington*, 48, citing to interview with Jerome Dick in 2004.

only seven years old he could hear the gun shots of Jews being killed as they were fleeing to Vilna because of the Pyetulra massacres.

Vilna was a hotbed of anti-Semitism, and when Golinkin studied law at the Stefan Batory University, he was forced to sit on "ghetto benches" and was often beaten by his fellow students. He understood how deeply Jews were hated in Eastern Europe: "Unlike many native-born Americans, my father believed that the Germans and their Polish and Ukrainian allies were perfectly willing and able to murder large numbers of Jews."[4] In 1938, when he finally realized he must flee Vilna, he was forced to stand in line every day for a year seeking a visa to escape Europe and go to the United States.

Noah's son David explained that, in the 1950s, synagogues tended not to hire rabbis with European accents. Noah's accent was unmistakable—one knew he was from the Old Country as soon as he spoke and, to some, this communicated a way of thinking about being Jewish that was as Old World as the country he came from—not modern enough for the Jews of the New World.

In 1950, the Arlington Jewish Center offered Golinkin a position as the congregational rabbi. Golinkin must have known, when he accepted this position, there was little evidence of an active Jewish community in Arlington. There was only one modest synagogue, barely out of the ground, and with little structure or grandeur: no Jewish day school, no deli in the neighborhood, and perhaps no place to buy kosher food—the most barren of communities. One block north was Fort Meyer, a large sprawling Army base on Arlington Boulevard: the Pentagon was nearby, as was a gentile country club on Lorcom Lane, and there were residential deed restrictions on selling homes to Jews and Blacks.

When he accepted the position of rabbi, Golinkin insisted that he be named principal of the Hebrew school. Golinkin came to Arlington with a fixed determination to restore interest in Hebrew literacy and its place in religious life. One of Golinkin's primary missions was to teach Hebrew to Jews, both children and adults, out of a concern that the language was dying. He saw much of the mystery and spiritual beauty of Judaism in the Hebrew language; but recognized it was a wall that steadfastly kept Jews from fully experiencing their faith.

Golinkin may also have seen a direct link between Jewish literacy and the survival of the Jewish people. One possible factor in the disappearing Jew was the disappearing Hebrew language. The American Jew does not flee from Judaism because there is any disagreement with its core values.

---

4. Medoff and Golinkin, *Student Struggle against the Holocaust*, 123–24.

American Jews flee, in part, because of Hebrew. Because they cannot read it, they find the services in *shul* tedious, incomprehensible, patriarchal.

Golinkin wanted to teach every child and adult how to read Hebrew; his goal was quite modest. He said that he wanted to make sure that when Jews came into the synagogue they could "just follow along with a service—to just follow the text along with her finger—to connect what is being heard from the pulpit to what is being read on the page is a tremendous experience."[5]

Here then, this new rabbi with a European accent, who had left Europe because Hitler had come to power, and because he had read *Mein Kampf* and was afraid that Hitler would do what he said he would do, came to a largely gentile, suburban community, fully prepared to revolutionize Jewish education and to make sure we Jews had access to our language, to our heritage, and to our own spirituality.

BAR MITZVAH TRAINING FOR RICHARD (1950)

If one walks across Arlington Boulevard, taking care to use the crosswalk, where it intersects with Filmore Street, six lanes wide and traffic moving at a high speed, one comes to the sprawling but modest Lee Gardens complex. Red brick units, three stories high, and without elevators. In the 1950s, it was the home to many returning servicemen and those who were stationed at the nearby Fort Meyer or the Pentagon. It also was the home of Noah Golinkin and his wife Dolly.

It was here, in 1953, at Lee Gardens, within its grassy courtyards, that Rabbi Golinkin met Richard, as well as Esther, and where, sitting on lawn chairs, taught Torah to my brother Richard. Unlike the fight Anna had earlier with Sol over Joe's bar mitzvah, no such struggle occurs here.

I am not certain exactly how it came to be that Esther and Joe, who had likely never joined a synagogue in Chicago, discovered and then joined the newly formed Arlington Jewish Center. But I suspect it was the same motivation that drives young parents today. Namely, they had a son, Richard, approaching bar mitzvah age, and a younger son, me, at an age where early Jewish education should start.

I recall watching Richard studying for his bar mitzvah. He still has the only "single" room in the house, the one facing Rockingham Street, and I see him with his small red printed book, pamphlet size, containing his Torah portion and *haftarah*, but with vowels under the Hebrew letters, unlike the Torah itself which is devoid of vowels. On his chest of drawers is a small

5. Andrew Siegel, "Rabbi Noah Golinkin, 89, Taught Hebrew," para. 11.

record player that plays both 78s and 45s. By listening to a record and following along in the red book, Richard is able to learn his required readings for the Saturday morning service that he will conduct. Richard is a good student: methodical, neat, organized. He is able to achieve whatever is asked of him. He does not cause trouble, does not ask for explanations, does not resist Esther and Joe. Richard is comfortable with authority, the one who goes along. I will resist and be troublesome.

Richard is bar mitzvahed on September 3, 1954. His bar mitzvah takes place in the lower floor of the new building, in what later becomes the social hall. There are no large parties for bar mitzvah celebrants, as there are today. Such an event would have been well beyond Esther and Joe's means in any event. The surviving black and white photogrpahs, taken that Saturday evening, perhaps at a modest reception, show Richard and Golinkin standing together, both looking proud of my brother's accomplishment.

To my knowledge, this ends Richard's religious training. There was no Hebrew High School and I do not think he would have been interested anyway. I have no recollection of ever seeing him in *shul* again. He is likely at a Passover seder or two. I don't recall him ever reciting the blessings in Hebrew. I do not believe he ever joins a synagogue, and later he will marry a young Catholic nurse while a sophomore at Johns Hopkins.

Richard's bar mitzvah may not have spurred his spiritual journey, but it may have been the start of Esther and Joe's. Richard's bar mitzvah, and his time spent on the lawn with Rabbi Golinkin at Lee Gardens is almost certainly the time when Esther and Joe start to develop their relationship with Rabbi Golinkin, and become more involved with the Jewish community. Golinkin was young, charming, and deeply empathetic; Esther and Joe would have found him appealing and a natural spiritual leader. So it seems possible that sometime during the early training for Richard's bar mitzvah, when they are meeting across the street, Golinkin may have mentioned to Esther that he needed secretarial help. And Esther, highly skilled at shorthand, and an experienced secretary, might have given some thought to returning to work, when her boys were older and further along in school. Three years later she became Golinkin's full-time secretary.

Once Esther and Golinkin had been working together for a while, I am guessing that Golinkin would have suggested that Joe get involved on the board, which was then still small. That Esther would be the one who would pull Joe into her career would not be surprising. Looking back now, I think I see how this all came about—this strange evolution of two secular first-generation Jews, into people who devoted much of their lives to the running of a synagogue. It is Richard's bar mitzvah that helps turn the corner in this family history—sitting in lawn chairs, on summer afternoons, watching the heavy traffic on Arlington Boulevard, the commuters coming and going, and studying Torah. That, and Esther's drive for involvement and purpose.

1956: HEBREW SCHOOL— WE BECOME CARPOOL JEWS

In the fall of 1956, when I am eleven years old, in fifth grade at Tuckahoe Elementary School, Esther and Joe decide I should start Hebrew school at the Center. It is the inevitable decision, given Richard's bar mitzvah, and the growing relationship between Esther, Joe, and Golinkin.

After coming home from Tuckahoe, and taking a fifteen-minute break, then it was time for the carpool to the Center. Steve Levenberg, Arthur Goldstein, Larry Lapidus, Neil Frommer, and me. Five of us stuffed in a car. We carry on like the children we are. We distract whichever mother is driving us. Two days a week, or was it three? No one now seems to recall for sure. Everyone I ask has a different version.

We arrive at the Center around 3:30. Upstairs then, to Mrs. Reinitz's classroom. Rachel Reinitz, from somewhere in Germany, teaches us to read the Hebrew letters and to learn a few of their basic meanings: no grammar and no verb conjugation. I remember sitting in Mrs. Reinitz's classroom, with a portion from the Shabbat service prayer book opened before us. Mrs. Reinitz would take out her watch and give us one minute to read; she would count the words, minus the ones we mispronounced. The prize went to the swift. The girls in the class raced through the text flawlessly; Joan Suskind, Patti Plaine, and Marilyn Cohen always read without error at a dazzling speed. Not me. Many years later, after she passes away, a classroom is named after Mrs. Reinitz.

But still, I learn the prayers, including the Shema prayer: "Hear O Israel! You shall love the Lord your God with all your heart, and with all your soul, and with all your might" (Deut 6:4), which becomes the centerpiece of my spiritual vision. The notion of hearing, of listening, of being able to respond to what is all around us; the spiritual energy and miracle of life. The translation of the Hebrew verb, to listen, is in the imperative form, and thus it means "you must hear," not merely "you may hear."

The distinction between heart, soul, and might appealed to me: that Judaism recognized the notion of a soul and a heart, each different, yet each needing to be fully involved. And what, after all, was might but the engagement of the mind, mediating between a soul that was connected to God, and a heart that gravitated to the world and the community of mankind? How much more than this did I need to see what religion was and what it was trying to say to me?

We learn the vocabulary words of a prayer book in biblical Hebrew. There are no textbooks as such, so Rabbi Golinkin writes his own. They are simple books with just a few words here and there; somehow the vocabulary, the memorization, comes easily to me. I am not a speed-reader but the words themselves and their meaning stay with me.

I see now that Mrs. Reinitz was doing exactly what Golinkin had hoped she would do—she was making sure that we could follow the text in our prayer book when the words were being chanted from the pulpit during a Jewish service, our finger moving across the page as the cantor or rabbi chanted the prayers. No longer a stranger to the ceremony, no longer resenting the tradition. Suddenly, the service was not a total mystery to us. The prayer book no longer a barrier to our being engaged.

Yet, I also see that there was much we did not learn. There was no introduction to the layered meaning of the great commentators who have told generations of Jews what these words mean, and why they matter. But for now, without a Jewish day school, and without existing textbooks, we still acquired a primitive and elementary skill set. The classes gave us at least the choice later in life to decide our own spiritual destiny, and gave us one tool to do so.

Here is what seems certain: had it not been for Noah Golinkin, my own Jewish life might not have had any serious Hebrew school. The Hebrew letters and its language would have rapidly vanished from my mind and become a barrier to an essential part of Judaism.

ESTHER GOES TO WORK FOR
RABBI NOAH GOLINKIN

How odd what happens next. In 1957, Esther goes back to work. She becomes Rabbi Golinkin's secretary, and later, an executive assistant, and in truth, his right-hand everything.

Besides, her boys are now sixteen, twelve, and nine years old. Time to be on their own, time for her to shine and use the administrative and secretarial skills she had so easily mastered as a young woman in Chicago. Time to take charge, both for herself and for Joe. None of us boys ever asked Esther to spend more time at home with us.

Esther ultimately becomes the one who runs most of the administrative operations at the Center. It seems to be her destiny: certainly, more so than staying at home with us. It is an odd pairing of the deeply religious with the barely religious, yet it is perfect for Esther. It is her natural place.

Esther never studied Hebrew, never had any Jewish education, was never confirmed, and could not tell you what was in the Torah. Esther, who may have known nothing about being Jewish except the bare fact that her family name was Cohen, now becomes the daily helpmate to a devoted and brilliant new rabbi. In some ways, Esther was just the sort of modern Jew that Rabbi Golinkin wanted to introduce to Judaism. I now wonder, whether in those quiet moments when the two of them were alone in the Center's office, he didn't encourage her to start her own Jewish journey. For years, she typed every word of every sermon, and commented on them. From our dinnertime conversations I know that he would practice parts of them for her, perhaps seeking her advice. Somewhere in this process, this rabbi from Vilna was having an impact on this young secretary from Chicago.

Esther brings to her job the same energy, skill, and leadership that helped her push Joe through his career. Once at a desk, once in an office, it is plain that Esther is in charge. She and her IBM Selectric typewriter are one. No one questions it; no one wants to. Esther is at her desk each day, five days a week, the office to the rabbi's study is within ten feet of her, and they become inseparable.

Esther leaves the house each day, leaving us home alone after school. It seems natural to have no one home when I arrive after the school day. I don't notice whether other mothers are home. But in truth, I am happy to find our house empty, no one to tell me what to do or what comes next.

My first job when I get home from school is to call Esther at the Center on our one black dial phone. She will tell me what to put in the oven, usually potatoes, which will then bake for hours so that the skin is burnt and tasteless, but I do not know it is supposed to be otherwise. It will be many more years before I discover that food has flavor.

At night, at dinner, we relive in detail Esther's day with the rabbi. Every night, the dinner talk is about the rabbi, and I drown in the details of running a synagogue. I learn about the janitor and getting the trash out, the lights on, the doors locked or unlocked, the *Chronicle* printed, the ads sold for the membership directory, the *Journal*, the minutes for the board; the list of subjects is endless. I come to see a synagogue as a business operation, certainly with more detail than I see in the Torah. Had I even seen the actual inside of the Torah? I knew better where the frozen hot dogs were stored in the Center's social hall kitchen, to be sold later on Sunday afternoons.

Esther did it all. It was Esther who assembled and ran the ticket distribution for the Jewish High Holidays. Long before computers, she would prepare a large white poster board chart with a space to write all the names of the congregants who had requested "tickets" to the High Holidays, and settle disputes about where everyone sat. I seem to recall she wrote the names in ink, and then, when fights erupted and changes were made, had to draw a fine line through one name, then add another. The fights over seats! No one wanted to be sent to the lower social hall, or sit too far back on the folding chairs.

Esther also organized the teams for selling advertisements for the *Journal*, which was the congreation's phone directory that was printed each year. Esther worked with the printing company to get it published and distributed. Later, when I am fifteen years old, that same printing company will give me a summer job selling advertisements for the programs for the local high school football games. Everything in my world is connected.

Esther's involvement is so complete that I do not distinguish the work world of the synagogue from the spiritual home the synagogue is meant to be. I am too young for subtle refinements. Esther and Joe are both immersed in synagogue administration and logistics. I know the names of the janitors, of the people who sell ads for the *Journal*. Now I learn lessons that even the rabbis cannot teach.

From Richard's bar mitzvah in 1954 until the end of Esther's time at the Center, Rabbi Golinkin was the center of our life, our dinner talk, and Esther's career. And yet, despite this, we never lit candles on Shabbat and never spoke a single word of Hebrew from the Torah in our home. We lived this odd mixture of a Jewish life: surrounded by everything touching the synagogue, and yet still very little of the deeper meanings and teachings. In the end, it was still Passover at Sears. It would be over fifty years until I read Rashi or studied in depth a Torah portion.

THE BAR MITZVAH CLASSES OF 1957
AND 1958: WE COME OF AGE

By the time I am twelve years old, in 1957, the responsibility for training bar mitzvah boys has been transferred from Rabbi Golinkin to a new teacher, barely out of his teens, named Hal Schlaffer. Rachel Reinitz was our Hebrew school teacher, but it was Hal who guided us through the learning of the Friday night and Saturday morning services.

I was part of the two Hebrew school classes that saw the Center in its new physical structure, with its upstairs main sanctuary, its classrooms, its permanent seats, its fully functioning air-conditioning. The upstairs sanctuary had been completed in time for the High Holiday services of 1955, although on that first High Holiday service, the air-conditioning was not working, and the permanent chairs in the sanctuary had not yet been installed. Still, 500 people attend. Stan Siegel had the first bar mitzvah in the upper sanctuary in September 1955,[6] and by then the Center had reached an early stage of maturity. The school was flourishing, the new sanctuary was completed, and the full-scale bar mitzvah ceremony could be performed in the larger sanctuary. And then the name of the synagogue was changed to the Arlington-Fairfax Jewish Center, reflecting that it had become a synagogue for both major counties in northern Virginia.

Our class of Hebrew school students dutifully attended each other's bar mitzvahs, and when it was not our turn we sat in the back rows as a group, and laughed and carried on, paying little attention to the service and the boring chanting. But even though we were immature, and not particularly attentive, still we witnessed the Jewish customs, we became familiar with the language of the Shabbat service, and we heard the words and the melodies of the entire service, both Friday night and Saturday morning. I assumed this was what all Jews did. The words of the service have never left me.

My bar mitzvah is on Friday night, August 29, 1958, and the following Saturday morning. Friday morning, there is work to be done; grass to be cut. We are a working family. There is company coming to our home on Rockingham Street for the celebration on Saturday night after services, and my job is to cut the grass so the house looks nice. I am wondering if this is part of my religious duty. A vague sense of resentment comes over me: *Is this what one does to get ready for this great moment of transition, a small household task?*

No matter. I cut the grass in very neat and careful rows and notice that when done exactly right the yard resembles the wonderful pure green of the grassy outfield in Griffith Stadium, where my Washington Senators play baseball, and I wonder who they are playing this coming week. Surely they will continue their unbreakable losing streak as I am chanting my *haftarah*. I prepare my backyard for our guests with the care of a groundskeeper at the stadium, and my resentment is gone. Now it is center field, neat rows of well-manicured grass.

While cutting the grass and thinking mostly about baseball, I have this boyish thought that how well the Senators do that day might well depend on how well I pay attention to my Jewishness. Is God looking? A sense of reward

6. *L'Dor v' Dor*, 10.

and punishment finds its way into the mind of a thirteen-year-old boy. Rachel Reinitz has made us all speed-read the shema prayers: the words, "And if you will carefully obey my commands which I give you today. . . . " We have raced over this, dismissed it, ignored it, and now suddenly it is there, inside us, like it or not. Will Allison or Killebrew play well that day, but only if I chant properly? If I don't daven, will Killebrew make an error at first base and let a run score? How deep or wide do these connections run, if at all? I cannot reach a decision, but I am careful to keep this in mind as the day goes on.

Friday night, I am on the *bema*, working my way through the entire Friday night service. I can probably see Sol and Anna in the synagogue and Esther and Joe, my brothers, and the others from my Hebrew class. Toward the conclusion of the Friday night service, Rabbi Golinkin says the benediction for the children: "May the Lord's countenance shine upon your face." Too young to understand, these words somehow find their way into my spiritual vocabulary; the beauty and imagery of this simple sentence stays with me for life, and it is now one of my favorite prayers.

Saturday morning is the longer and more difficult service to learn. It is the 13th and 14th of Elul on the Jewish calendar. I chant the two traditional services, *shacharit* (the morning introductory prayers) and *musaf* (an additional group of morning prayers) and read my Torah portion and *haftorah*. The family is all there, in coats and ties, and the women dressed up as well, another tradition now mostly gone in progressive synagogues, where any form of casual clothing is the norm.

My Torah portion is from Deuteronomy 21:10, "Ki Teitzei." I don't recall discussing with Rabbi Golinkin what this portion was about, nor do I recall preparing a *d'var torah* (discussion about a Torah portion) to be read to the congregation, which now seems to be the fashion. I was glad my *haftorah* portion, Isaiah 54:1 (a biblical selection from the Book of Prophets read each week) was one of the shortest. Although I read it, I did not truly become engaged with the meaning of the prophet Isaiah, nor did I know where he fit into the great tradition of Jewish prophets.

As is the custom then, at the end of the service, the president of the Sisterhood gives a gift. I am given the Sabbath and Festival Prayer Book, published by United Synagogue of America, with my full name on the front, in Hebrew. This is signed by Mrs. Morton Stiefel, "Sisterhood President, 1958–59." She writes: "Our fondest hopes that you will use this prayer book to further your knowledge of your people's prayers and traditions."

Rabbi Golinkin also gives me a gift on the *bema*: a copy of the Holy Scriptures, published by the Jewish Publication Society. My name is engraved on the front, and on the inside cover Rabbi Golinkin writes this:

God blessed you with a lovely name, a lovely family and a lovely heritage. May you always try to live up to the challenge of your name, to the expectations of your family, and to the greatness of your people's heritage.

There it is again—the name thing. I wonder now if I have been true to either inscription. I have, at least, preserved their words and kept the books close to me always, never further away than my law books, my secular reading. Both are on my shelves: my two selves, each competing for time and attention, each calling out. Still, even now.

What were Sol and Anna thinking as they sat there that day, all three hours of the overly long Jewish Shabbat services, then in their early sixties, having come from Europe to this strange place called Arlington? Did they have some sense of satisfaction that the journey they had started sixty years ago had now come to fruition? That they had left Vilna to save not only themselves but some essential part of Judaism? The millions who emigrated had saved enough of Judaism for future generations. Maybe saving Judaism was a gradual act, that "one brick at a time" that builds a cathedral, as I once heard John Roberts, later Chief Justice of the Supreme Court, say of his religious views.

BAR MITZVAH GIFTS

That evening, we had a small bar mitzvah party in our basement on Rockingham Street. There were gifts piled up in my bedroom, and I remember slipping away to my bedroom and going through them, mixing up the cards and the gifts, so I would not be able to thank the right person for each gift. Joe came up to rescue me and brought me back to the party.

The traditional gift from the sisterhood was a clock radio, the first one I had ever owned. Every member of our Hebrew school class would get one. Mine lasted for decades, and I am sorry later when it no longer works. For a long time, it stayed by my bedside and provided me with many hours of quiet nighttime listening to the Washington Senators, my soul-like journey to an orderly world where good was rewarded and my attention to duty honored, the biblical rules of baseball working well.

The true gift, of course, was that I learned Hebrew, though just barely enough so that sight reading was easy for me, even if comprehension was not. Today, I feel great affection for the language, and I love its look and feel on the printed page. I am amazed at the complexity of the verb roots, and the nuance hidden so carefully within the layers.

For this, I remain grateful to what Noah Golinkin brought to Arlington—gentile Arlington, which had almost certainly never had a rabbi before him who insisted its members learn Hebrew. Yet, it may be that Golinkin's insistence on Hebrew was both too much and too little. To some extent, Golinkin was ahead of his time. Years later, other institutions would take up the issue of Hebrew and textual literacy. The interest in Hebrew today is in a modest revival. We see this in the recent publication of an entirely new English translation by Robert Alter, who has spent over ten years retranslating the Hebrew Bible. It is Alter's view that the prior translations were insufficiently true to the meaning of the Hebrew language, and that the King James Version had a shaky sense of Hebrew.[7]

Not all rabbis agree that Hebrew is key or that synagogue attendance and participation matter that much. Some leading rabbis decry the modern synagogue as having adopted rituals and structures for services that drive away members. Rabbi Sidney Schwarz, who founded the synagogue I attend today, has written highly regarded books that question the approach of the modern synagogue, as well as the traditional format of three hours of chanting, mostly in Hebrew.[8] He documents what he calls the "turnoff of the postwar suburban synagogue," noting that synagogues built in the 1950s and 1960s "offered impressive facilities and a wide array of services, [but] the boomer generation raised in these synagogues remember them as cold and austere."[9]

Rabbi Schwarz believes synagogues have failed the Jewish community in many respects. Yet I wonder whether it isn't also true that we Jews have failed our synagogues by our unwillingness to undertake the hard work and discipline to become engaged in learning and textual study. We've disconnected belief from discipline. Or is it acceptable that only a few remain "observant" while the rest do what they can when they can?

If Noah Golinkin had not come to Arlington, the Jews who settled on Rockingham Street might merely have been an odd coincidence—a small collection of Jewish families who moved to a convenient location, but whose interest in things Jewish was minimal, and decreasing daily, so that what made them Jewish was drifting away with each secular day. It is only now that I appreciate what Rabbi Golinkin gave us then. It was his love of Hebrew, and his willingness to write the first Hebrew primers we studied that changed us from hopelessly secular to something Jewish.

---

7. Alter, *Hebrew Bible*, 1:xiii–xiv.

8. See generally, Schwarz, *Finding a Spiritual Home.*

9. Schwarz, *Finding a Spiritual Home,* 20.

But how much of this would last after he left us, when we were on our own and responsible for our own lives? Would we always be hanging by that same insubstantial thread?

CHAPTER 17

From Colonial Jews to
Synagogue Jews (1958–1960)

WE BECOME COLONIAL JEWS:
WILLIAMSBURG JUNIOR HIGH

IN THE BIBLE, THERE are two different versions of the creation story.[1] How odd, I have often thought, that this basic narrative of God's most important work would be described in two different ways. And then, while in exile in suburban Virginia, I would learn of yet another creation story, the creation of God's city on a hill, that is, the American creation story, a story deeply rooted in Colonial America, and in particular, in Virginia.[2]

My indoctrination into this view of history begins in earnest in September 1958, a few weeks after my bar mitzvah. I return to Williamsburg Junior High School, now in eighth grade. I think of this period as one in which we went from being carpool Jews to being colonial Jews, American colonial, Southern, but without the confederate flag. It is during this period that our education is dominated by the colonial history of Virginia, and the

1. Compare Gen 1:1 with Gen 4:1. Robert Alter notes these two different versions including the different names for God and a different notion of how things came into being (Alter, *Hebrew Bible,* 1:13).

2. The phrase "A City Upon a Hill" is derived from the parable of salt and light in Jesus's Sermon on the Mount (Matt 5:14). It has been used in our history to refer to America standing as a "beacon of hope" for the world. It was supposedly first uttered in America by the Puritan John Winthrop in "A Model of Christian Charity."

166

tradition and teachings of Thomas Jefferson and the other founding fathers. I begin to see the colonial period as experienced in Virginia as yet another variant on the creation story; the true rebirth of civilization: the birth of democracy, something as important as our Jewish heritage.

John Glenn, a Marine pilot, has moved in across the street from Williamsburg Junior High School. We see his home each morning when the school bus drops us off. Next year, in 1959, Glenn will be selected as one of the Mercury Seven, a group of test pilots who will become the nation's first astronauts. Later, on February 20, 1962, Glenn will fly the Friendship 7 mission, becoming the first American to orbit the Earth, and the fifth person and third American in space. But, for now, in 1958, his son is a classmate at our school, and we do not yet know what an astronaut is or what he does. We are having enough trouble keeping our feet on the ground below us.

Even though the summer has ended, baseball lingers through the fall, and for a few more weeks baseball remains at the core of my life. Then, and now, my thoughts return to *Damn Yankees,* the twentieth-century version of the Faustian myth—the notion of a deal made with the devil—that looks good when made, but ends poorly. Still, I would make this deal, I am sure: trade my soul for a slot on the team and the chance to win the pennant. Why wouldn't the fictional character, Shoeless Joe from Hannibal, Missouri, make such a deal? A soul for fame, for love, for recognition? How different, after all, is that deal from the one we make daily? How different from the reward and punishment of religious life? And given Judaism's mostly indifferent belief in the notion of some form of eternal damnation, the odds seem better.

The Senators are 61 and 93 in 1958, and in last place, where they always seem to be. We needed Shoeless Joe. I needed him. There is a limit to one's suffering. The Yankees will win the World Series as they always do. Calvin Griffin is the manager of the Senators. Eddie Yost, Roy Sievers, Bob Lemon, Bob Allison—all of whom are later to be joined by Harmon Killebrew—are the key players. Pascal and Ramos pitch. Bob Lemon is the worst left-fielder in baseball history, and he often would be booed when he took the field because he could always be counted on to make an error, kick the ball, or simply let the ball fly over his head. I loved this team. This was suffering as it was meant to be.

While attending Williamsburg, I can look out the classroom window and see, about a mile or so away, the tall cranes working on the construction of our new high school; actually, the renovation and transformation of Yorktown from an old elementary school to a vast new high school: antiseptic, clean, new. Each new school, even more than the last, embeds in us the firm conviction that here in Virginia is where the world is made right.

We become indoctrinated and immersed in the history of Virginia, of Williamsburg, Yorktown, and the founding fathers. I listen, learn, and become intensely proud of my Virginia heritage, and will not discover for many years the darker side of that heritage. Even more years will pass before I realize that, while we have been surrounded by the secular world of America, the city on a hill that brought democracy to the rest of the world, I have only gained a small foundation in the study of Jewish texts. Whatever role Judaism has played in moving civilization alongs its rightful path is out of sight for the moment. We have no sense of this imbalance; nothing in our daily lives cries out for change. The forces in the world that make things happen are political and secular. This is as it should be: dull, steady, safe. The 1950s in the suburbs: breathing at a slow rate.

Arlington is intent on teaching its students about the history of Virginia and its colonial roots. Everything focuses on the birth of the nation, on colonial Williamsburg, and, indeed, the highlight of seventh grade comes in the spring when large Greyhound buses pull up to the front of the school and our class is taken for an overnight visit to colonial Williamsburg. We stay in the Williamsburg Inn and visit both Yorktown and Williamsburg.

The Rockefellers have spent tens of millions of dollars reconstructing Williamsburg over its old foundations and have rebuilt the town exactly as it looked in the late 1700s, although later I learn that the streets were not tree-lined when Jefferson and Benjamin Franklin walked them, and that the trees were added later to conform to our modern concept of beauty and to provide much needed shade in the hot summer months.

I came to see human history—at least the parts that were most worthy—as not truly starting until the American Revolutionary War, and I saw Virginia as the place where most everything good happened. I walked the same streets as Thomas Jefferson, John Adams, George Washington, Benjamin Franklin. I inhaled this history, and it informed my consciousness: the American religion of democracy. I went to the court building where Patrick Henry uttered his famous cry of "Give me liberty or give me death!" Patrick Henry was here, and I felt his reality. More than Moses, even.

I studied Jefferson intensely, and later in life visited his home at Monticello on numerous occasions. It became clear to me that the separation of church and state was key; I am taught that Jefferson did not believe in God, or at least not in any organized religion. But, later I learn he was busy cutting and pasting together his own bible, "a collage of verses from the New Testament—*The Life and Morals of Jesus of Nazareth*."[3] Jefferson was searching

---

3. Parker, "Reading Thomas Jefferson's Bible," 94.

for the precepts of religious ethics, but "minus the mumbo jumbo" of God.[4] President George Washington, however, spoke of the centrality of religion in his Farewell Address of 1796: "Of all the dispositions and habits which lead to political prosperity, religion and morality are indispensable."[5]

What we see as teenagers in this suburban world is that the nation was built on an odd mixture of separation and adulation; one nation under God, but yet one nation where God could not be forced upon us. The pushing and pulling, one nation under God as long as it is my God and not yours.

This part of American history, the part with our founding fathers, became a key part of how I viewed the world. The culture of America is overwhelming and persuasive. Jewish culture was more in the background; submerged. Here, in Arlington, there were no smells or sounds of Shabbat on the streets, no Shabbat candles in every window, no one rushing home to prepare the Sabbath meal, no memory of Vilna. Friday night is football night at the local high school. That I had another founding father, Abraham, who changed the world's civilization by tearing us away from the worship of idols, values which surely transcended even the critical thinking of Jefferson and Hamilton, could well have slipped away forever at this point—but for what happened next.

THE KUNEY FAMILY: WORKING AT THE CENTER

While Arlington was doing its best to convince me that the civilized world rotated around Virginia, the Center still remained a key part of my life, as it did for Esther and Joe. When I was fourteen and fifteen years old, the Kuney family seemed to always be at the Center, one way or another, working to run the synagogue and its many functions. And although I remained actively involved with the Center, the connection was more administrative or logistical. I had yet to delve into the sacred texts, and certainly never carried with me, at that stage of my life, a sense of their daily importance.

During this period, Esther, Joe, Steve, and I make the twenty-minute drive from Rockingham Street to the Center every Sunday. Richard is now at Johns Hopkins, and I take over his job as the clerk for the Sunday school.

4. Parker, "Reading Thomas Jefferson's Bible," 94.

5. "Washington's Farewell Address," para. 27. President Washington stated as follows: "Where is the security for property, for reputation, for life, if the sense of *religious* obligation deserts the oaths which are the instruments of investigation in courts of justice? And let us with caution indulge the supposition that morality can be maintained without religion. Whatever may be conceded to the influence of refined education on minds of peculiar structure, reason and experience both forbid us to expect that national morality can prevail in exclusion of religious principle" (para. 27, emphasis added).

There we are: the Kuney family hanging around the office. Joe attends adult education on the upper floor, Steve is in class, Esther is behind her desk, and I am running errands and making sure each teacher has his or her supplies.

We would remain at the Center from about 10:00 until 12:30, sometimes followed by bowling on Columbia Pike, other times followed by pepperoni pizza at Esther and Joe's favorite pizza place, Mario's on Wilson Boulevard, still standing all these decades later. Not unlike Sol, who loved the freshly fried shrimp sold at the wharves near Lake Michigan. Other times, we made do with the kosher hot dogs sold in the social hall by the Center's sisterhood on Sundays.

I worked as the school clerk for Herbert Hoffman, who was the Sunday school principal. In real life, Herb was a high-ranking political appointee at the Department of Justice (DOJ), where he had a huge office. I fell in love with the very name of the building: *Department of Justice.* A life of justice. My life must connect to this building somehow. I had enough disagreements with Esther and Joe that I felt a need to speak up; unfair things were all around me.

In a year or two, Herb Hoffman will help me get a summer internship (mostly as a clerk-typist and errand runner) with the DOJ, and I will have the chance to see President John Kennedy in the Rose Garden. Robert Kennedy is the Attorney General. During my time at the DOJ, I see, almost daily, three summer interns from different law schools, who are in the Justice Department's honors program, and I watch them writing legal memos in the law library. There are no computers; all their work is handwritten on legal-size yellow pads. I watch. I yearn. I connect. Whatever it is they are doing, they are *writing*, and on pads, surrrounded by books and on long desks. Even then, I sense that whatever it is they are doing is what I must do. This is where the wrongs in the world are made right; it is the power of writing. It is all about words. There is no way to understand this; some things have an obvious quality when lived, and yet resist explanation.

But for now, on Sundays, I dispatch supplies at the Center, and collect the weekly *keren ami*—the small charitable donations made by the students of nickels and dimes—and I count the coins, add them up, roll them up, and make sure they are deposited. Later, when I leave, Steve will take over my job, so there will be three Kuney brothers who seemingly hold this job in perpetuity.

Esther and Joe were growing much closer to the Jewish community and becoming an essential part of it. That Joe was attending the adult education lectures every Sunday surely signified his own growing interest in things Jewish; and yet, not once did he ever tell us about these lectures, what he had learned, or what had been discussed. Still, we were there, firmly planted in the daily and weekly life of of the Arlington-Fairfax Jewish Center. We had become a fixture; three brothers passing down the role of clerk; a secretary; and a board member. By this time, Esther was essentially running the administration of the Center. In that sense, our family was key, and yet we had never seen the inside of a Torah scroll, nor once discussed the teachings of Moses Maimonides.

HEBREW HIGH SCHOOL

I was now at a turning point for so many Jews, that moment when bar mitzvah is over, and there is the chance to lay it all aside, all the Jewish learning, and turn instead to career, ambition, and learning a trade.

Rabbi Golinkin was deeply committed to the notion that something must be done with this group of young people, now bar mitzvahed and past the typical course of Jewish education. So, he developed the concept that Conservative *shuls* should continue with the education of their teens beyond bar mitzvah, and he added a Hebrew High School to the Center's progam. To my knowledge, this had not been done elsewhere, or if so, only on a smaller scale. While the idea has since spread, in the 1950s it was new. Yet, it may be this decision, along with the rabbi's insistence on teaching Hebrew to adults, that ensureed Golinkin's lasting impact.

The Hebrew High School program was for two years. I am almost certain that I attended Hebrew High classes at least once a week when I was fourteen. My memory is less clear about whether I finished the second year. I was grateful for the program and felt comfortable in it. Looking back, I see now that there were important subjects we never studied: for example, we never once studied the great commentator Rashi. Still, I was connected, and the program ensured that the syngagoue would become an essential and permanent part of my life. Life without it is not one I can imagine.

Hal Schlaffer, who was then a graduate student at American University and only in his early twenties, became our Hebrew High School teacher, a faculty of one. Yet, Mr. Schlaffer almost single-handedly made Hebrew High School a place of joy for all of us. Mr. Schlaffer was young and poor. He told us about the time his students took him to a men's clothing store to buy him a suit so that he had something to wear at their bar mitzvahs.[6]

Mr. Schlaffer's classes were raucous. Jackie Pevenstein, now a highly regarded doctor, was then a teenager who became known to us as the "flying Pevenstein," presumably because of his desire to jump off desks and pretend he was flying around the classroom. Mr. Schlaffer's typical punishment for

6. *L'Dor v' Dor*, 25.

misbehavior was that the miscreant had to write a composition. Years later, Mr. Schlaffer recalls that Jackie's composition set a record. "It was so many sheets. We stapled it together and we hung it in the hallway and it covered the entire hallway of the school section."[7]

Mr. Schlaffer believed that how he treated the students was part of the key to Jewish survival:

> The most important thing that Arlington taught me is that if you approach kids right about Jewish education, then they will continue with you, they will stay with you. It's my opinion that the teens are the most important time because the kids don't have to be there; they're there because they really want to learn and the world is just really starting to open up for them.[8]

The Hebrew High School classes of 1957 and 1958 made up much of this new experiment in Jewish education outside of the Jewish day schools. The classes were frantic and crazy; there was mischief and bad behavior, but there was above all else a sense of love and happiness at being at the Center, now with no bar mitzvah to worry about, simply the joy of being with our Jewish friends.

The Center also had a youth group for its teenagers: United Synagogue Youth, or USY. This was for both young boys and girls. Blanche Davidson devoted years to running this program and, as I recall, it was the center of our social life. Friday night services were when girls my age showed up for services, presumably to meet boys at least as much as God. We boys did the same. For this kind of event, I had no trouble getting Esther and Joe to let me use the older of the two cars we then owned. I was allowed to drive to the *shul* and back home. Friday night became my core Jewish tradition. Not to mention an opportunity to be with girls.

Friday night services brought together USY and Hebrew High School. By the time we were fifteen and sixteen, the Center had become our home away from home, a place where we saw our friends and had our core social life. As my friend and classmate, Danny Siegel, remembers it, "Friday night we were packed with kids, or Shabbat morning bunches of us were here. This is where you were, this is where you hung out, where you did your activities."[9]

Danny, today a Jewish scholar and national leader in his own right, reflected on the experience:

7. *L'Dor v' Dor*, 25.

8. *L'Dor v' Dor*, 23.

9. *L'Dor v' Dor*, 26.

It was a good place to be. . . . [W]e learned when we were kids that the synagogue is three different places: a Beit K'nesset just to get together, a Beit Midrash to study, and a Beit T'fillah, to daven [to pray]. I wanted the kids to know that this is the place you want to be, just to be with people because it's a Jewish atmosphere, a place with Jewish values, a good place, a place where you can be appreciated.[10]

Danny went on to quote from Rabbi Rossman, who wrote an article called "Everything I Needed to Know I Learned in Synagogue." Rabbi Rossman said: "University elevated me on my grades, here I'm elevated on my deeds, who I am as a person."

Michael Dick, whose father was one of the most influential original members of the synagogue, remembered the joys and the fun beyond the formal learning:

We had a two-year Hebrew High School, and it was more than just going to school. We had our football team and a softball team. We had our own newspaper. We started a formal dance called the Hebrew High Ball, which was wildly successful. . . . There was a band at that time called the Party Makers, and it was kids who went to our high school and they were the hottest band around. We had over three hundred people stuffed in the social hall for our dances.[11]

Years later, Rabbi Sidney Schwarz, who founded the Adat Shalom synagogue in Bethesda, Maryland, wrote in his book, *Jewish Megatrends*, that synagogues have failed the Jewish community in many respects.[12] Perhaps. But the Arlington-Fairfax Jewish Center was not failing us at that stage of our lives. Things were left out for sure; a more serious and thoughtful reading of texts needed to be part of the program, and this failure cannot be overlooked. But the failure that Rabbi Schwarz seemed to note was not the lack of more serious education, but somehow an absence of meaning, something lost in the veneer of the modern suburban synagogue. But we did not feel that same alientation from our synagogue. And at least we had the ladder on which to climb the slope and to get over the daunting barrier of learning Hebrew. We were not blind and deaf to the harder learning that would come later.

Danny Siegel questioned the notion that synagogues necessarily must fail us, and indeed argues that what we had at the Center is not just

10. *L'Dor v' Dor*, 41.

11. *L'Dor v' Dor*, 23.

12. Schwarz, *Jewish Megatrends*, 3–39.

nostalgia, but a model of what we should have now. In his interview for the Center's congregational history, he speaks at length on this subject, noting in particular the obligation to join a *shul* and to be part of the community:

> One of the things I got from Arlington Fairfax is you belong to a community, you join a synagogue; it's as simple as that. I've been around the country a few times. There are literally thousands of people who would give their right arm to have one more Shabbat like they had at USY camp, or at NFTY camp, or have a Shabbat like the ones we had with Rabbi Golinkin, or a time with an excitement about going to Hebrew High School class. That's real. For people to knock it down and say, "Well those are the old days and they're never gonna come back," I say, "No excuse, we're supposed to try, to recreate that kind of a thing. . . ."[13]

Danny's formula is study, pray, and join, then add in basketball and football, a prom, a summer camp, and make it last through the mid-teens, right up to the time before college. Can this possibly be enough? Perhaps. But, for the truly observant Jewish parents, it is only the Jewish day school that will be adequate. For the rest of us, the modern Jew with little history of observance or orthodoxy, we must make do with a thinner slice of Jewish education and exposure. But the Center did in fact work its magic at least to the extent of what Golinkin thought it could achieve. We would always be able to attend a Shabbat or holiday service, and in Golinkin's words, point with our finger to where we were in the text.

Mr. Schlaffer added another dimension. Mr. Schlaffer speaks thusly of both love and prayer: "But as competitive as they were that's how supportive of one another they were. The kids could daven, they could lead the Sabbath morning service. We fell in love with one another and we got extremely close and we still are close. At our reunion several years ago, it was like coming home."[14]

Of course, that was many years ago now. Some have stayed, some have left the Center. I am one of those who moved to other side of the Potomac, here in Maryland. Yet, one day, about fifteen years ago, I was standing in a deli in Potomac. Hal had come in for something. We had not seen one another in decades. He saw me and recognized me, despite the signs of aging. He said, with the same smiling firmness as he had when I was fifteen and had failed to do some assignment for class, "Don't you owe me a composition?"

What did I take from Hal's classes? I do not have any notes from those classes, and I do not even recall there being a textbook. Yet, I still see Mr.

---

13. *L'Dor v' Dor*, 42.

14. *L'Dor v' Dor*, 24.

Schlaffer behind the teacher's desk with his five-by-seven-inch note cards from which he lectured. I remember his joy and love. I remember the touch football we played before class. I remember thinking that this synagogue was a part of my life, an unquestioning bond that would make the thought of not joining a synagogue years later unthinkable. We had USY, Hal, touch football, and a modest amount of Jewish instruction. We met as friends and enjoyed each other's company. What is it exactly we were being taught other than that *this place* is where I belong?

Hal Schlaffer passed away prematurely from a rare disease on September 17, 2017, shortly before I started work on this memoir. It was sad news. But, now I know for sure that he was right. We did fall in love with one another. And those of us on Rockingham Street owed him much. We did not have Rashi and Soloveitchik, but at least we had the rare connection between Jewish learning, a meaningful social life, and the joy of late-childhood play. Whatever was left out—and there was much—it was possible to recover later in life, in large part because of what we had been given when we were young. We may have been colonial Jews, but in truth, as I now see it, we were at long last synagogue Jews. And from this there would be no turning back—try as we might.

So Hal might have been right after all—maybe I did owe him a composition and, if so, then this memoir is just that.

CHAPTER 18

Joe as President of the Center
The Bland Sixties (1960–1963)

JOE BECOMES PRESIDENT OF ARLINGTON-FAIRFAX JEWISH CENTER

BY 1960, HEBREW HIGH School is over and our days of Jewish education at the Center have ended. Whatever is left undone, unread, and unknown remains so.

But Esther and Joe will continue to work at the Center for many more years. Each day, Esther is downstairs in the Center's office, sitting behind her desk. She is the same person she was in Chicago. Coffee-drinking, chain-smoking, and hard-driven, she is lightning fast on her IBM Selectric, and able to organize her way out of any problem that arises. She works with Molly Pevenstein, the treasurer, and makes sure the bills for dues are sent, the sermons are typed, and each piece of the rabbi's correspondence is typed to perfection. She is perfection itself.

It is during this period that Joe also begins to take a more active role in the running of the synagogue. Sometime in the 1960s, Joe agrees to serve on the Board for the Center. He had organizational and executive skills, which were needed, and membership on the Board did not require him to be observant or learned, which he was not—at least not then. Board duty required the ability to sit through long meetings and debate the many issues that confront a synagogue. Contracts to renew, budgets, curricula for the school—the list was endless. Joe progressed through the typical roles in such organizations, first serving as vice president of the Board of Directors in 1960, and then becoming president of the Board a year or so later.

So, even though my formal Jewish education was over, I continued to see Esther and Joe at the Center for one thing or another. This was how I saw them: always working, always together. Just as Esther had become a key part of the ACS, and had gone with Joe to most major ACS meetings across the country, so too did the two of them become fixtures at the Center.

Once Joe becomes vice president and then president of the Center, the phone at our house is always ringing. The black phone—only one model is offered by AT&T—with the round dials, is in constant use. I remember our number: Jefferson 4-3398. (JE 4-3398). When I walk by the kitchen, I see Joe on the phone, talking to a board member, or to a congregant, arguing or debating, but always making sure the Center is functioning properly, the community has what it needs. He complains about the calls, but I think he actually likes them, and he does the work dutifully for years. Joe is always about duty; less so, affection. Joe is their president, and he has the energy and skill to work on problems; ever the patient engineer, the umpire.

Watching this over the years, I come to believe that service on a board is the right thing to do as a member of the community. I also see Joe teaching me, without any words, that accepting one's role in the community is required. Joe's lesson about Judaism, the truth he is always driving home, is that we are a people, not just individuals. In Judaism, the notion of a community is holy. This is why we pray only in a group of ten, only when we have a *minyan*; prayer requires a communal voice.

Years later, when I follow suit and take up a similar role on the board in my synagogue, I find that, unlike Joe, I lack the patience for it, and the board work does not seem to make good use of my talents, whatever they are. Yet, I see now, even in my efforts to push away from him, I was still seeking to emulate him. This was the contradiction I lived with for the rest of his life: there was so much of him I admired, and yet the two of us could never fully embrace one another, neither physically nor emotionally.

Perhaps I should not have been surprised at what happens next. It is during this period that Joe becomes more interested in Jewish learning. He goes to the Center every Sunday with Esther. She is at her desk, helping to run the Sunday school and, while she is working, Joe attends the adult education lecture in the double classroom on the second floor. The Center had developed a well-regarded adult education program under Harold November, who started the program in 1955 and served as its chairman through the mid-1990s. The program announcements are still available in the archives maintained by the Capital Jewish Museum.

Joe was an intellectual, and I am certain he found the lectures by well-known Jewish thinkers and scholars intriguing and stimulating. He was hearing disucssions about Torah and Israeli culture and politics that had never been part of his life before. I believe these lectures were instrumental in Joe's movement toward a deeper belief in things Jewish.

And then there was another change. I barely notice, but around this time, Joe starts attending weekday *minyans*—the short morning prayer service. I think Joe was beginning to feel a greater need for religious content, for the daily prayers, although his Hebrew was still too weak to follow the prayers fluidly. He joins a few of the older members twice a week for a short morning service and some Torah study. They have coffee and bagels while they talk. I go with him once, but feel the service is too remote from me and the men too old. But still, I *see* my father doing this and, once you see these things, they acquire a legitimacy that cannot be forgotten. We believe what we see.

I wonder if Sol went with Joe to any of these *minyans*. I like to think he did, and that perhaps now, for the very first time in their lives, they began to share something Jewish. I hope so. I do not know for certain what Sol thought about his son becoming the president of the Arlington-Fairfax Jewish Center, when he, Sol, had pushed back so hard on Joe's Jewish education years earlier, but I am guessing he felt some regret, as well as new feeling: a sense of pride in his son's accomplishments.

So now, looking back, I see what I missed. This was the time when Joe was willing to engage his spiritual side more deeply. I don't think he was ready to give up bacon and shrimp; he would still work on Shabbat, and would never daven at home, but he was moving closer to a desire to know and read Torah, despite his lack of training, as did Sol, the two of them—one from Vilna, where he had refused to attend shul, and one from Chicago, where he had little if any Jewish involvement. Yet there they were together, in this suburban *shul*, trying as best they could to follow the service in Hebrew, in whatever way they could manage. Maybe Sol's Jewish soul was always present, eager to find its voice, but whatever he had seen in Vilna had made its expression too hard—living in a world where Jews were hated and murdered. But now, safe in suburban Virginia, he could forgive God. Now, here in Arlington, he could start to let his Jewish soul breathe a little.

CLASSES START AT YORKTOWN HIGH SCHOOL

I start tenth grade in September 1960, at Yorktown High School. There are five, maybe six Jewish students out of about 1,200 students. While I knew this, it was of no significance to me or my Jewish classmates that we were in the minority. The difference between a nonobservant Jewish student and a modestly observant Christian student was hard to discern. We all played football on Friday night.

In many ways, Yorktown represented the pinnacle of academic success in the secular suburban world in which I lived. Yorktown was a school of high-achievers, including those who saw themselves as future political leaders or high-level government officials. Almost all graduating students were headed to college. There was a strong belief in civic involvement, and many I knew looked to careers in public service, the military, and government.

All of this success and striving was part of the suburban gentile experience. The achievemenets of some of my classmates are now on display in a small atrium at the school in which there is a glass case, designated as the Hall of Fame, with pictures and short biogophries of those who went on to acquire some national recognition.

One of these students was a classmate of mine, Joe Kruzel. He and I sat together in the last row of a large English literature class. Joe was clearly on the path to something important and later he would attend the US Air Force Academy. I read about Kruzel in George Packer's book, *Our Man: Richard Holbrooke*, the story of an American diplomat. Packer tells the story of how Joe's life and career ended. Kruzel had become the Deputy Assistant Secretary of Defense for Euopean Affairs and was accompanying Holbrooke on a diplomatic mission to pursue a Balkan peace plan. He and Holbrooke were in a convoy driving on a narrow, winding road in Sarajevo, when Kruzel's vehicle plunged down a ravine, caught fire and exploded. Kruzel's vehicle, right behind Holbrooke's Humvee, was the only vehicle to go over the cliff. So Holbrook survives and Kruzel dies.

Joe Kruzel was, for me, what gentile Yorktown was all about. Secular striving, a modicum of Christian prayer, and a career in the military or government. There is no revolution for us; no cultural revolution. After his death, a corridor at the Pentagon is named after him and he is buried in Arlington Cemetery, which was once the home of Robert E. Lee.

In Arlington, the sexual and cultural revolution of the early 1960s passed us by with hardly a glance. We had careers to attend to. Arlington was the suburban bedroom of the Pentagon and the military establishment in Washington, DC; not just a few officers here and there, but ubiquitous. Uniforms wherever you looked. Both the Center and Rockingham Street were filled with the military and civilians who worked for the military. Just as colonial history formed my thinking, so, too, did this exposure to those who wore a uniform every day and those who worked for our military as civilians. No one in Arlington worked on Broadway. No one was an investment banker. No one was a captain of industry. We were the rock-solid middle, drained of all distinctive features. Father knew best, I suppose, because there was not much that one needed to know.

Yorktown was my parallel universe in the secular gentile world. I was surrounded by synagogue talk at home, and had attended Hebrew High School, and yet my daily life was mostly devoid of anything Jewish. True, I knew Esther was running the Center on a daily basis, and Joe was running the Board, but my daily anxieties, the things I needed to do, were not framed by Judaism. The Jewish education I had been given did not penetrate my consciousness sufficiently; I was not trying to work out the problems of late teenage life in any way that was framed in Jewish learning. Try as the Center had to educate us, my friends and I were still, at this point, illiterate Jews when it came to the wisdom of Judaism. It would take many more years for this to change.

1960S: ON DATING NON-JEWISH GIRLS

One thing changed sooner than I anticipated. When the question of dating non-Jewish girls surfaced, the parallel universes of the secular and the religious began to be less comfortable with one another.

At first, the secular world and the Jewish world seemed to coexist, neither one giving much notice to the other. One could be both gentile-like and a Jew in suburban Arlington. At times, I bragged that at my school I was one of five Jewish students. I was secretly proud that I fit right into this gentile world. I was learning how they spoke, what I would sometimes call their "code." Words that meant one thing for them and another for us Jews. It had not yet occurred to me that my Jewish identity needed more. Yet, this peaceful coexistence would change when girls, cars, and dating became part of our life.

Growing up Jewish on the Broyhill Plantation ultimately led to the true crisis of my teenage years: Would I be allowed to date non-Jewish girls? This of course would be the prelude to the ultimate question of whether I had to marry a Jewish woman. Now, for the first time, Esther and Joe seemed to notice that living in suburban Arlington, and immersion in its secular world, could have consequences they might not have considered.

Along with my first thoughts about girls came cars. Back then, Arlington had fairly relaxed rules on driving, which meant that we could get our driver's licenses at fifteen. So girls and cars seem to enter life at about the same time. The most important course for all of us in high school is driver's education, as this is a requirement for obtaining our licenses. It is taught by the high school wrestling coach. Three of us sit inside a large Dodge sedan and drive around the hills of Arlington during sixth period. Joe and Esther offer no resistance to my getting my license at fifteen.

Dating in the 1960s meant driving. And dating in the 1960s usually meant taking girls to the movies, bowling, or one of the evening parties held at friends' homes. There were no internet dating services and we were too young for bars. We had to suffer through the ritual of asking a girl out, sometimes in person and sometimes by phone. And once in the car, we were on our own, and suddenly there was a new sense of freedom and a chance to explore.

Cars and girls are the beginning of my migration away from my family. I grow restless and want to be with my friends. Obtaining a driver's license plainly outranks my bar mitzvah as the true coming of age, at least as seen through my teenage eyes.

Once girls enter my life, the Jewish question becomes more pressing. I see this now as a kind of dividing line—those parents who insist that their sons only date Jewish girls, and those who did not. How odd then that Joe, son of Sol, the one who brushed it all aside, and joyfully ate shrimp on the pier in Chicago, would suddenly take the side of faith. Now Joe would have to explain to me what it meant to be Jewish and why here, in suburban Arlington, surrounded mostly by gentile girls, I had to limit my dating pool to Jewish girls. How could he, who barely had a bar mitzvah and certainly had never seriously studied Torah, explain any of this to me, much less to himself? Now Joe would have to explain more than he truly knew.

I remember standing with Joe one afternoon in our small hallway on Rockingham Sreet, while he is trying to make me understand why I could date only Jewish girls. Joe's argument was that the Jews had survived for 2,000 years, and that because of this, I should and must be attentive to my Jewishness and date only Jewish girls.

Joe's argument made little sense to me. At age fifteen, there was no contest between the history of the Jews and a pretty girl with green eyes who I wanted to date. I was not equipped to deal with either. I knew too little about girls and too little about my need for Judaism. Joe's argument seemed unconvincing, but the car keys belonged to him, and there was no way past this hurdle. So, in a way, it was my need for the car that kept me away from non-Jewish girls.

Looking back, I don't think there was much Joe could have added at the time to convince me he was right. When your family has Passover at Sears, and Friday night is football night, and the weekly Torah portion is never once discussed at the dinner table, and when Mario's pepperoni pizza is still one of your parents' favorite meals, then surely a non-Jewish wife will not alter one's fate. I suspect this inabilitiy to explain the "why" of Judaism is precisely why the intermarriage rate across the globe today is almost 60 percent.[1]

---

1. Pew Research Center, "Chapter 2." "Among respondents whose current, intact

In retrospect, Joe was feeling something that neither he nor others were able to explain well. Scholars have noted the Jewish resistance to destruction, and claim it is based on the mysterious foundations of our Jewish destiny.[2] But such arguments, even if Joe had found the words, would not have carried the day. What did it matter if we had resisted destruction now that we were here, safe in exile, safe on the Broyhill Plantation, attending a high school with five other Jewish students? Assimilation felt fine. The foundation of our Jewish destiny seemed too remote, too mysterious, too abstract—just an idea with nothing concrete for me to hold onto.

In the end, I largely conceded this fight with Joe, and ironically, as it turned out, the girls who wanted to date me usually were Jewish. This led me to look for girls among the young Jewish teenagers who attended Friday night Shabbat services at the Center or those who were active in USY. This worked well enough. The Center, its USY program, and its Friday night services provided me with ample opportunity to meet Jewish girls, even if they were from other parts of northern Virginia. As Danny Siegel would later write, part of what made the Center something we would remember the rest of our lives was that it was a place where we wanted to hang out together, a place where we could see and meet Jewish girls, make friends, date.[3]

Esther and Joe's insistence on my dating Jewish girls, however, does not work entirely. Oddly, of the three brothers, I am the only one who will heed their insistence, as each of my brothers will marry outside our faith. And then, later, so too will our oldest son. Sometimes the control of the car keys is not enough.

And so it is that assimilation glides over us, comfortable and reassuring, and we hardly notice that whatever made the Jewish soul unique and whatever reasons there might be to remember our Jewishness were quietly being erased here in the cozy and soft landscape of Robert E. Lee and the Broyhill Plantation.

My classmates and I talk often about where we should go to college. None of us is intimidated by the process; our parents stay on the sidelines, offer no help on forms; no guidance counselor or other similar mentor. We just manage the process without any fanfare. I know so little about one school or the other. Joe drives me to Penn State on a snowy Saturday, and we sit in the large football stadium and watch a part of a game. We see the academic

marriage took place in 2005 or later, 58% have a non-Jewish spouse" (para. 1).

2. Sacks, "God Who Acts in History (Vaera 5779)," 11:13, citing Nicolai Berdyaev.

3. *L'Dor v' Dor*, 26.

buildings on the main campus, the dorms, and other facilities that provide for student life. I don't ask which schools have Jewish students, which do not. Some of my friends apply to Harvard and Duke and seek early admission, but my grades are not good enough. I spent my high school years being too easily distracted by one thing or another, never quite able to apply myself, letting whatever intellectual skills I might have remain undeveloped. I am impulsive and unfocused, and now, looking back, it's little wonder that Esther and Joe were at a loss to understand me. So, for me, going to college meant only leaving them, being free, and it was this quest for freedom that I felt far more than the question of which college to attend.

Joe says I should go to the University of Virginia because I am an in-state student and it will not be expensive. We must have taken a drive to look it over. I am relatively certain that, even on my first visit, I found the colonial architecture of the university to be exactly what I knew I wanted; everything I learned at Yorktown and Williamsburg about our history was now manifest in this gorgeous lawn and campus. I did not need Abraham, Issac, or Jacob, or the patriarchs of Judaism to guide my thinking. Thomas Jefferson was more than enough. After all, isn't this exactly what I had been taught ever since seventh grade? This, the second creation story—America, the city on the hill, was more than enough for me.

Yorktown, then, made Charlottesville inevitable, and more deeply rooted me in Virginia, something Southern, and something that would make Thomas Jefferson and the University of Virginia so critical to my younger self. And although I saw no connection between this genius of American democracy and Judaism at the time, I would begin to knit them togther in the coming years, and would see how Jefferson's views on learning, on reading, and on democracy would fit in with Judaism's teachings. Today, I will sometimes refer to myself as a "Jeffersonian Jew," trying to bring together the American colonial experience, with its charm and core Jewish values. I did not anticipate that I would fall in love with Charlottesville and the university, and yet I did. If I would later turn to a more serious notion of being Jewish, at this point in my life I only wanted to preserve my love of what I saw in Charlottesville.

I graduate from Yorktown High School in June 1963. I do not see a future that includes a war, the military, nor a life outside of Arlington. Next stop is Charlottesville, where I cannot find a Conservative Jewish synagogue, much less a bagel.

CHAPTER 19

A Jeffersonian Jew (1963)

"I cannot live without books."

—THOMAS JEFFERSON[1]

SEPTEMBER 1963: THE UNIVERSITY OF VIRGINIA—A DIFFERENT KIND OF GHETTO

IN SEPTEMBER 1963, ESTHER, Joe, and I drive the two hours, down Route 29, Lee Highway, to Charlottesville for the start of classes. Esther and Joe drop me off at one of the university's first-year dormitories, Humphrey Hall, Room 303. My roommate is Randy Rankin, a classmate from Yorktown. I have a few bags and not much else. Esther and Joe unpack the car and then are on their way. They do not come up to my room to make sure everything is in order; we do not have lunch together—I am on my own, like Sol in Antwerp as he boarded his ship for America. If someone cried, I missed it. I am free at last. Maybe Esther and Joe felt the same relief themselves.

I soon fell in love with Charlottesville and have never fallen out of love with it. It is "The Lawn" that captures me, considered by many to be an architectural masterpiece.[2] Jefferson believed that architecture was the heart of the American ideal and, in his mind, "a building was not merely a walled

1. Thomas Jefferson to John Adams, June 10, 1815, *Papers of Thomas Jefferson*, 8:523.
2. "Thomas Jefferson's Architectural Village," para. 1.

structure, but a metaphor for American ideology . . . that would embody the fulfillment of civic life of Americans."[3]

Brick serpentine walls wind around the Lawn, surrounding a large grassy and treed area that cascades down from the Rotunda, toward Cable Hall. The students' quarters are small one-bedroom units, attached one to the other and forming a long rectangular structure within the walls, with the Rotunda at one end and Cable Hall at the other. Jefferson's eye for architecture captures the symmetry of nature, with the graceful, elongated rectangular shapes offset by Grecian columns. The rooms all open on to the Lawn, and have rocking chairs and firewood sitting outside the black wood doors. Doors are left open in the fall and spring, as the Honor Code makes theft in Charlottesville virtually unheard of.

Interspersed every ten units or so is a larger structure, two stories high, where the university professors are housed. This "Academical Village,"[4] as Jefferson thought of it, is where students and professors live and learn together. Jefferson envisioned daily contact between students and faculty, out of class as well as in class, with frequent meals together and a continuing dialogue.

Virginia and the Honor Code were, to me, synonymous. There was one sanction only—withdrawal for those found guilty of lying, cheating, or stealing. One or two witnesses were usually required. Each year, a few were told to leave. There were debates about whether the one sanction was too severe, but in my years there, it was not a serious issue on campus. The ethical foundation of the honor system seemed entirely correct to me; I could never understand what would make a person lie, cheat, or steal. I never understood the impulse to be evil. I may have suffered from other forms of uncontrolled impulse—but not cheating or stealing. One's word mattered. Others may be savvier, more cunning, and move more quickly in the corporate world, and even in the law world, but I could never shake the conviction that the Honor Code was one of the most important values I learned at Virginia. The Honor Code reflected much of what being Jewish meant to me.

During my first week on campus, I make a trip to the "Corner" bookstore, located in a small strip of two-story retail stores on University Boulevard, many of which have been there since the 1920s. I see the neatly arranged rows of paperbacks, both modern and Victorian, and I am amazed that this is what college is all about—buying and reading these wonderful

3. "Jefferson and the Politics of Architecture," para. 3.

4. https://www.virginia.edu/visit/grounds.

books. I cannot wait. It takes only a few short weeks in Charlottesville before I begin to feel that somehow my life must be like this always.

For years, I say that this is where I want to live, and where I want to be buried. It is here that I find myself. Everything is perfect, ordered, temperate, honest, and quiet. I see exactly what Jefferson was trying to create, driven by his "inexplicable, but powerful yearning for order, simplicity and centrality."[5] I am away from home just reading books.

JUDAISM: MY SILENT PARTNER AT MR. JEFFERSON'S UNIVERSITY

Yet, in many ways, the university was just an extension of everything I had seen and lived in suburban Arlington—the ever-present military and an absence of Jewish life. I see now that I was continuing to move in a distinctly Southern, gentile world, with only modest Jewish involvement. I had come from a high school with five Jewish students to a university where it was rumored that there was a strict Jewish quota of no more than 10 percent in any one class.[6]

Even the daily presence of the military was similar to Arlington. The dorm live-in counselor was a third-year student named Barry Fake, who was a rising star in the Navy ROTC. Barry had a full Navy ROTC scholarship and was in a program that gave him the same class status as midshipmen attending the Naval Academy in Annapolis, Maryland. He would go on to a long and successful career in the Navy. Like Colonel Blackburn and Major Carpenter, Barry was simply further confirmation to me of all that Arlington had validated: that adult life was connected to our government, our military, our history. Prompted by Barry's example, Randy and I would both join the Air Force ROTC, and once a week would wear our blue Air Force uniforms on campus with hardly a thought about what any of this meant, nor whether I was even suited for the military life.

Barry and Arlington become even more connected when Randy introduced Barry to Elizabeth Cornell—"Bibber" to me—who lived across from us on Rockingham Street. They dated steadily and upon graduation, they married.

My Jewish life had a submerged quality to it. I was dating Rose, a Jewish girl from a nearby high school in Arlington, but I had not yet come to any decision on how my life would, or would not, embrace any form of

---

5. "Jefferson and the Politics of Architecture," para. 9.

6. "Encyclopedia of Southern Jewish Communities—Charlottesville, Virginia," para. 22.

observant Judaism. Judaism was present, silently, but it made no demands on me, and did not change much in my world. My secret sharer, in a sense. There, in my mind and soul, but not yet given its full voice.

In the early 1960s, Charlottesville had only one synagogue: Beth Israel, constructed in 1882 and still a Reform synagogue today. Beth Israel conducted its services entirely in English and did not require men to wear yarmulkes—the traditional head covering. An organ accompanied a choir—neither of which I had ever heard in our Conservative synagogue at home. Charlottesville had no need for a second synagogue. In 1947, the Jewish population in Charlottesville was 106.[7] Indeed, during a fifty-year period ending roughly in the 1940s, there was only one bar mitzvah ceremony.[8]

I remember that September day when I first set foot in Beth Israel. It was Yom Kippur, and I had been fasting. I went back for the afternoon session at 4:00 p.m., thinking that the service would last until sundown when Jews are supposed to end their fast. But at 5:00 p.m., with the sun still shining in its last summer vigor, services ended, and I realized that all in attendance were headed home to break the fast before sundown.

This was the first time I became aware that not all Jews fasted on Yom Kippur, and that some who did, ended their fast early. Or, perhaps had a morning coffee to get through the headache of not eating during the fast day. I could not help but think that this was no different than our tradition of Passover at Sears. And yet, I judged it as wrong, for whatever reason. I see now I had started the process of picking and choosing, doing whatever parts of Judaism seemed right or convenient, and disregarding the rest.

I made a few visits to Hillel House, a place for Jewish students to gather, with a Jewish "chaplain." But there was no Jewish learning and, to my knowledge, no way to find it. My Jewish classmates and I were probably not all that interested in any event. No one davened; no one observed Shabbat when Friday night or Saturday morning arrived. Not even one Jewish student could be seen on the grounds with a yarmulke.

THE JEWISH FRATERNITY SYSTEM

Nevertheless, there was one place on campus where male Jewish students could congregate. The university had a system of segregated fraternities. There were the Jewish houses and all the others. The rule against Jews

7. "Encyclopedia of Southern Jewish Communities—Charlottesville, Virginia," para. 19.

8. "Encyclopedia of Southern Jewish Communities—Charlottesville, Virginia," para. 17.

joining the other houses was mostly unwritten, but well understood. AEPi, Phi Epsilon Pi, and ZBT were the big three national Jewish houses. ZBT had rich Jews with big cars. AEPi had middle-class Jews who wanted to be lawyers or doctors, and everyone in PhiEp was from New Jersey, so that was out of the question for me. My friends from the Center seemed content with this segregation—none of us saw it as anti-Semitism. None saw it as part of our exile.

The rush season is in the fall of 1963, and I am selected as a pledge— the status one is given pending initiation into the brotherhood the following year. Esther and Joe were fine with my joining AEPi, and agreed to pay the additional costs for dues and meals, because they saw what I saw: that the young men from the Center were also joining: Steve Zimmet, Larry Evans, all the well-respected Jews from home. Esther and Joe were willing to pay the extra costs just to keep me around other young Jewish men. They must have thought this would keep me on a Jewish path, whatever that meant, and however inadequately this was understood. I think they saw that these were young people of ambition and determination, and they wanted me to be among them.

The Jews of UVA (University of Virginia) came mostly from Richmond, Norfolk, New Jersey and Northern Virginia. A few came from New York. We huddled together in segregated fraternities and never thought a thing about it. I liked being around Jews. I had no desire to be in one of the other more prestigious gentile fraternities. The Jewish fraternity felt much the same as USY had felt at the Center: a place to hang out and be with other young Jews. That we were segregated seemed of no importance. We happily accepted our exile, and I moved into the Jewish fraternity, our small and safe ghetto, with satisfaction. If there was a revolution coming just around the corner, neither I nor my friends saw it.

Although we were a Jewish fraternity, there was little, if anything, that stood out as distinctively Jewish. No one mentioned Shabbat or keeping kosher, but at least most went home for the Jewish holidays. For whatever reason, that felt Jewish enough to me.

What did stand out was ambition. Studying was key. We took it seriously. There was active competition among the fraternities for the highest grade-point average, and AEPi was always among the top two or three. We studied hard, days and nights in the library carrels. We exchanged notes from classes with our more senior fraternity brothers who had taken the courses earlier and done well. The coat-and-tie tradition was unquestioned. It would be a few more years before the war in Vietnam would puncture this serenity.

We seemed to settle down to our adult life early—ready for marriage and a business career. Many of my fraternity brothers would later marry the same young women they were dating at the time, including me. Most of the relationships were serious. Our female dates would arrive on the major party weekends, often by train from Alexandria or points south. As was the practice, we would find rooms for them in the local motels.

We dated and we studied. We wore our coats and ties, shared our notes, and attended our parties. There was no sexual revolution here; no feminist movement, no peace movement, no protests, no graffiti. There were simply manners and quiet decency. Just what Jefferson had envisioned—orderliness.

In September 1964, during my second year at the University of Virginia, I was initiated as a brother in AEPi. I moved out of the dormitories and into a rented house across the street from the Rotunda. Three of us—Art Lazerow, Charlie Sachs and I, newly minted fraternity brothers—rented an apartment at 123 Chancellor Street, one block from the corner. It is still there today, looking exactly the same as it did then, except now it has the name of the fraternity on the front porch, and Zillow lists its value as $2.5 million for the six-bedroom home.

I had my desk on Chancellor Street next to a window looking out on the porch, and Art had a small desk behind me in the corner. Art, like Barry, was in the Navy ROTC. We both studied quietly at night, often with classical music playing. We had typewriters and wrote our papers without computers. We both tried pipe-smoking. It was serene.

Our apartment was one block from ElJo's and Stevens Shepherds, the two leading clothing stores, which prospered during the era of coats and ties. We mostly frequented ElJo's, where we bought our dress shirts, ties, sport coats, and Bass Weejuns' penny loafers for ninety dollars. El and Jo Hyman had come down from Baltimore and opened this store, which they ran for decades. A new sport coat cost thirty-five dollars, and I remember the first one I purchased and either El or Jo agreed to let me pay ten dollars monthly. Gant shirts, still made today, were beloved, especially the ones with the button on the back of the collar, at a cost of fifteen dollars. Next to ElJo's was Mincer's pipe store, which sold records, pipes, tobacco, and magazines. I worked there for many months. And next to Mincer's was the Virginian, where we ate many of our meals.

Life was good; we had all we needed. We may have stopped by the Hillel House once or twice, and Esther and Joe visited a few times but usually

I called home on Sunday afternoons and reported that all was well. The conversations were short.

MARRIED AS AN UNDERGRADUATE

During the summer of 1965, between my second and third year, Rose and I decide we will get married in the fall. I have been dating Rose since my junior year in high school, and I feel ready to be married and to settle down, despite being barely out of my teens.

Rose, one year behind me in high school, does not go to college. She is working for the government and is also ready to be married. We are both ready for adult life. I want a job in which I sat at my desk, read, and write stuff, and am dropped off at the office by my wife, and then picked up for dinner. I am done with childhood and being a teenager. I may have been done with that since I was ten. I am twenty, and am told by everyone that we are too young, but I pay no heed. A quiet married life in Charlottesville with books and literature and the Corner and the Lawn, is all I want and will ever need, or so I think.

Rose's parents are in favor, and are warm and loving, and I find a sense of comfort and love within their family. They are happy to pay for a large Jewish wedding. Rose's parents are thrilled that their daughter will be married to the son of the synagogue president.

Esther and Joe initially think we should wait until graduation, but are not seriously against the marriage taking place two years earlier. In some ways, I am off their hands, and in their view, I am now more focused and settled, so maybe marriage is a good idea.

In September 1965, when I have just turned twenty, we have a large Jewish wedding ceremony at the Conservative synagogue, B'nai Israel, which is then located on 16th Street in Washington, DC. Two hundred people attend. This includes my Jewish friends from the University of Virginia, all of whom wonder why I wanted to get married so young. After the ceremony, Rose and I drive off in a new Volkswagen, our wedding gift from both sets of our parents, and head for our honeymoom to historic Williamsburg, Virginia, now fully restored by the Rockefellers to look as it did in Colonial times.

Little do I know that the wedding is one week too late.

In July 1965, President Johnson announces he is ordering an increase in US military forces in Vietnam, from the present 75,000 to 125,000 troops, and will order additional increases, if necessary. In order to meet this increase in military manpower needs, he says the monthly draft calls will be raised from 17,000 to 35,000. Johnson also announces that the marriage deferment will end for all men married after September 1, 1965.

Shortly after this announcement, Rabbi Golinkin calls me to discuss the end of the marriage deferment and to suggest I move the wedding date up by a week. He suggests two ceremonies: one private ceremony in August and the larger wedding in September. I have never heard of two ceremonies, and it doesn't seem quite right. I ignore the rabbi's advice. Some bad decisions have an endless half-life.

I frankly have never given any thought to Vietnam. I assure Rabbi Golinkin that I don't need to worry, nor do I need to rely on the marriage deferment because I will have the graduate student deferment. I tell him I will be going to law school or graduate school in two years, and by the time my graduate deferments are over, the war will be over.

I might have listened to the rabbi had I been following the news more carefully, or if reading it, had understood what it really meant. But no one I know is talking about being drafted out of graduate school. So, I ignore Golinkin's advice, and we are married on September 6, 1965, just a few days after the marriage deferment has ended. And so it is, a few years later, that I find myself on a plane headed to Vietnam with my Marine Corps buddies.

ENGLISH HONORS PROGRAM

In September 1965, I started my third year at the university, having married Rose just before classes began. My mind was not on the Vietnam War, nor was it on the thought of being drafted. I was ready to immerse myself in the study of literature. I was selected for the English Honors Program that started in September. I was also part of the Ford Foundation's three-year MA program. The Honors Program let me lead the kind of adult life I had wanted. I could spend my days reading and writing, while Rose was at work for the Social Security Administration. She would pick me up from the library at the end of the work day, and we would go home, where Rose would cook dinner. I was content.

Starting in my third year, I was only required to take six credit hours of standard course work during the next two years; all the rest was literature seminars and tutorials, taught in small groups of ten students, and in the case of tutorials, there were only two of us. There were no exams, just papers and writing, and even the papers were not given official grades. So, for two years, I had to take only one regular class a year. I still recall them: one was Shakespeare and one was accounting. This two-year program gave me exactly the kind of life I wanted to be living. Typical college life fell away. I had my freedom and my work.

I picked accounting because, despite my love of literature, I had some vague notion that I might go to law school. Each day, I would walk past Clark Hall, where the law students (almost entirely men at that time) had their classes in those days, and see the law students dressed in coat and tie carrying their briefcases, many being dropped off by their wives. This was adult life here in Charlottesville, where everything was ordered and beautiful. On a few days, despite my love of literature, I slipped into Clark Hall to see what the law students were doing. I opened a few of the books and saw the cases and the doctrines, and I could already feel the tension between a life of literature and one in law. I loved books, but I had seen the young lawyers in the Honors Program during my summer at the Department of Justice, and this memory lingered and began to pull me toward the law. The notion of working on issues of justice, protecting those who could not protect themselves, was urging me toward a different kind of work.

But, if truth be told, and despite being drawn to law school, I met myself in literature. Before the University of Virginia, there was no real me. I lacked substance. Before college, I barely knew the meaning of literature. The courses at Virginia gave to reading a legitimacy that I had failed to recognize previously. This was serious business, and it was timely and current. The gifted professors at UVA awoke in me the intellectual excitement of ideas and writing. Professors Douglas Day, Robert Kellog, and others shaped my thinking, and I was convinced that whatever I did in life would grow out of this immersion in literature and writing. The magic of words flowing onto paper enthralled me. This was the emotion I had felt in Joe's office when I was ten, standing in the supply room, looking at the beautiful boxes of yellow wooden pencils and paper writing tablets, wanting to write, but not yet knowing what it was I was supposed to write.

Charlottesville was where I first understood that there were serious writers who wrote about life as I then understood it; writers and professors talking about the anxiety and pain of the twentieth century. For the first time, I saw that writing mattered, that writing was a worthy profession, that literature was worthy. I was a serious student. I wanted to work at a desk and read stuff and write things. I had seen Joe do that, and it seemed like what a person was meant to do. When I learned that you could read literature and teach it for a living, I was tempted.

Part of my study focused on modern American literature, and I read deeply into Hemingway and Faulkner. Ultimately, it was Hemingway who tugged at me, and I did my honor's thesis on his notion of the private war.

Mostly, it was the rhythm and cadence of a Hemingway sentence that stayed with me forever: short, understated, ironic.

Yet, oddly, what I was reading during those two years was in some ways pulling me away from observant Judaism. While I did not fully appreciate it, I was being exposed to the great twentieth-century authors who had come to doubt much about religion and God, and who had separated themselves from organized religion. While I was reading the authors as a form of emancipation from the anxieties of my early twenties, they were writing in a context that was not all that different from the one in which Chaim Grade was writing: intimations of a Godless universe. It would be decades before I would come to see that what had felt liberating then was a view that I would discard and reject as I matured.

Douglas Day taught the course in modern Europen literature. We read Albert Camus, Franz Kafka, Thomas Mann, Rainer Rilke, and others. I heard for the first time the notion of existential angst, the discomfort of life, and permanent anxiety. When Franz Kafka writes, in *The Metamorphosis*, that he awoke one day to discover he was a large bug,[9] I knew that he lived with a permanent sense of Jewish angst, not even able to hold onto his own image of himself, lacking in confidence, confused by an arbitrary and indifferent world.

What I did not fully realize was Kafka, Camus, and Mann were part of a general movement in Europe that was casting away much of religion. In a sense, they were an extension of the Jewish enlightenment that Sol and Anna had seen in Vilna. Traditional views were giving way to the secular.

The experience of being Jewish in Germany and Austria had led to much of this sense of modern anxiety. The universe was too disordered and arbitrary to serve as evidence of a Jewish God who took care of the world. Kafka did not embrace his Jewishness. Toward the end of his life, in a *Letter to His Father,* Kafka wrote, "I could not understand how, with the insignificant scrap of Judaism you yourself possessed, you could reproach me for not making an effort . . . to cling to a similar, insignificant scrap."[10]

Like many young students, I found solace in the discomfort of the great writers, and a plausible excuse for my own sense of rebellion, however quiet. I, too, could push thoughts of religion aside if the notion of a benevolent God was no longer the accepted wisdom. Hemingway's war was private because he was no longer connected to the larger society and thus he could leave the battlefield, leave the army behind, and try to make a separate

---

9. https://theboar.org/2016/01/the-top-10-opening-lines-in-literature/.
10. Roth, "Franz Kafka," para. 5.

peace. All of this was an excuse to retreat inward—a view that I also would later discard, but which I grasped then.

These writers and their books appealed to me as a twenty-year-old who was still trying to figure out why it was that some part of my life did not feel right, despite all I had. And now I wonder if my marriage at age twenty was simply my own small revolution, my decision to leave Esther and Joe, to leave Rockingham Street, to set out on my own, and to settle my own private war.

But others were fighting a war that was not so private. I don't think I paid much attention to the beginning of antiwar protests, or to the growth of groups like the Student Nonviolent Coordinating Committee (SNCC). SNCC had gotten started in early 1960, and by 1965 had become active on some campuses, but as I recall, we barely paid any attention to it at the university. In late 1965, SNCC issued its position paper on the Vietnam War and declared its opposition to the war.[11] No, I did not pay attention; nor did most of my classmates or fraternity brothers. The fraternity brothers made fun of Art in his Navy ROTC uniform when he wore it to the fraternity house on ROTC day—typically a Tuesday.

Jefferson and UVA kept me sheltered from the tumult of the 1960s. Whatever was driving others outside of the university to revolt and to demand change had not found its way to Charlottesville; like a virus perhaps, its path was uncertain and some of us were far too resilient to change. I still wore a coat and tie to class. I still loved every new Gant shirt, fresh out of the package. We had the Honor Code. It all meant something. We were men of honor; the word "gentleman" could be used without derision or irony at the university. We were careful; you could trust us and believe us. We were idealistic; we wanted to preserve institutions. We would not take well to the revolution of the 1960s—that is, until we learned, a bit too late, that it was our very lives that were at risk. Vietnam was about to turn our world upside down.

I graduated from the university in June 1967 and I was awarded a Bachelor of Arts with High Honors. I had done well on my oral exams, and my thesis on Hemingway was well received. I tried to undertand what it was that made Hemingway's characters leave the arena, as Joe would put it, and deal only with their private war.

But my essential self was starting to come into being: a love of literature, and yet a pull toward engagement, toward justice, toward something

11. See "Student Nonviolent Coordinating Committee Position Paper on Vietnam."

that still connected me with the notion that we Jews were supposed to do good with our lives. The tension between law and literature had weighed on me throughout my last two years as an undergraduate. Rose was encouraging me to puruse a legal career, in part because she felt she would be uncomfortable in an academic environment.

My love of literature seemed to define my feelings toward Esther and Joe. I saw myself as fighting my own private war, still feeling isolated and somewhat apart, not fully connected to them. Our family life on Rockingham Street had been too emotional, too crazed for me. I could never satisfy Joe—the engineer and chemist, and me with my lesser skills. I was not really what he had bargained for. I needed to be free from both of them, no matter how dutiful and responsible they had been. I was unmoored from the family, uncomfortable, and longing to be on my own.

Like Sol, I had drifted away from observant Judaism, although not consciously. The secular world of Arlington and the notion of being a colonial Jew was now who I was, or so I thought. I was a Jew who had grown up in the shadow of the Pentagon. The existential writers of Europe had made me question whether life was orderly and guided by a benevolent, Jewish God. The world of literature and the impact of the American revolution, of Jefferson, had left my sense of Judaism in a neutral position, like a state of repose.

For now, I had my books and I had the wonderful world of Jefferson. What I did not know was that I would not have any of this much longer. I ignored the war, and it me.

It is June 1967. I will have one more year of peace in Charlottesville, and then nothing will ever be the same again.

CHAPTER 20

The End of the Rockingham Era (1965–1968)

WE ALL MOVE AWAY: RABBI GOLINKIN LEAVES ARLINGTON-FAIRFAX JEWISH CENTER

WHILE I AM AN undergraduate at the University of Virginia, playing golf at Keswick Country Club, reading Hemingway and Thomas Mann, and letting my Judaism drift into neutral, I do not notice that things are changing at the Arlington-Fairfax Jewish Center. I do not notice that things on Rockingham Street are changing. Such is the price of self-absorption. We lose track of history even when we are living it. And when I was not looking, the 1960s ended almost everything I might call my youth.

In 1965, Rabbi Golinkin decides to move on to a larger stage. He resigns as rabbi of the Arlington-Fairfax Jewish Center. Mayer Smith suggests he is leaving because he is unhappy the board would not give him a lifetime contract that other rabbis are sometimes offered. But his son, David Golinkin, tells me he leaves in order to become the first director of the Board of Jewish Education where he is responsible for forty-five Jewish schools in the Greater Washington area. But if the Center declined to give Golinkin a lifetime contract, I see it now as a serious mistake, and as a failure to understand the importance of his work—a fatal flaw, if you will.

Mistake or not, Golinkin served as the founding director of the Board of Jewish Education of Greater Washington, from 1965 to 1970. Later, he became president of the National Institute of Hebrew Literacy in Columbia,

Maryland, and he assisted an estimated 200,000 American Jews in their efforts to read the Hebrew of prayer books. Rabbi Golinkin continued his efforts as a leading advocate for the teaching of Hebrew sufficient enough to enable Jews to understand in some modest way the language of prayer books and the liturgy of Sabbath services. Or at least, as he had put it, to be able to point with their finger to the place in the prayer book where the service was being chanted.

Rabbi Golinkin's journey from Vilna to Arlington had come to an end. He never forgot Vilna, and always carried with him a love of Vilna, despite the pogroms and violence he had seen there when he was young, back when Sol and Anna were still two young teenagers. In 1939, only one year after he had arrived in America, he wrote an article describing his love of Vilna, the Jerusalem of Lithuania. In it, he wrote:

> On mountains and valleys lies, spread out, the favorite city of today's Poland, Vilna. It is an incantation for the lovers of nature as for the lovers of culture. Each contributed its part here; each tied her hopes to here. But no one had found a more beautiful, pet name, which breathes more love and respect, than the Jewish name: Yerusahalayim d'Lita, the Jerusalem of Lithuania.[1]

When Golinkin passes away, his son, Rabbi David Golinkin, delivers the eulogy. David writes about his father's passion for saving the Hebrew language, but more broadly, about his effort to resurrect the notion of Hebrew literacy. David knew that, in his father's mind, an inability to read Hebrew meant that assimilation would be more pronounced, would take us one more step away from being able to understand, to explain—to ourselves or our children—why we were Jewish.[2]

Rabbi Jonathan Sacks also wrote that our ability to read the texts shapes our entire Jewish being: "What is at stake is not just biblical interpretation but the moral life itself. How we read a text shapes the kind of person we become."[3]

Even though Rabbi Golinkin moved on from the Center, and took his life mission to a national scale, he had left his mark on the Center and on Rockingham Street. And then, as in all things in life, our time on Rockingham Street also came to an end.

1. YIVO Institute for Jewish Research, "Center of Jewish Scholarship," para. 12.

2. Medoff and Golinkin, *Student Struggle against the Holocaust,* 138.

3. Sacks, "Was Jacob Right to Take Esau's Blessing? (Toldot 5775)," 0:23–0:32.

LAW SCHOOL: SEPTEMBER 1967

I still planned to head to graduate school, and perhaps one day teach English literature. I was enrolled in the "Three Years Master's program" sponsored by the Ford Foundation. Had I wanted, I could have obtained my master's in English literature in one more year of course work, with my junior and senior years counting as the first two years toward the master's degree.

I had come to believe that language is about morality and empathy.[4] It is through words that we achieve a just society. Words we can trust, spoken by those who are trustworthy. What is a nation of law but a nation of words? What I was learning at Virginia was that morality is the soul of literature, that there are truths that only good writing can convey. Writing is the means to empathy, which in turn is the pathway to justice, so that in the end, a love of justice and a love of writing are one and the same.

Yet, for reasons that may have reflected my Jewish instincts about justice, I decided instead to become a lawyer, hoping that, in this way, I could be of value. The summer in the Department of Justice, the brief meetings with John Kennedy and Robert Kennedy, Clark Hall, all of those moments provided me with an image of that future life. Literature still sustained me, but it would not be my career.

So in September 1967, I started law school at the University of Virginia, thinking that I would graduate in 1970. As a married student, I was living off the grounds in a one-bedroom apartment on Park Street, overlooking a public golf course. I got part-time work at Leggett's Department Store selling shoes and men's clothing. Ed Golf was my neighbor and a credit manager. Jim Smith, who taught gym at the local high school, lived in the unit two doors down. Red Dennis, a tall, lean, star golfer whose day job was as a traveling shoe salesmen, lived next door. These were my best friends.

I enjoyed the retail world and my friends. Am I Sol, a Jewish peddler selling clothes? Later, I changed jobs and became a writer and researcher for the Research Group and wrote a legal memo each week; ten hours a week, probably making twenty-five dollars a week. Four memos paid the monthly rent of $100 on Park Street.

Esther and Joe came to visit us but, without much to do in Charlottesville, they were bored. So they paid my dues of thirty-five dollars a month to join the Keswick Country Club, and when they came to see us, we often played golf together. How could I fail to see what a privileged life I was

---

4. Bharara, "Stay Tuned." "It has occurred to me that good writing is a kind of morality, honest communication, thoughtful use of words. I think the way we talk to one another, the way we write to one another, is about how we are interacting with one another, and an attempt at basic human decency" (0:34–0:42).

leading? But the point was not lost on my neighbors, only one of whom attended college. Not until I was about to move out and join the Marine Corps did they confess with some embarrassment that they had resented all I had, though less so when they saw how poorly I played golf. I was not offended, but surprised at the comment. I had not noticed how good I had it. That is, until I joined the Marine Corps and life as I knew it ended.

JUNE 1968: VIETNAM, MARINE CORPS, THE END OF THINGS

One day in June 1968, everything changed. The day before was still an age of innocence. June 6, 1968: I was taking my final exam in contracts law in Clark Hall, when Professor Hardy Dillard gave us the news of the shooting of Robert Kennedy. We still had to finish our exam, but my heart was broken.

Yet, even before then, we knew our youth was coming to an end; that something dark was fast approaching. News of the end of the graduate draft deferment had shattered the law school. A headline in the *Cavalier Daily*, the student newspaper, showed a picture of students in the law school with this headline: "Who Will Be Here Next Year?"

Not me, was the answer. I knew that I would not be among those who would return for their second year of law school. I had seen this coming, even before the terrible news of June 1968. By January, as my first semester was coming to an end, I realized I was likely to be drafted during the summer unless I could make my way into Officer Candidate School (OCS).

I gave no thought, nor did my classmates, to things that others considered later—ways to avoid the draft through medical deferments or other means. I was neither against the war nor for it. I just accepted it as reality and tried to find a way to deal with it. I thought about whether I could survive in the military. I thought back to Chip Carpenter, the Marine major who lived next door, and to Colonel Blackburn, and those in Arlington who seemed to be the kind of normal people who I hoped represented what the military was like.

Some of my law school friends were going to wait to be drafted. But I knew I wanted to head for officer candidate school. The pay was better for an officer than it was for an enlisted man; a private in the army made about $1,200 a year; a lieutenant made $5,000 a year, and while serving in Vietnam, the salary was exempt from federal income tax. I suppose it was somewhat odd to be thinking about the salary given what was at stake, but I did. Am I like Joe, terrified about not having enough money, collecting old newspapers for a few extra dollars?

I talked to my law school friends who were veterans. They too seemed normal, thoughtful people I could relate to. *It cannot be so bad*, I concluded. They survived, although they tell me about the "Bouncing Betties," the land mines that explode when stepped on and what they do to your body. I found it hard to keep this image out of my mind. So, I started training, running, and weightlifting.

In January 1968, I signed a government enlistment contract, agreeing to serve for three years in the US Marine Corps, provided that I graduate from OCS. Rose and her parents accepted my decision to join the Marine Corps without much anguish, at least none they shared with me. I did not consult Esther and Joe beforehand, and when I did tell them, they seemed to accept it as well. Decades later, I wondered why they had not cautioned me against such a reckless decision; didn't they know that the mortality rate of new officers in Vietnam was strikingly high? Were they not concerned that I was not suited to be among the Marines who considered themselves "warriors?" Where was the advice that might have taken me on a different course?

We gave up our apartment on Park Street, and Rose moved back in with her parents on Columbia Pike in Arlington. On a summer day in July 1968, Rose drove me to Quantico, dropped me off, and left me to try to figure out where on the base I was supposed to report. Thus, I began my three-year tour of duty. That was the end of my youth. What was I doing in the Marine Corps? Rarely did a Jew find a less appropriate place than the Marine Corps. Hadn't Arlington been enough of the non-Jewish world? The influence of Colonel Blackburn and Major Skip Carpenter may have given me a flawed sense of what this was all about.

Until then, I had led the typical life of a post-teenager from suburbia. I was self-absorbed, unconnected to history or to any of the political movements then afoot. And now, without having asked for it, I was to become part of the dark history of Vietnam. A Jew in the Marine Corps. A Jew from suburban Arlington. What had I done? Had I not been paying attention?

I suppose I could have let the US Army draft me and stayed in Charlottesville until the very last moment. Even if I were a basic draftee, with the rank of private, the Army might have found some safe desk job for me, or would have realized that a first-year law student could be useful in some office in the Pentagon. Nor did I understand that there was a major difference between how the Marines and the Army were funded; the Army had modern equipment and the latest technology; the Marines were severely underfunded and, hence, every facility and piece of equipment was outdated and dingy. But it was too late for such thoughts.

The OCS program runs for ten weeks. I begin, like everyone else, as a private. About one-third of the class will drop out and will be sent to Paris Island for training as an enlisted Marine; those who graduate will become second lieutenants. Oddly, I do not find officer candidate school particularly difficult—only lonely and depressing. I do not belong there. My class is a special class made up of about one-half formerly enlisted Marines. Many of my classmates come from poor backgrounds and know things I do not know, like how to take a car engine apart—the very same skill that will make them able to disassemble and reassemble the various weapons we are required to master. None of my classmates have come from law school; none are Jewish.

Still, I can outrun most of them, can easily do the rope climb and the confidence course without much difficulty. I am lost in the subjects that are more suited for engineers, but I stumble through them. In September, with just a few weeks left, the Jewish High Holidays arrive, and our platoon sergeant asks me if I want leave to attend services. I say yes and attend services at the Center with Esther, Joe, and Rose. We look for a new car during the break from services in the early afternoon. Some traditions do not change: the Jewish holidays and shopping after services always feel right.

I graduate from OCS in the early fall of 1968, and receive the gold bars of a second lieutenant. As we leave the graduation ceremony, our drill sergeant gives us our first salute as officers, and, in keeping with tradition, we hand him a silver dollar. Everyone is there this time: Sol and Anna, Esther and Joe, Rose and her parents. It still seems benign—we understand so little of what it all means.

After graduation from OCS, my classmates and I are ordered to our next duty station, which is the Basic School, also at Quantico. I move with Rose to Woodbridge, Virginia, about forty-five minutes from Quantico. Now at the Basic School, our training becomes more intense. The Marines insist that "every Marine is a rifleman," meaning, in short, that regardless of what you might do later in the Marines, you first learn to be part of the infantry, even those who will become lawyers and pilots. We learn to assemble, disassemble, and fire a variety of weapons—machine guns, M-16 rifles, and .45-caliber pistols. I have never fired a weapon in my life before this. Yet, for some inexplicable reason, I find I shoot well and earn an expert's badge with the .45-caliber pistol, which is the pistol that officers carry as their standard sidearm. I have always assumed my ability to shoot well was due to the eye-hand coordination I had inherited from Esther, who made me take typing in seventh grade, and turned me into one of the fastest typists in any law firm I would later join.

I graduated from the Basic School in April 1969. Prior to graduation, we were asked to list our preferred MOS—military occupational speciality. I asked to be a supply officer, and the Marine Corps agreed. I don't think anyone saw me as leading a rifle platoon.

For my next duty station, I am sent to Camp Lejeune in North Carolina and attached to the Marine Air Wing. My primary duties include maintaining, storing, and distributing spare parts for Marine helicopters and other aircraft. Outside my office, which is part of a large warehouse, are dozens of spare helicopter rotors, each about twenty yards long, that are used as replacements.

Not all of my classmates live much longer. Some of my Basic School classmates are sent to Vietnam almost immediately, following a short additional training session for "03s"—the designation for infantry among the occupational specialties. Gary Letson, who was close to number one in our class, is shot in the head on his twenty-seventh day in country, on June 18, 1969, in Quang Tri Province, while serving with Company C, 1st ballation. John LaRose, who never paid attention in class, thought he knew enough to fly, crashes his plane in a training exercise and is killed shortly after graduation from the Basic School.

I hoped that my tour of duty in Camp Lejeune, North Carolina would last a long time. Rose and I decided to take the risk of trying to have a child, hoping that I would not be sent to Vietnam anytime soon. But the Marines had other plans, and were insistent that all new officers serve in Vietnam.

Robert Michael Kuney was born on October 30, 1969 at the Camp Lejeune hospital, and, shortly thereafter I received my orders to report to "WestPac," which is Marine jargon for the Western Pacific command area; or, in other words, Vietnam. Danang to be exact. The Marines granted me a thirty-day delay, so that I could spend time with our new son. After that, I would not see Robert for an entire year.

My life as I had known it, and everthing about the 1960s, ended for me in December 1969, when as a Marine lieutenant I landed in Okinawa, on the way to Vietnam. I packed my personal belongings in a cardboard box for storage and shipping to next of kin in case of death, and put my dog tags in my boots so that I could be identified if body parts became separated. It would be exactly one year before I saw Rockingham Street again—or Robert or Esther and Joe. Rose was able to join me once during the year, in Hawaii, for the standard six-day "R&R" provided for Marines in Vietnam.

In Vietnam, I learned that a year is forever. We were cut off from the world, from everything we knew—wood floors, flushing toilets, paved streets, a house to call your own. My life was back in that cardboard box in Okinawa. Vietnam was another world where we lost our souls, whether we lived or died, and I was no exception. And if I died, if we all died, there would be remarriages and new families, but in the end, it would have been for nothing. We would have gone for nothing. We knew this for a certainty. And that knowledge shattered whatever sense of innocence was left. It did little for our sense of decency as well. Somewhere in all of this was the end of my marriage, but that would be later.

Vietnam is where Rockingham Street ceases to exist. I am no longer in the world. I am in a place that has no reality, no values, no sense of time. What is Rockingham Street now, in 1969 and early 1970, when I am in another world? The two worlds do not connect. It is just an address where I send letters from Danang. I go out to inspect the lines at night; a young marine locks and loads and asks me for the password. I forget and say my name and rank: "Lieutenant Kuney." He believes me for some reason.

I send home recordings on small cassette tapes, knowing my family will listen to them in Arlington, at dinner or later, or going to the club, or having a root beer float and wondering about their agenda for tomorrow. But my tomorrow has a different agenda: I will fly in a Huey helicopter gunship over the DMZ, the "Demilitarized Zone," a narrow band of terrain extending from Laos to the coast, about five kilometers on either side. At times, it is the most dangerous part of Vietnam, but it is less active as the war winds down. The pilot is a twenty-something Marine, carefree and careless, indifferent to risks, who tells me to put my flak jacket on the seat to protect my genitals from ground fire; he smiles, and tells me no one gets shot in the chest when flying a helicopter. On our headsets, we listen to rock and roll music from Monkey Mountain, a location where the Marines have set up a radio station. Because the pilot can barely read the navigation maps or the instruments because he, like me, can only wonder what he is doing here, we just follow the dirt road below us. How we survive is a miracle. Flying over the DMZ, I cannot help but wonder if I will ever see Rockingham Street again. I have no idea what brought me here, but for a while, when I return, I will not like anyone who was not here with me. These Marines become my family and, for a time, that is all there is.

Halfway through my tour of duty in country, another lieutenant tells me he has requested and been approved for a split tour, which means he will spend his second six months in Okinawa and not Vietnam. I am told

I need only submit a form called an Administrative Action request to start the process. I dismiss this as unlikely and too good to be true, but I fill out the form and my commanding officer endorses it and sends it somewhere—Washington, perhaps.

And then one day, my company commander says, without much fanfare, "Your orders are here." Travel orders to Okinawa in a week. I left Vietnam in June 1970, with no regret, glad to be alive. I had done enough to say to myself, and others, that I could do this. But my instinct to survive was paramount.

I spent the next six months in the relative security of a large Marine camp–Camp Courtney and Camp Hansen, both close together—where I mostly supervised a large warehouse of Marine Corps clothing items and a team of Marines who kept track of the inventory and made sure we had enough on hand for the Marines in country. I was also in charge of operating a series of retail stores where Marines stationed in Okinawa could purchase basic uniform items. Here, in Okinawa, I received my best fitness report, with my supervising officer saying I was perhaps the best Marine lieutenant he had worked with. I seemed to have returned yet again to the work Sol did.

But the safety of Okinawa did nothing to erase the feelings of being in Vietnam. To this very day, the names of the camps, and any mention of Vietnam or Okinawa still haunt me. That there was actually a December night in 1969 when I got off an airplane and set foot in Danang, and saw the flares along the mountain ridges so that the night sentries could better see Viet Cong trying to breach the fence, has left its mark on my soul and my point of view on how one faces hardship and deprivation and the ordinary, everday risk of knowing someone in the countryside is paid to kill you. That first step on the tarmac in a country where I was the enemy worked some fundamental shift that simply will not let go of me.

It is not until December 1970 that, at last, I am given orders and permitted to fly back to Dulles Airport. The plane has a stopover in Hawaii, and I call Rose to tell her I am coming home—news she had not known. For a moment she is silent, and then I hear her drop to the floor, phone in hand, weeping.

Then at last, an unfathomable year is about to end. Looking down at Dulles Airport and the serene Virginia countryside is too much to grasp; I had left this world utterly and totally, and now coming back is a compromised embrace.

Esther and Joe are not very emotional the day I return, and I, for one, have the same hollow feeling most of us who have taken this strange journey away from the world experience. I feel empty, detached. *Why did you send me?*, I wondered. *Why did you let me go?*

1971–1973: "HOW GOES THE WAR?"

After Vietnam, I was sent to Norfolk, Virginia—my last duty station. I remember learning during Passover in 1971, while still stationed at Norfolk, that Anna had died. I don't recall that she had any serious illness, nor that she suffered. She was entitled to a peaceful parting. I don't believe I saw then that this was the beginning of the end of the Rockingham era for our family.

During my time in Norfolk, during those last few months of active duty as a Marine, I found I did not like anyone other than those of us who served and had spent time in country. I had earned a Vietnam campaign ribbon, which I wore each day on my uniform prior to release from active duty. I was arrogant about my own willingness to risk my life for this, even though I had tried to protect myself. I had no connection to the protests and, in truth, knew little about them. I had done what I thought was my duty, for better or worse, whether qualified or not. Some of us lived, some died. I had seen the aluminum caskets stacked ten high and five wide at the Danang airport awaiting transport to their final resting place. I would never be the same. My sense of life and its hardships were now engraved on my soul.

Now at last I knew what Joe had meant when he would ask me, "How goes the war?" I would always be a Marine, even if not well-suited for it, whether I liked it or not.

I was released from active duty in June 1971, and I returned to law school that September. I had been away for three years, and I had forgotten the hard study skills that school required. My second-year grades fell into the solid middle of the class, and now, what had seemed like a shot at Law Review was gone. But this was all my own doing; neither history nor politics was to blame. It was simply my own inability to see where I stood in the midst of this maelstrom.

Later, while on the required three years of inactive reserve, the Marines promoted me to Captain. I had always wanted to wear the silver insignia of a captain—another symbol of another fantasy. But I had chased enough illusions. I sold my Marine Corps sword and gave away my flight jackets. I would not see my Marine classmates from The Basic School until 50 years later when we celebrated our reunion.

THE SALE OF OUR HOME ON ROCKINGHAM STREET

1973 brought about too many changes. When I look back and think about what happened, I find myself wishing I could stop the chronology, make everyone rethink what they were doing, and then put the narrative into a new trajectory. I have had the same feeling when rereading a tragic novel and hoping I can change the ending if I read more slowly. But I cannot.

Somehow, by the end of 1972, Joe knew he wanted to leave the ACS and to move on to another positon. The boxes from Jackson contain only hints of why Joe made this change, but there is some suggestion that he was not happy with senior management. To my mind, Joe had the perfect job at the ACS. After he left, Joe received dozens of letters, all of which reflect that, to many, the ACS and Joe were synonymous. It is here, at this point, that I wish Esther and Joe had thought this through, and perhaps tried harder to make things work at the ACS.

Having decided to leave, though, Esther and Joe sold our home on Rockingham Street. On December 17, 1972, they signed a contract of sale, agreeing to sell our home to Browning Associates for $41,000. Settlement was scheduled to occur on February 16, 1973, at the law offices of Fried, Fried, Klewans & Lawrence. The closing took place, and with it the Rockingham Street era for our family ended.

Then Sol did the same with his home. Now that Anna had passed away, and Esther and Joe had decided to leave Rockingham Street, Sol also decided the time had come for him to leave Arlington. Sol signed a contract for the sale of his home on 26th Street, on May 31, 1973, and he moved to Florida, where he would live for the remaining seven years of his life.

I do not think Sol was glad to see the end of our time together on Rockingham Street. Surely, being close to the family gave him a quiet satisfaction. I never see him again, but I talk to him at least once shortly before his death. He tells me he is the "invisible grandfather." I assume he meant that no one was paying much attention to him, and I certainly deserve some of the blame. All those years together on Rockingham Street, and still the bonds are so fragile.

Had Joe asked me, I would have told him not to leave the ACS—more, I would have told him not to sell our home on Rockingham Street; that once the house was gone, and part of our history uprooted, nothing would be the same. I would have told Joe what he had often told me: to stick it out and deal with the problems at the ACS, whatever they were. Nothing would change by moving, because *we* are always the issue. Hadn't Joe been the first to preach the truth of the comic book character of the 1960s, Pogo: "We have met the enemy and he is us?"[5] Joe had so often warned me of this: "Everywhere I go, there I am." It is never "they" that cause the pain, but only us.

5. "36. We Have Met the Enemy and He Is Us."

In my mind, I create an entirely different outcome—one that I wish had happened. What if Joe and Esther had never moved away from Rockingham Street? What if Sol and Joe had started going to *minyan* and Saturday morning Shabbat services together? Sol would not be invisible. Couldn't Joe ride through the turmoil of a difficult boss—the problem of being undervalued, and ignored, or whatever was causing the pain?

But no one asks my advice, and I am powerless to change the events, no matter how often I replay them. Joe and Esther move to White Plains, New York for his new position at Wiley. Joe is the manager of the Journal and Encyclopedia Department. But it is not longlasting, and Joe leaves Wiley in 1974. It is also during this period that Esther is diagnosed with one of her two bouts with cancer.

Esther and Joe then move back to Virginia, where everything had started. In September 1975, they purchase a unit in a newly constructued garden apartment condominium in Oakton, near Westwood Country Club. At least here they are close to an essential part of themselves, a world of activity and sports, and the kinds of friends they once had in Chicago and then later in Arlington.

Joe continues to work for the next several years, and from what I can see, does moderately well. After coming back from New York, Joe is hired by Informatics Inc. as Vice President and General Manager of the NASA Scientific and Technical Information Facility. This job takes him to a facility near the Baltimore-Washington Airport. A few years later, Joe retires from Informatics. He becomes the publisher/editor of *Chemcyclopedia*, an annual directory of commercially available chemicals. He now works out of his modest home office. He teaches a course titled "Use of Information in a Democratic Society" at the University of Maryland, Baltimore County. His resume notes, "I also play softball twice a week during the season." His love of baseball never ends. He would be Shoeless Joe in a heartbeat, if given the chance.

1973 is also my last year at the University of Virginia. I graduate from the law school in June 1973 and accept a job at Miles & Stockbridge in Baltimore. I am assigned to the banking section, and mostly focus on closing commercial loans. It will later prove to be a valuable experience in learning how contracts are negotiated and the meanings of words in a contract. But I do not belong in Baltimore, and two years later, I accept a new position in Washington, DC at the law firm of Melrod, Redman and Gartlan. Lippy Redman and Joe had been close colleagues on the Board of Directors at the Center and, although Esther and Joe are now in New York, my job application to the new firm is accepted within a few days. Later, Cathy will join the same firm after she graduates from George Washington Law School.

Meeting Cathy at Melrod turns out to be the most important event in my life, and we will marry a few years after we meet.

JANUARY 6, 2001: JOE'S SECOND BAR MITZVAH

After Esther and Joe return from New York, and move to Oakton, Esther continues to work at the Center on a part-time basis. When Rabbi Golinkin leaves the Center, Rabbi Marvin Bash becomes the new rabbi and he calls on Esther from time to time over the years to work for him. Joe will drive her to the Center and often will wait there until her day is done. She is never able to pull herself away from the Center. Until Joe passes away, it is an essential part of her life. Rabbi Bash will later say the eulogy at Esther's graveside funeral.

Despite, or perhaps because of, all these passages, Joe moves toward a more meaningful embrace of his Judaism. As Joe is nearing his eighty-third birthday, he decides to follow the Jewish tradition of having a second bar mitzvah celebration on the seventieth anniversary of his earlier bar mitzvah. But this time, Joe insists he will read in Hebrew from the Torah scroll, for which he prepares for many weeks.

Joe reads the Torah portion called Vayigash. In some ways, it is his story as well. The biblical Joseph has a confrontation with his brothers, whom he has not seen in many years. They do not recognize him, in part beause he has become the Viceroy of Egypt, second in authority only to Pharoah. At this moment of confrontation and revelation, Joseph says to his brothers, "I am Joseph." But it is a statement of disclosure to both himself and his brothers who had failed to see who he was. Now, both he and his brothers see him for who he truly is; not an assimilated Egyptian, second in command, but as a member of the Hebrew tribe, a few generations before the giving of the Torah.

So, too, our Joseph, who was ready to recognize his own Jewish soul, the soul that had been transmitted to him from Sol and Anna, and the hundreds of generations that preceded him. Now he could say to himself and the community, "I am Joseph."

Joe asks me to come to the Center the day before his bar mitzvah, where he is practicing, to take photographs, which I do. I still have these color photos, now assembled on a poster board by a kindly secretary, and they show him with the pointer on the Torah scroll. He is smiling brightly and, in one picture, has raised his hand in the victory symbol, which is what he will do when he finishes reading from the Torah the next day. He knows he has met this last challenge of his life, and that what he helped build, this enduring Jewish community, will now come to celebrate, although seventy years later, his Jewish manhood and achievement.

So, there he is, a child of immigrant parents from Vilna, who never learned Hebrew as a child, and probably thought little of it, but who, in Arlington, in the South, comes to understand what he needs to do to build a Jewish community, and to build his own Jewish soul. He had done the same thing when he built our modest basement on Rockingham Street: learned how to do things he had never done before, and then done them well, until at last he tackled the hardest challenge of all—to learn Hebrew and read from the Torah.

Joe will only live a few months more. In April 2002, lying in a bed in a nursing home, he will announce to no one in particular, "I want to get out of here," and so he does. He was entitled to pick his own time. He had done enough, and even if the path had its moments of anger and distress, what he left for the rest of us was an unshakable sense of duty, the same that Sol and Anna had passed on to him. He was still the son of a tailor. Still thimble and thread.

CHAPTER 21

Closing the Boxes

Now, more than fifteen years after Esther and Joe have left us, after I watched her being rolled into the black limousine, I have mostly finished going through the boxes sent from Jackson, have spoken to those who are still here, and have gleaned as much as I can from the historical records. I am ready to close the boxes and return them to the shelves. Retirement from the active practice of law gave me the time to look into them, and I am grateful for that time.

But before I close the boxes, before I try to assess what I have learned, I feel obliged to see where some of my former friends and classmates from the Center have gone. Did they remain Jewish? Did they marry within the faith? What did the Center and Arlington mean to them?

I go back to Etz Hayim in the spring of 2019, and I see the building yet again transformed. The permanent seats have been taken out, although I loved them, and in their place are removable seats. The raised *bema* is gone and now the pulpit is on the same level as the seats. I liked the older version better. Why the need for this modern look? I am guessing this is part of the trend away from the notion of a service as a performance on a stage by the clergy and an effort to make it more participatory. Still, I think we may be kidding ourselves to think this is possible. Performance is exactly what many want, and showing up for most is the highest level of participation. It strikes me as tinkering at best, and without regard for root causes.

Who remains? Who still comes to services at the Center these decades later? The Zimmets and Gondos still attend; so, too, do Jerry Jacobs and the

Okins. But I also sense the memory of others—Esther and Joe in the office, next to the sanctuary where Rabbi Golinkin and Esther spent decades working; and upstairs, Hal Schlaffer and Rachel Reinitz, who taught us Hebrew. Their memories are fixed into the walls. It is all still there. And so are we.

Some, in their youth, like Ricky Okin, had parents who were liberal and modern, for whom religion did not seem all that important. Ric drops out of Hebrew school, but later in life picks up where he left off. He becomes very active at Etz Hayim, and in 1981 becomes the president of the *shul*. Indeed, he serves again in 2001–2003. He, too, seems to find the Center tugging at him even late in life. But then, during the course of writing this memoir, in May 2020, Ric falls, and is hosptialized. Within one day, he is infected with COVID-19, all part of the pandemic that has gripped our lives, and is dead in twenty-four hours. His wife Sonya, his family, and his many friends are devastated. Rockingham Street is floating away from me faster than I can write down its slender history.

Others—too many—have already passed away. My list is not complete. Arthur Goldstein and Neil Frommer, my carpool mates have left us. Steve Levenberg? I do not know.

Marsha Teichman was a student of Rachel Reinitz five years after our class of 1957 had moved on. I ask her for her thoughts on Etz Hayim. She and her parents were barely once-a-year Jews. Now she reads from the Torah at our synagogue, Adat Shalom, and is a scholar in her own right. She says you either have the spark or not. I wonder if this isn't the best summation of all, leaving all complexity behind and getting down to brass tacks.

There are so many different views on what makes education work or not. The words of Rabbi David Golinkin come back to me. You cannot educate Jews with two days a week of Hebrew school as an afterthought. Is it just, as Marsha has suggested, for those who have the spark, or do you need more help along the way to help capture those for whom the spark is less visible?

The words of Rabbi Holtzman, from Adas Israel, come back as well. As he said one day in our Torah class, the Jewish religion is a religion of observance, but only a few observe. I thought I heard in this a suggestion that there is something inevitable about how this turns out, no matter what we do. That only a few will show up, only a few will have the spark. For the rest, participation as viewers of the well-intentioned performance is the best we can do.

Abe Golinkin, brother of David Golinkin, wrote that his father, Noah, thought Arlington was a model community. "God says it is not because of your great numbers that I have chosen you to be my people, but because of the special qualities of you and your ancestors, and likewise we could say [the same] about our congregation. This is what my father always saw in the congregation. He considered Arlington a model community."[1]

Did Arlington truly become a model community, after starting in a shoe store, and contending with the Broyhill Plantation, the Catholic Empire, and so many other non-Jewish influences?

Hal Schlaffer, Rachel Reinitz, Noah Golinkin, Sol and Anna, Esther and Joe—all are gone now. Still, we must tread lightly on this history and be careful of the conclusions we draw. It is hard to know what makes some turn toward religion and others against it. Marsha Teichman says it is either there or not, in the soul, and the *shul* matters less. Maybe, but I think there is more to it than that.

And for me? I have tried to learn what I did not learn the first time around. I have tried to master the language, examine the texts, see the mysteries of Jewish learning and understand what makes some civilizations and peoplehood last for 4,000 years while others disappear. Each morning, I return to the very same prayer that Mrs. Reinitz made us speed-read, the parts of the Shema that remind us of the covenant with God and the notion that it is the love of God and the laws of Judaism that will bring us joy and satisfaction in life, provide a guide to all things we do. Perhaps it is not easily understood, nor readily grasped, but it is worth the effort, worth a life of learning.

I cannot judge whether I have been any better than Esther and Joe and Sol and Anna in trying to transmit any of the Jewish tradition to our children. Time will tell. I was divorced when Robert was eight years old, and my involvement in his daily Jewish life was not as substantial as it should have been. But Rose remarried a wonderful man, and a devout Jew, so Robert saw up close what an observant life is like. I have urged Robert, who is now over fifty years old, to join a congregation and to make a commitment to a Jewish community. I hope he does. And Rose has remained a good friend of ours and our children, so this has made the continued celebration of festivals as one family a joyful time.

Daniel and Jessica, the children from my marriage to Cathy, have an obvious and strong sense of being Jewish. When they were starting elementary school, we enrolled them in the Charles E. Smith Jewish Day School, and my fondest hope was that this would give them what I had missed. But, through no one's fault, a day school education was not appropriate for either of them.

And while they are only modestly observant, they do observe, and even seem to enjoy the major holidays with varying degrees of interest and

1. *L'Dov v' Dor*, 41.

enthusiasm. Jessica has many Jewish friends and frequently goes to group Shabbat dinners. And when the Covid-19 pandemic hit us, she was on Zoom and attending services.

Daniel married a wonderful Jewish woman, Dana Klinghoffer. They had a beautiful, traditional Jewish wedding ceremony. At the moment, they are overwhelmed with the duties of new parents, but I am hopeful. Dana had a bat mitzvah, and Daniel a bar mitzvah. When Dana visits with Daniel, and we light the Friday night candles, Dana joins in the blessings in Hebrew and shares in the joy of Shabbat. They both know of my interest in Judaism, and I think over time they may increase their involvement. Their first-born son, Joshua Foster Kuney, has a Hebrew name, Maimon—the name of the father of Moses Maimonides—intended to honor Cathy's mother, with whom Daniel was very close.

Joshua is now the youngest member of our family, the youngest Kuney. He was only a few months old when most of this memoir was written. And we have many pictures of him facing the camera with his blue eyes, wide, inviting, and thoughtful. In one picture, he is holding a baby toy that oddly has the shape of a scroll, with two rounded ends, ball-like. Sometimes, in my own private fantasies, and given his Hebrew name, I think of this picture as his way of saying to us, to all of us, that he will hold to the Jewish tradition, will hold tight to the Torah scrolls, and will carry on in a way that continues and enlarges the journey that Sol and Anna started more than 100 years before his birth.

All of this is because of Sol and Anna and Esther and Joe. Flawed, but critical. Everything builds on something else. I do not know if we can succeed, but having watched those who went before me, and having felt the magnitude of the effort, I must at least try. The bare, irreducible minimum of Jewishness may have been enough for a moment or two of human history, but surely, we will need more now.

Sol and Anna's voyage means something. Something good but incomplete. They gave us life and saved us from extinction at the hands of our enemies. They gave us our heritage and then they gave us America. The work of two tailors who agreed on little about being Jewish and whose own children went from a soft indifference to an embrace with a sense of duty and devotion.

I should know more, perhaps, but I do know this: we were young once, and this was how we lived our life on Rockingham Street.

Bibliography

"300 Jews Die Daily in Warsaw Ghetto." *The Sentinel*, August 21, 1914. http://www. idaillinois.org/digital/collection/p16614coll14/id/68624.

"$3,000,000 in 30 Minutes." *The Sentinel*, December 29, 1916. http://www.idaillinois.org/ digital/collection/p16614coll14/id/17037.

"36. We Have Met the Enemey, and He Is Us." https://library.osu.edu/site/40stories /2020/01/05/we-have-met-the-enemy/.

"Abraham Verghese." *Literary Arts*, April 12, 2012. Podcast. 51:31. https://literary-arts. org/archive/abraham-verghese/.

"Albert Speer, On the Nazi Invasion of Poland—Sept. 1, 1939." *New York Times*, August 31, 1979. https://timesmachine.nytimes.com/timesmachine/1979/08/31/issue.html.

Alter, Robert, trans and ed. *The Hebrew Bible*. 3 vols. New York: Norton, 2019.

Altman, Avraham, and Irene Eber. "Flight to Shanghai, 1938–1940: The Larger Setting." *Yad-Vashem Studies* 28 (2000). https://www.yadvashem.org/odot_pdf/Microsoft%20 Word%20-%203234.pdf.

Apelbaum, Laura Cohen, and Wendy Turman, eds. *Jewish Washington: Scrapbook of an American Community*. Washington, DC: Jewish Historical Society of Greater Washington, 2007.

"Appliances: The History and Advancements of the Washer and Dryer." https://www. easyapplianceparts.com/resources/History-and-Advancements-of-the-Washer- and-Dryer.aspx.

Balkelis, Tomas. "Opening Gates to the West: Lithuanian and Jewish Migrations from the Lithuanian Provinces, 1867–1914." http://ces.lt/en/wp-content/uploads/2012/03/ EtSt_Balkelis_2010.pdf.

"Beginnings of the Vilna Community: The Jews of Vilna at the Beginning of the 20th Century." https://www.yadvashem.org/yv/en/exhibitions/vilna/background/20 century.asp.

"Behind the Nazi Ghetto Walls of Warsaw." *The Sentinel*, August 21, 1941. http://www. idaillinois.org/digital/collection/p16614coll14/id/68617.

Berger, Joseph. "Inna H. Grade, Fierce Literary Guardian, Dies at 85." *New York Times*, May 12, 2010. https://www.nytimes.com/2010/05/13/nyregion/13grade.html.

———. "In Yiddish Author's Papers, Potential Gold." *New York Times*, May 17, 2010. https://www.nytimes.com/2010/05/18/books/18grade.html.

Berlin, Adele, and Marc Brettler, eds. *The Jewish Study Bible.* 2nd ed. Oxford: Oxford University Press, 2014.

Beschloss, Michael. *Presidents of War: The Epic Story, from 1807 to Modern Times.* New York: Crown, 2018.

Bharara, Preet. "Stay Tuned: The Laws of Language (with Ben Dreyer)," June 6, 2019, in *Cafe Insider*, podcast, 1:05:18. https://cafe.com/stay-tuned/stay-tuned-the-laws-of-language-with-ben-dreyer/.

Brook, Daniel. "Double Genocide." *Slate*, July 26, 2015. https://slate.com/news-and-politics/2015/07/lithuania-and-nazis-the-country-wants-to-forget-its-collaborationist-past-by-accusing-jewish-partisans-of-war-crimes.html.

Carroll, James. "Abolish the Priesthood." *The Atlantic*, June 2019. https://www.theatlantic.com/magazine/archive/2019/06/to-save-the-church-dismantle-the-priesthood/588073/.

"Charles Lindbergh Makes 'Un-American' Speech." *History Unfolded: US Newspapers and the Holocaust.* https://newspapers.ushmm.org/events/charles-lindbergh-makes-un-american-speech.

Chernow, Ron. *Grant.* New York: Penguin, 2017.

Colletta, John P. *They Came in Ships: A Guide to Finding Your Immigrant Ancestor's Arrival Record.* Nashville: Turner, 2008.

"Commonwealth of Poland." *Encyclopedia Britanica Online.* https://www.britannica.com/place/Poland/The-Commonwealth.

Cutler, Irving. *The Jews of Chicago: From Shtetl to Suburb.* Chicago: University of Illinois Press, 2009.

Diner, Hasia R. *The Roads Taken: The Great Jewish Migrations to the New World and the Peddlers Who Forged the Way.* New Haven: Yale University Press, 2015.

"Drag Jews from Hospitals to Go to Nazi Galicia." *The Sentinel*, August 21, 1941. http://www.idaillinois.org/digital/collection/p16614coll14/id/68646 .

"Encyclopedia of Southern Jewish Communities—Charlottesville, Virginia." https://www.isjl.org/virginia-charlottesville-encyclopedia.html.

Engel, David. *The Holocaust: The Third Reich and the Jews.* 2nd ed. London: Routledge Taylor & Francis, 2013.

"Ephraim Oshry." https://en.wikipedia.org/wiki/Ephraim_Oshry.

Fishbein, J. I., ed. *The Sentinel: History of Chicago Jewry: 1911–1986.* Chicago: Sentinel, 1986.

Fredriksen, Paula. *When Christians Were Jews: The First Generation.* New Haven: Yale University Press, 2018.

Freedlander, A. A. "The Epochal Roosevelt-Churchill Conference." *The Sentinel*, August 21, 1914. http://www.idaillinois.org/digital/collection/p16614coll14/id/68620.

"Germans Capture Vilnus and Warsaw." *HistoryCentral.com.* https://www.historycentral.com/ww1/VilniusFallstoGer.html

Goldsmith, Emanuel S., et al., eds. *The American Judaism of Mordecai M. Kaplan.* New York: New York University Press, 1990.

Golinkin, David. "A Wonderful Life: Rabbi Noah Golinkin (1913–2003)." https://schechter.edu/a-wonderful-life-rabbi-noah-golinkin-zl-1913-2003/

Golinkin, Noah. "The Center of Jewish Scholarship—A Portrait of Yivo in 1939." https://www.yivo.org/the-center-of-jewish-scholarship-a-portrait-of-yivo-in1939.

Grade, Chaim. *My Mother's Sabbath Days: A Memoir of Chaim Grade.* New York: Knopf, 1986.

————. *The Sacred and the Profane*. Lanham, MD: Rowman & Littlefield, 1997.

————. *The Yeshiva*. Translated by Curt Leviant. Indianapolis: Bobbs-Merrill, 1967.

Grade, Inna Hecker. "Foreword." In *My Mother's Sabbath Days: A Memoir of Chaim Grade*, by Chaim Grace, vii–xvi. New York: Knopf, 1986.

————. "Foreword." In *The Sacred and the Profane*, by Chaim Grade, vii–viii. Lanham, MD: Rowman & Littlefield, 1997.

Greenbaum, Marsha. *The Jews of Lithuania: A History of a Remarkable Community (1316–1945)*. Jerusalem: Gefen, 1995.

Hevesi, Dennis. "Joel T. Broyhill, 86, Congressman Who Opposed Integration, Dies." *The New York Times*, October 4, 2006. https://www.nytimes.com/2006/10/04/washington/joel-t-broyhill-86-congressman-who-opposed-integration-dies.html.

"Hold Public Bonfire of Books in Kovno." *The Sentinel*, August 21, 1941. http://www.idaillinois.org/digital/collection/p16614coll14/id/68646.

"The Holocaust in Lithuania." https://en.wikipedia.org/wiki/The_Holocaust_in_Lithuania.

Jamadi, Mariana. "The Paris of Siberia, According to Checkov." https://fathomaway.com/paris-siberia-according-chekov-russia/.

"Japs Condemn Program as Jewish Plot." *The Sentinel*, August 21, 1914. http://www.idaillinois.org/digital/collection/p16614coll14/id/68646.

"Jefferson and the Politics of Architecture." http//xroads.virginia.edu/~CAP/JEFF/jeffarch.html.

Jefferson, Thomas. *Papers of Thomas Jefferson: Retirement Series*. 17 vols. Princeton: Princeton University Press, 2004.

Kafka, Franz. *The Metamorphosis and Other Stories*. Translated by Stanley Appelbaum. Dover Thrift Editions. New York: Dover, 1996.

Kaplan, Mordecai M. *The Greater Judaism in the Making: A Study of the Modern Evolution of Judaism*. New York: Reconstrucitonist, 1960.

"Kaunas Pogrom." https://en.wikipedia.org/wiki/Kaunas_pogrom.

Kimmel, Thomas. "Interview of Tom Kimmel on the Pearl Harbor Attack & Admiral Kimmel." *YouTube*, August 3, 2017. https://www.youtube.com/watch?v=jzOsSi-ZTRs.

L'Dor v' Dor in Arlington County: An Oral History of Congregation Etz Hayim. Written transcript available from the Congregation of Etz Hayim.

Leviant, Curt. "Chaim Grade's Centenary." *Jewish Action* (Winter 2011). https://jewishaction.com/jewish-world/people/chaim_grades_centenary/

————. "Translating and Remembering Chaim Grade," *Jewish Review of Books* (Winter 2011). https://jewishreviewofbooks.com/articles/272/translating-and-remembering-chaim-grade/.

Library of Congress. "From Haven to Home: 350 Years of Jewish Life in America: A Century of Immigration, 1820–1924." https://www.loc.gov/exhibits/haventohome/haven-century.html

"Lindbergh Accuses Jews of Pushing U.S. to War." https://www.jewishvirtuallibrary.org/lindbergh-accuses-jews-of-pushing-u-s-to-war.

Liulevicius, Vejas Gabriel. *A History of Eastern Europe*. Chantilly, VA: Great Courses, 2015.

Lively, Penelope. *Dancing Fish and Ammonites: A Memoir*. New York: Penguin, 2013.

Lustiger, Arnold, ed. *Chumash Mesoras Harav, Sefer Shemos*. New York: Oxford Univeristy Press, 2014.

Martin, Doug, "Ephraim Oshry, 89, a Scholar During the Holocaust." *New York Times*, Oct 5, 2003. https://www.nytimes.com/2003/10/05/nyregion/ephraim-oshry-89-a-scholar-in-secret-during-the-holocaust.html.

"Mass Expulsion of Jews from Lublin Reported from Nazi Poland." *Jewish Telegraphic Agency,* August 18, 1941. https://www.jta.org/1941/08/18/archive/mass-expulsion-of-jews-from-lublin-reported-from-nazi-poland.

"Mass Expulsion of Jews from Lublin Reported from Nazi Poland." *The Sentinel*, August 21, 1941. http://www.idaillinois.org/digital/collection/p16614coll14/id/68637.

"Maurice Samuel Makes First Chicago Appearance at K.A.M. Temple." *The Sentinel*, November 27, 1941. http://www.idaillinois.org/digital/collection/p16614coll14/id/49585.

"McCalla II (DD-488)." *Naval History and Heritage Command.* https://www.history.navy.mil/research/histories/ship-histories/danfs/m/mccalla-ii.html.

McCullough, David. *Truman.* Simon & Schuster, New York: 1992.

McIndoe, Dominique. "Married Men to Get Draft Deferment—For Now." *World War 2.0* (blog), June 26, 1942. https://blogs.shu.edu/ww2-0/1942/06/26/married-men-to-get-draft-deferment-for-now/.

Medoff, Rafael, and David Golinkin. *The Student Struggle against the Holocaust.* Jerusalem: Schecter Institute of Jewish Studies, 2010.

Merriman, John. *A History of Modern Europe.* Vol. 2. 3rd ed. 2 vols. New York: Yale University, 2010.

M. J. L. "What Are Kohanim, or Jewish 'Priests?'" *MyJewishLearning.com.* https://www.myjewishlearning.com/article/kohanim-jewish-priests/.

Mnookin, Robert. *The Jewish American Paradox: Embracing Choice in a Changing World.* New York: Hachette, 2018.

"Napoleon Named Vilnius 'Jerusalem of the North.'" *VilNews*, November 9, 2011. http://vilnews.com/2011-01-napoleon-named-vilnius-'jerusalem-of-the-north'.

"Nazis Prohibit Jews to Eat Vegetables, Swedish Newspapers Report." *The Sentinel*, August 21, 1941. http://www.idaillinois.org/digital/collection/p16614coll14/id/68624.

Nusbaum, Hermien D., compl. *Our Baby's First Seven Years: The Mothers Aid of the Chicago Lying-in Hospital.* Chicago: The University of Chicago Press, 1928.

Ober, Lauren. "How Racial Covenants Shaped D.C. Neighborhoods." *WAMU 88.5 American University Radio*, Jan. 17, 2014. https://wamu.org/story/14/01/17/how_racial_covenants_shaped_dc_neighborhoods/.

Oshry, Ephraim. *Annihilation of Lithuanian Jewry.* Edited by Bonnie Goldman. Translated by Y. Leiman. New York: Judaica, 1995.

Parker, James. "Reading Thomas Jefferson's Bible." *The Atlantic*, November 2020. https://www.theatlantic.com/magazine/archive/2020/11/peter-manseau-jefferson-bible/616476/.

Pew Research Center. "Chapter 2: Intermarriage and Other Demographics." https://www.pewforum.org/2013/10/01/chapter-2-intermarriage-and-other-demographics/.

Plaut, W. Gunther, ed. *The Torah: A Modern Commentary.* Rev. ed. New York: Union for Reform Judaism, 2005.

Porat, Dina. "The Holocaust in Lithuania: Some Unique Aspects." In *The Final Solution: Origins and Implementation*, edited by David Cesarani, 159–74. New York: Routledge, 2002.

Reeves, John. *The Lost Indictment of Robert E. Lee: The Forgotten Case against an American Icon.* Lanham, MD: Rowman & Littlefield, 2018.

Roberts, Andrew. *Churchill: Walking with Destiny.* New York: Viking, 2018.

Roth, Matthue. "Franz Kafka: The 20th Century's Realest Surrealist." https://www.myjewishlearning.com/article/franz-kafka/.

Rothman, Lily. "This Is What Eleanor Roosevelt Said to America's Women on the Day of Pearl Harbor." *Time Magazine*, Dec. 7, 2016. https://time.com/4584910/eleanor-roosevelt-pearl-harbor/.

Sacks, Jonathan. "Anger Management: (Chukkat 5775)." Podcast series, *Covenant & Conversation: Judaism and Torah,* June 24 2015. http://rabbisacks.org/anger-management-chukkat-5775/.

———. "The God Who Acts in History (Vaera 5779)." Podcast series, *Covenant & Conversation: Judaism and Torah,* December 31, 2018. https://rabbisacks.org/wp-content/uploads/2018/12/CC-5779-The-God-Who-Acts-in-History-Vaera-5779.pdf.

———. "Was Jacob Right to Take Esau's Blessing (Toldot 5775)?" Podcast series, *Covenant & Conversation: Judaism and Torah.* November 19, 2014. https://rabbisacks.org/jacob-right-take-esaus-blessing-toldot-5775/.

Schwarz, Sidney. *Finding a Spiritual Home: How a New Generation of Jews Can Transform the American Synagogue.* San Francisco: Wiley, 2000.

———. *Jewish Megatrends: Charting the Course of the American Jewish Future.* Woodstock, VT: Jewish Lights, 2013.

Seltzer, Robert M. *Jewish People, Jewish Thought: The Jewish Experience in History.* New York: Macmillan: 1980.

Shepard, Richard. "Chaim Grade, Yiddish Novelist and Poet of the Holocaust, Dies." *New York Times,* July 1, 1982. https://www.nytimes.com/1982/07/01/obituaries/chaim-grade-yiddish-novelist-and-poet-on-the-holocaust-dies.html.

Siegel, Andrew. "Rabbi Noah Golinkin, 89, Taught Hebrew." *Baltimore Sun,* March 4, 2003. https://www.baltimoresun.com/news/bs-xpm-2003-03-04-0303040304-story.html.

Singer, David. "Zakhor: Jewish History and Jewish Memory, by Yosef Hayim Yerushalmi." *Commentary Magazine,* July 1983. https://www.commentarymagazine.com/articles/david-singer-4/zakhor-jewish-history-and-jewish-memory-by-yosef-hayim-yerushalmi/.

Soloveitchik, Joseph B. *Days of Deliverance: Essays on Purim and Hanukkah.* New York: KTAV, 2007.

"Stocks Collapse in 16,410,030-Share Day, but Rally at Close Cheers Brokers; Bankers Optimistic, to Continue Aid." *The New York Times,* October 30, 1929. https://archive.nytimes.com/www.nytimes.com/library/financial/103029crash-lede.html.

"Student Nonviolent Coordinating Committee Position Paper on Vietnam." http://www2.iath.virginia.edu/sixties/HTML_docs/Resources/Primary/Manifestos/SNCC_VN.html.

Taylor, Keith. "Our Damaged Nobel Laureate." *The Los Angeles Times,* March 31, 2002. https://www.latimes.com/archives/la-xpm-2002-mar-31-bk-taylor31-story.html.

Teutsch, David A., ed. *A Guide to Jewish Practice: The Life Cycle.* Wyncote, PA: Reconstructionist Rabbinical College Press, 2014.

"Thomas Jefferson's Architectural Village: The Creation of an Architectural Masterpiece." https://www.upress.virginia.edu/title/3601.

"Trans-Siberian Railway in the World History." http://www.irkutsk.org/fed/transsib.html.

"US and Japs at War. Bomb Hawaii, Philippines, Guam and Singapore." *The Chicago Tribune*, December 9, 1941. https://newspaperarchive.com/chicago-daily-tribune -dec-08-1941-p-1/.

"Washington's Farewell Address." https://www.ushistory.org/documents/farewelladdress .htm.

Weeks, Theodore R. "From 'Russian' to 'Polish': Vilna-Wilno 1900–1925." https://www. ucis.pitt.edu/nceeer/2004_819-06g_Weeks.pdf.

"What are Kohanim, or Jewish 'Priests?'" https://www.myjewishlearning.com/article/ kohanim-jewish-priests/.

Yad Vashem World Holocaust Remembrance Center. "The Invasion of the Soviet Union and the Beginnings of Mass Murder." https://www.yadvashem.org/holocaust/ about/final-solution-beginning/mass-murder-in-ussr.html.

"YIVO Institute and the National Library of Israel Jointly Acquire the Estate of the Late Yiddish Writer, Chaim Grade." https://www.yivo.org/The-YIVO-Institute-and-the-National-Library-of-Israel-Jointly-Acquire-the-Estate-of-the-Late-Yiddish-Writer-Chaim-Grade.

YIVO Institute for Jewish Research. "The Center of Jewish Scholarship – A Portrait of YIVO in 1939." https://yivo.org/the-center-of-jewish-scholarship-a-portrait-of-yivo-in939.

"Yorktown High '68." https://yorktown68.myevent.com.

"Young Nazis Burn Cross at Noted Rabbi's Home." *The Sentinel*, August 21, 1941. http:// www.idaillinois.org/digital/collection/p16614coll14/id/68645.

Zalkin, Mordechai. "Vilnius." http://www.yivoencyclopedia.org/article.aspx/Vilnius.

Made in the USA
Middletown, DE
15 September 2021